This Bible was given to

First published in 2023 by Floris Books, Edinburgh. www.florisbooks.co.uk
British Library CIP data available ISBN 978-178250-865-6
Printed in China through Leo Paper Products Ltd

Printed on sustainably sourced FSC® certified paper. Uses plant-based inks which reduce chemical emissions.

The Discovery *Illustrated Family* Bible

Retold by Christian Maclean
Illustrated by David Newbatt

Floris Books

Contents

Old Testament

The Old Testament

Beginnings

The Creation

In the very beginning, God created the heavens and the earth. The earth had no shape or form, and there was only water and darkness. The spirit of God hovered over the waters, radiating warmth.

God said, "Let there be light." And there was light. It flooded out when God spoke. God saw that the light was good, and he separated the light from the darkness. He called the light "day" and the darkness "night". And there was evening and there was morning. It was the first great day of creation.

God said, "Let there be an arching roof to separate the waters above from the waters below." And, having spoken, God made an arching roof called the "heavens". And there was evening and there was morning. It was the second great day of creation.

God said, "Let the water under the heavens come together, and let dry land appear." And, having spoken, it was so. God called the dry land "earth" and the waters "seas". Then God said, "Let the earth grow plants and fruit trees that give seeds." And, having spoken, it was so. God saw that it was good. And there was evening and there was morning. It was the third great day of creation.

God said, "Let there be lights in the arching roof of the heavens to separate day from night, and to give light on the earth." And, having spoken, it was so. God made two great lights: the sun to rule the day and the moon to rule the night. He also made the stars. God saw that it was good. And there was evening and there was morning. It was the fourth great day of creation.

Then God said, "Let there be many living creatures in the waters, and let there be birds that fly above the earth." And, having spoken, it was so. God made great sea creatures and every living thing that moves in the teeming waters, and all kinds of winged birds to soar in the roof of the heavens. And God saw that it was good. God blessed the creatures, saying, "Be fruitful and multiply. Fill the waters of the seas and the skies on the earth. And there was evening and there was morning. It was the fifth great day of creation.

Then God said, "Let there be living creatures upon the earth: cattle and creeping things and wild beasts. And, having spoken, it was so. And God saw that it was good.

Then God said, "Let us make a human being in our image, like God, to rule over the fish of the sea, the birds of the air, the cattle and creeping creatures and wild beasts that live on the earth." And, having spoken, it was so. God blessed the human being, saying, "Be fruitful and multiply, fill the earth and give it order. Rule over the fish of the sea, the birds of the air and every living creature that moves on the earth."

Then God said, "I will give you every plant and fruit tree that gives seeds, and they shall be your food. And to every bird of the air and every living creature that lives on the earth, I will give green plants for food." And, having spoken, it was so. God saw that everything he had made was very good. And there was evening and there was morning. It was the sixth great day of creation.

In this way the heavens and the earth were completed, in all their great variety.

On the seventh day, God finished all the work of creation and rested. God blessed the seventh day and made it holy.

Adam and Eve

The Garden of Eden

God planted a garden in the east, in Eden, and he made all kinds of trees. In the middle of the garden stood the Tree of Life and the Tree of Knowledge of Good and Evil. And a great river flowed from Eden and divided into four streams that flowed around the whole earth.

From the dust of the earth, God formed a person and breathed life into him. The person became a man called Adam, which means "earth". God put him in the Garden of Eden to take care of it. He commanded Adam, "You are free to eat from any tree in the garden, but you must not eat from the Tree of Knowledge of Good and Evil, for if you eat from that tree, you will certainly die."

Adam did not know what this meant, for nothing that God had created had died yet.

God brought all the animals on the earth and the birds in the sky to Adam, and asked him to name them. Adam gave names to all the cattle, birds and all the wild animals.

Adam could speak and he could think, but he had no one to speak to, so God said, "It is not good for Adam to be alone. I will make another person as well." God made Adam fall into a deep sleep, and while he was asleep God created a woman from one of Adam's ribs, and named her Eve.

When he woke, Adam looked at Eve with wonder, and he saw that she was different from him, but in many ways the same. They felt as if they belonged together. They had everything they needed in the Garden of Eden. A golden light glowed all around them, and they had every kind of fruit to eat. It was paradise.

The Fall

A crafty serpent came to see Eve one day, to persuade her and Adam to disobey God. The serpent asked her, "Did God really say that you must not eat from any tree in the garden?"

She answered, "We may eat fruit from all the trees in the garden, except one that stands in the middle. God said, 'You must not eat from it, or you will die.'"

Eve did not really understand what "die" meant, so the crafty serpent said to her, "Oh, you will not die. God knows that if you eat from that tree your eyes will be opened and you will be like God, understanding good and evil."

Eve looked at the fruit of the tree. It looked pleasing and good, and she wanted to know what it was like to have her eyes opened like God's, and to understand more about good and evil. So she took some of the fruit and ate it, and also gave some to Adam.

Suddenly everything changed. The golden heavenly light that glowed all around them was gone; now when they looked at each other, they saw they were naked. They felt ashamed and hid themselves among the bushes.

That evening, in the cool breeze, God was walking in the garden. He called out to Adam, "Where are you?"

Adam answered, "I am hiding, because I am naked."

God asked, "Who told you that you are naked? Did you eat from the Tree of Knowledge of Good and Evil?"

"Eve gave me some fruit from that tree and I ate it."

Then God asked Eve, "What have you done?"

And she replied, "The serpent tricked me, and I ate fruit from the forbidden tree."

God said to the serpent, "Because you have done this, you will be cursed, and crawl on your belly eating dust for all the days of your life. And you will be an enemy of all people – they will try to crush your head when you bite their heels."

And God said to Eve, "When you give birth to children, it will cause you great pain."

And to Adam he said, "From now on, the ground will be cursed and will

produce thistles and weeds. You will have to work hard to grow food from it. And when you die, you will return to the ground from which you were taken."

God gave Adam and Eve clothes made of animal skin so that they would no longer feel naked. Then he said, "You and all people have become like God, understanding good and evil, but you must not also eat from the Tree of Life and live forever."

So God banished them from the plentiful Garden of Eden to work on the bare earth. A Cherubim, one of God's mightiest angels, drove them out of the garden with its flaming sword, and stood guard over the pathway to the Tree of Life.

From that time onwards, Adam and Eve lived on the bare earth and worked hard to grow their own food. They had children, then many grandchildren. Their lives were busy, yet often very happy.

Cain and Abel

Adam and Eve's firstborn son was called Cain and their second called Abel. When the boys grew up, Abel kept flocks of sheep and goats, and Cain worked the soil to grow food.

One day Cain made a stone table to use as an altar. He put some grain and vegetables that he had grown on the altar as an offering to God. Abel also brought the firstborn lamb from his flock.

God looked with favour on Abel's offering, but ignored Cain's, which made Cain jealous and very angry. God said to Cain, "Why are you angry? Why is your face downcast? Always do what is good, or your anger and jealousy will gnaw away at you. You must be strong to conquer that."

Cain's heart was so filled with jealousy that he didn't listen to God's advice. Instead, he said to Abel, "Let's get back to work."

When they were in the fields, Cain's heart was still so full of anger that he attacked Abel and killed him. Then he heard God's mighty voice: "Where is your brother, Abel?"

"I don't know," Cain replied in fear. "Am I my brother's keeper? Am I to look after him?"

God ignored Cain's lie and asked, "What have you done? I see and hear your brother's blood crying out from the earth. You will be punished. When you work the soil, it will no longer yield fruit and crops for you. You will wander the earth restlessly."

Cain was deeply ashamed of what he had done, wishing he had acted differently. He replied, "The punishment is too hard for me to bear. Wherever I wander, someone will find me and kill me."

But God said, "I will put a mark on you, so that anyone who kills you will be punished seven times over."

From that time on, Cain no longer heard the voice of God.

During his wanderings, Cain married and had a son, who had many children and grandchildren. Some became skilled smiths of iron and bronze, while others learnt how to make musical instruments like harps and flutes, which reminded them of how Cain had described the voice of God.

But Cain continued to wander the earth, never again hearing God's voice, though he kept seeking it.

Noah and the Flood

Noah builds the ark

When people had been living on the earth for a long time, they forgot the time of paradise in the Garden of Eden. They were so busy working the land to grow food that they forgot God and could no longer hear his voice. Gradually they became more and more wicked, telling lies and fighting one another. Even the animals seemed to copy people and fight with one another. God was saddened by what he saw and regretted that he had ever created human beings.

But there was one family that was good and felt close to God: Noah, his wife, their three sons and their wives. So God said to Noah, "I am going to put an end to all people, for the whole earth is filled with violence because of them. Build yourself an ark of cypress wood and coat it with tar."

Noah wondered what an ark was, but he could not ask because God continued to speak. He listened carefully. "The ark should be three hundred cubits long, fifty cubits wide and thirty cubits high. Make a roof over it, leaving an opening all around. Put a door in the side of the ark and make a lower, middle and upper deck."

Noah knew what a cubit was – the length of an arm from fingertip to elbow. Three hundred cubits was enormous... but he did not have long to ponder on this, for God continued, "I am going to bring floodwaters on the earth to destroy almost all life under the heavens and almost every creature that breathes."

Now Noah realised that the ark must be some kind of ship, which would float on the floodwaters.

God said, "I will make a promise to you. You and your family must enter

the ark, and you must bring two of all living creatures, a male and a female, and keep them alive with you in the ark. Take every kind of food, and store it for you and all the creatures."

At last Noah had time to think about everything God had said to him. It would be a great task to prepare for: to explain God's plan to his family; to cut down many cypress trees to have enough wood to build this enormous ark; to dig for black, sticky tar; to catch a pair of all the animals, especially the wild ones; and to gather up all the kinds of food that they would need.

Noah and his family did as God had commanded them. As they were building the ark, their neighbours came by and laughed at them – why were they building a boat in the middle of dry land? But Noah and his family just steadily kept working.

At last, the ark was built and they coated it with tar. Then they set about catching a pair of all the animals and gathering up all the food they would need. The neighbours now thought that Noah and his family were quite mad – were they going to start an animal market in their strange wooden contraption?

God spoke to Noah again and told him to gather not just one pair, but seven pairs of animals that can be eaten. Then he said, "Go into the ark, you and all your family, because you have been good and obedient. Seven days from now I will send rain on earth for forty days and forty nights, and I will wipe every living creature I have made from the face of the earth."

Noah did as God asked him. He and his family stored all the food in the ark, and then they entered it. All the animals they had caught followed them inside, from the greatest beasts, like elephants and the giraffes, to the smallest creatures that crept along the ground, like ants and beetles. All the birds took shelter under the roof of the ark. All this took seven days.

The Great Flood

As soon as Noah and his family were ready, the heavens opened and it rained. All the springs in the depths of the earth burst forth and water gushed everywhere. Great puddles formed that quickly turned into ponds and then lakes as the waters rose all over the earth. The ark began to lurch, and then floated. All the little cracks between the timbers had been coated with tar to keep the water out, so Noah, his family and all the animals remained dry.

The waters covered the fields and bushes, leaving only the treetops showing. But soon they too disappeared, and still it rained. It didn't stop raining for a week, and even the mountaintops disappeared under the waters. Every living creature on the earth and all the people drowned in the great waters. Birds who could fly also died, because they couldn't find anywhere to rest.

And still it went on raining for ten days, for twenty days, for thirty days. Then, after forty days, it stopped. The rain no longer drummed on the roof of the ark, and there was a great silence. Outside, the waters stretched in all directions and there was no land to be seen.

The earth remained flooded for a hundred and fifty days. There was nothing else to do for Noah and his family but to keep sailing on the oceans. Then one day there was a gentle bump as the ark came to rest on the top of Mount Ararat. The ark stayed perched there until finally, after another three months, the tops of other mountains appeared like little islands in the great sea.

After another forty days, Noah sent out a raven, and then a dove, but they couldn't find anywhere to perch, so they returned to Noah in the ark.

After seven days Noah sent the dove out again. When it returned in the evening there was a freshly plucked olive leaf in its beak, so Noah knew that the waters had receded from the earth. After another seven days, the dove flew out again but did not return, so Noah knew that it had found dry land to rest on.

Exactly a year after the flood began, the waters had dried up from the earth. God said to Noah, "Come out of the ark, you, your wife, your sons and their wives. Bring out every living creature that is with you – the birds, the cattle and the wild beasts – so that they can be fruitful, multiply and fill the earth."

And Noah did so. And after every kind of animal had left the ark, Noah found stones and built a flat-topped cairn as an altar to worship God and make an offering.

God's blessing

God was pleased with Noah and with the offering he had made, and he said in his heart, "Never again will I curse the earth because of humans. As long as the earth exists, seedtime and harvest, cold and warmth, summer and winter, day and night will never cease."

Then God blessed Noah and his sons and their wives, and said, "Be fruitful, multiply and fill the earth. I will make an agreement with you and your descendants, and with every living creature on earth. Never again will there be a great flood. Never again will I destroy all living creatures on earth."

And God said, "As a sign of this agreement, I have placed a rainbow in the clouds. Whenever a rainbow appears, I will see it and remember my everlasting agreement with all living creatures on the earth."

As Noah and his family looked up, they saw a great shining rainbow stretched in a mighty arc high in the sky. And from that day on, whenever they looked up and saw a rainbow, they remembered the agreement that God had made with them.

The Tower of Babel

After a long time, the number of people on the earth had increased greatly, and they had moved to the flat, fertile plains in the Land of the Two Rivers. There were no rocks there, and so there was no stone to build with. Instead, they baked clay in the sun to make bricks. For mortar, they used black, sticky tar, like Noah had used for sealing the ark.

In those days everyone spoke the same language: the one Adam had used when naming all the creatures. They told each other tales of the Garden of Eden, and when they heard the stories, they almost felt they had been there themselves. People longed to see the Garden again, so they said to each other, "Come, let us build a city with a tower that reaches up to the heavens, so that we can see as far as the Garden of Eden, and so that we will become famous for building such a tall tower."

With great skill, they built a tower from baked bricks. Its steps reached to the very top, and it was the highest building ever made.

But when God saw the tower he was angry, because he could see the pride of its builders, how they wanted to be admired for creating such an amazing sight. He called his angels together and said, "Come, let us destroy this tower and scatter these people across the earth. Let us confuse their language so that they will not understand each other and be able to come together to build such things."

With great flashes of lightning and tremors of the earth, the angels destroyed the great tower, and the people fled in terror.

When the people gathered together to see the ruins of their city and its tower, they suddenly found that they could not understand each other. They were confused, as everyone now spoke different languages. So the city was renamed Babel, which means "confusion". Since that time, people no longer felt themselves to be part of one united humanity; instead, they were split into different nations and peoples.

The Patriarchs

Abraham

Abram travels to Canaan

Many years later, a man called Abram lived with his wife Sarai and his nephew Lot in a city called Haran, in the Land of the Two Rivers.

One day, as Abram was in his fields with his servants, God spoke to him: "Leave your country and your people and go to the land I show you. I will make you the leader of a great nation, and I will bless you and make your name great. I will bless those who bless you, and curse those who curse you. All people on earth will be blessed through you."

Abram was puzzled. Where was he to go, and what did God mean? But he obeyed God's command. He took Sarai and Lot, gathered his servants and possessions, and they set out. At every crossroad or fork in the path, he heard God's voice telling him where to go.

After a long journey, they arrived at the land of Canaan. Abram and his family continued travelling until they found a great oak tree at Shechem, in the centre of the land. At this holy place, God appeared to Abram and said, "I will give this land to your offspring." So Abram built an altar there to worship God.

Abram and Lot separate

Abram kept travelling through the land of Canaan. He built another altar at the edge of Judea and named the place Bethel, which means "house of God". In that land, Abram became wealthy. He had plenty of livestock, silver and gold, as well as many servants. His nephew, Lot, also had great flocks and herds and several servants. But Judea was a stony, dry part of Canaan, and it was difficult to find land with enough plants to support their vast flocks. Abram's and Lot's herders quarrelled over which pastures they could use and from which springs their herds were allowed to drink.

So Abram said to Lot, "Let's not quarrel, because we are family. Let's part company instead, for the whole land is before us. If you choose to go north, I shall go south; and if you choose to go south, I shall go north."

Lot looked around from the heights of the sanctuary (the holy place) of Bethel and saw the whole valley of the Jordan River far below. It was well watered, like the Garden of Eden and the Land of the Two Rivers, so Lot chose to go south to the valley of the Jordan, to the city of Sodom. And Abram remained in the hill country of the north.

God said to Abram, "Look around you, to the north and the south, the east and the west. I will give all the land that you see to you and your offspring for ever. Your children and their children will be many: they will be as uncountable as grains of dust on the earth. Go and walk the length and breadth of the land."

Abraham wondered how this could happen, because he had no children. But he obediently followed God's word. After walking the length and breadth of the land, he settled under the sacred oak trees at Mamre, near Hebron, where he built another altar to worship God.

Abram rescues Lot

The people of Sodom and the neighbouring cities in the valley of the Jordan had turned their backs on God. One day, they fought against the armies of four kings from the east, but they were defeated. The four kings captured all their women, servants, flocks, goods and food. They also captured Abram's nephew Lot, along with his family and all their possessions.

A good man who had escaped came to visit Abram at the oaks of Mamre and reported what had happened. That night, Abram called all three hundred and eighteen men in his household together, and they followed the armies of the four kings. In the night, Abram and his men attacked the sleeping armies of the four kings and chased them to the far north of Canaan. In their haste, the four kings left behind all the women, servants, flocks and goods that they had captured. To his great joy, Abram found Lot and his family unharmed, and they returned home together.

On his way back home, Abram, his followers, Lot and all the freed people passed through a valley where there lived a wise, quiet king, Melchizedek, priest of God Most High. Melchizedek means "king of righteousness", and he was king of Salem, the place where the city of Jerusalem (which means "city of peace") was later built.

Melchizedek the priest-king came out when Abram and his company passed by, and invited them to rest. He brought bread and wine and made an offering to God. Then he blessed Abram, saying, "Blessed be Abram by God Most High, creator of heaven and earth."

Deeply moved, Abram swore an oath – a sacred promise – to God Most High, creator of heaven and earth, that he would not accept any reward for freeing the people of Sodom. Then he gave Melchizedek a tenth of all his food and money, and left feeling happy and peaceful.

When the king of Sodom heard that Abram had defeated the four kings, he sent messengers to Abram, saying, "Give me my people back, but keep all the goods for yourself."

But Abram replied, "I have sworn an oath that I will accept no reward. I will take nothing that belongs to you, not even a thread or the strap of a sandal.

That way you will never be able to say, 'I made Abram rich.' I will accept nothing except what my men have eaten while we were in your lands."

God's promise to Abraham and Sarah

When Abram was ninety-nine years old, God appeared to him and said, "You will no longer be called Abram. Your name will now be Abraham." Abram means father of the heights, but Abraham means father of a multitude. And God breathed his breath of life over Abraham.

God continued, "I will keep the promise I made to you. I will make you a father of nations and of kings. I will give you and your descendants the whole land of Canaan, where you now live as a foreigner."

God also said to Abraham, "And your wife, Sarai, will now be named Sarah. You will have a son with her." Sarai means my princess, and Sarah means princess of many. And he breathed his breath of life over Sarah.

Abraham fell face down and laughed. "How will my wife have a child at the age of ninety?"

God replied, "Sarah will bear you a son, and you will call him Isaac." Isaac means "laughter".

God visits as three angels

Soon after this, God appeared to Abraham while he was at home, sitting in the shade of the oaks of Mamre.

Abraham looked up and saw three men nearby. He did not know who they were, but it was the custom to welcome strangers, so he walked over to them and bowed low to the ground. He said, "My lords, if it would please you, let me bring you some water, so you may wash your feet and then rest under this tree. Let me get you something to eat, so you may feel refreshed and then go on your way."

"Very well," they answered.

So Abraham quickly went into the tent and asked Sarah to take the finest flour and bake some bread, for they had guests. Then he hurried to his herd, selected a tender calf and gave it to a servant to prepare.

He soon brought the three men some curds and milk, then the meat that the servant had prepared, and placed everything before them in the shade of the trees.

"Where is your wife, Sarah?" they asked.

Abraham was surprised they knew his wife's name, but he answered, "There, in the tent."

One of the men replied, "I will return to you this time next year, and Sarah will have a son."

Now Abraham began to feel that these men were perhaps not just ordinary passers-by, for they were repeating God's words to him.

Sarah had been listening at the entrance to the tent, just behind Abraham, and when she heard what the stranger said, she laughed to herself. "I am far too old to have a child," she thought.

Then God – for it was God who appeared as the three strangers – said to Abraham, "Why did Sarah laugh? Is anything too hard for God? I will return to you this time next year, and Sarah will have a son."

Coming out of the tent, Sarah was afraid, so she lied and said, "I did not laugh."

But God replied, "Yes, you did."

When the men had finished they got up to leave, and Abraham walked alongside to show them the way. From the heights of Mamre, they could see the fertile plain of Sodom and the neighbouring town of Gomorrah, whose people had turned their backs on God.

God said, "I have heard that the people in Sodom and Gomorrah are very wicked. I will go down and see for myself, and if what they have done is as bad as the outcry that has reached me, then I shall utterly destroy them."

When Abraham heard this, he was sure that it was God appearing to him as three men. As they turned away and headed towards Sodom, Abraham thought of his nephew Lot and his family. He approached God and asked, "Will you sweep away good and honest people with the wicked? What if there are fifty good people there? Will you really sweep them all away? Surely you would not do such a thing, treating the good and the wicked alike?"

God said, "If I find fifty good and honest people in the city of Sodom, I will spare the whole place for their sake."

And Abraham was satisfied for a moment, but then he began to wonder if there really would be that many good people in Sodom. What if there was only Lot and his family? It would seem selfish to plead just for them... but perhaps if he approached it slowly he might be able to. So Abraham spoke up again.

"Now that I have been so bold as to speak to you, Lord God, though I am nothing but dust and ashes, what if the number of good people is five fewer than fifty? Will you destroy the whole city for the lack of five people?"

"If I find forty-five there," God said, "I will not destroy it."

Once again Abraham spoke. "What if only forty are found there?"

God said, "For the sake of forty, I will not do it."

Then Abraham said, "Please do not be angry, Lord, but what if only thirty can be found there?"

God answered, "I will not do it if I find thirty there."

And Abraham asked, "And what if only twenty can be found there, Lord?"

And God replied, "For the sake of twenty, I will not destroy it."

Then Abraham said, "Please do not be angry, Lord, but let me speak just once more. What if only ten can be found there?"

And God answered, "For the sake of ten, I will not destroy it."

This time, when God had finished speaking, he left.

Abraham returned home.

The destruction of Sodom and Gomorrah

In the evening, God arrived at Sodom in the form of two men. Lot was sitting in the gateway of the city. When he saw the men, though he did not know them, he got up to meet them and bowed down with his face to the ground.

"My lords," he said, "I am your humble servant. Please come to my house. You can wash your feet and spend the night, then go on your way early in the morning."

"No," they answered, "we will spend the night outside."

But Lot insisted so strongly that they went with him to his house. There he prepared a meal for them, and they ate.

The neighbours had seen Lot going into his house with the strangers. They were curious and jealous, because Lot was a stranger to them too, and they were afraid that he would become richer and more powerful than they were. Before Lot and his guests had gone to bed, all the men of the city, young and old, came and surrounded the house. They called to Lot, "Where are the men who came to your house tonight? Bring them out and leave them with us."

Lot came out of his house and shut the door behind him. "No, my friends," he said. "Do not harm these people I have welcomed. You know our custom – when people are staying at our homes, they are under our protection."

But the crowd became angry because, though they knew that guests should always have the protection of their host, they hated Lot.

"Get out of our way!" they replied. "You came here as a foreigner, and now you want to play the judge! We'll treat you even worse than them."

They pushed and shoved Lot, and moved forward to break down the door. Just then, the two men inside reached out, pulled Lot back into the house and shut the door. Then they struck the men outside with blindness so that they could not find the door. The crowd fumbled around, hitting each other or bruising their hands on the rough walls, until they stumbled away.

In the quiet of the house, the two men said to Lot, "If you have family or any servants in the city, get them out of here. The outcry against the wicked people of this city is so great that the Lord God has sent us to destroy it."

In the dark of night, Lot went out and spoke to the young men who were pledged to marry his daughters, and warned them. "Hurry, leave this place, because the Lord God is about to destroy the city!" But the young men thought he was joking and refused to leave.

Just as the sky was lightening in the east with the coming of dawn, the two men urged Lot to leave: "Hurry! Take your wife and your two daughters now, or you will be swept away when the city is punished."

Lot hesitated, so the men grasped his hand and led Lot and his family safely out of the city. One of the men said, "Run for your lives! Do not look back or stop anywhere on the plain. Escape to the mountains or you will be swept away!"

But Lot replied, "My lords, you have shown great kindness by sparing my life and the lives of my wife and my daughters. But I cannot run all the way to the mountains; this disaster will overtake us and we will die. Look, over there is a small town near enough to run to. Let us escape there instead."

One of the men said to him, "Very well, I will grant you this request and will not destroy that small town. But run there quickly, because I cannot do anything until you reach it. And do not look back."

Just as the sun was rising, Lot reached the little town and heard an almighty roar. He saw that the whole sky was red, as fire and burning sulphur rocks rained down on Sodom and Gomorrah. Lot saw that God had wiped out those cities and the entire plain, destroying all those living there as well as everything growing on the land.

Then Lot noticed that, in the confusion, his wife had disappeared. As the great fire began to die down, he went looking for her. He found her facing back towards the city, but she had become a pillar of salt. She had disobeyed the men's warning to not look back.

Early the next morning Abraham got up and returned to the place where he had stood before God. He looked down towards Sodom and over the plain, and he saw dense smoke rising from the land. Abraham was saddened that there were not even ten good and honest people in the city to stop its destruction, but he rejoiced when he heard that Lot and his daughters were safe.

Isaac

The sacrifice of Isaac

A year after the three angels visited Abraham, Sarah gave birth to a son. They called him Isaac, as God had told them. Since God had given them the breath of new life and new names, Abraham and Sarah felt younger again. When Isaac was a young boy there was a drought in the hill country of Judea, so Abraham and all his followers moved south to the plains of the Negev and settled at Beersheba, which means "well of seven".

When Isaac was about twelve years old, God decided to test Abraham to see if he was worthy of being the father of many descendants. God said to Abraham, "Take your son Isaac, whom you love, and go to Moriah, to a mountain I will show you. There, sacrifice him as an offering to me."

Abraham was shocked by God's request, but he felt deeply that he must obey God's word. With a heavy heart, Abraham rose early the next morning, before Sarah and the rest of the household. He woke Isaac and two of his servants, and they cut enough wood to make an offering. They loaded the wood onto a donkey then set off for Moriah. Like Abraham's earlier travels, at every crossroad or fork in the path he heard the voice of God telling him which way to take.

It was a long journey from Beersheba to the mountain. The whole time, Abraham pondered the word of God, wondering how he could have descendants if he sacrificed his only son. But he knew that God's will was not always easy to understand.

On the third day, Abraham looked up and saw they were close to the mountain. He told his servants, "Stay with the donkey while I go over there to worship with my son. We will return soon."

Abraham took the wood and gave it to Isaac to carry, while he carried a knife and a little oil lamp to light the fire. They walked for a while in silence, until Isaac asked, "Father, the fire and the wood are here, but where is the lamb to burn for the offering?"

It was the question that Abraham had been dreading. Eventually, he simply said, "God will provide the lamb for the offering." And Isaac was content with the answer his father had given him.

They continued until they arrived at Moriah. Together they built an altar from stones and wood, ready for the sacrifice. While Isaac laid the last piece of wood on top, Abraham seized him, tied him up, laid him on the altar, and held his knife, ready to sacrifice him. Isaac was too surprised to say anything.

Just then, God spoke through an angel, who called from heaven: "Abraham, Abraham!"

Abraham replied, "Here I am."

And the angel said, "Do not lay your hand on the boy. Do not do anything to him. Now I know that you respect and obey God, because you were willing to sacrifice your only son."

Abraham looked up, and there in a thicket he saw a ram caught by its horns. He captured the ram, untied Isaac and sacrificed the ram as a burnt offering. Everything had happened so fast that Isaac had been in a daze, but he saw that his father's words had come true: God had provided the animal for the offering.

The angel of God called to Abraham from heaven a second time, saying, "Because you were willing to sacrifice your son for me, I promise that I will bless you and make your descendants as numerous as the stars in the sky and the sand on the seashore. Your descendants will take possession of the cities of the land, and through your offspring all the people on earth will be blessed, because you have obeyed me."

Full of joy, Abraham returned with Isaac to his servants, and together they set off back to their home in Beersheba.

Isaac and Rebekah

When Abraham was very old he called his faithful servant Eliezer and said, "I want you to promise by the Lord God that you will not find a wife for my son, Isaac, from the people of this land. Instead, go to my country, the Land of the Two Rivers, and my own relatives to find him a wife."

Eliezer asked, "But what if the woman is unwilling to come with me? Shall I then take your son back to the country you came from?"

Abraham calmly replied, "Do not take my son back there. The Lord God told me that he will send an angel to help you find a wife for my son. If the woman is unwilling to come back with you, then you may return without her."

So Eliezer made the promise to his master Abraham and prepared for the long journey to Haran, the city in the Land of the Two Rivers where Abraham's family had come from. Eliezer and his men loaded ten of his master's camels with all kinds of gifts as well as provisions for the journey, then they set out.

When, after many days' journey, Eliezer reached the town, he made the camels kneel near the well outside the city walls. It was almost evening, the time when the daughters of the townspeople came to draw water.

Eliezer prayed, "Lord, God of my master Abraham, show kindness to him and make me successful today. When I ask a young woman, 'Please, could you give me a little water,' and she says, 'Drink, and I will draw water for your camels too' – let her be the one you have chosen for your servant Isaac."

Before he had finished praying, a young woman called Rebekah came out with her jar on her shoulder. When she had finished filling her jar from the well, Eliezer hurried to meet her and asked, "Please, could you give me a little water from your jar?"

"Drink, my lord," she said, taking the jar off her shoulder and giving it to him. Then she said, "I will draw water for your camels too."

Rebekah emptied her jar into the animal trough and ran back to the well to draw more water. She had to make several trips, for after a long journey the camels were very thirsty.

When the camels had finished drinking, Eliezer took out a gold ring and two gold bracelets and placed them on her finger and arms. He asked, "Please tell me, is there room in your father's house for us to spend the night?"

She answered, "We have plenty of straw and fodder, as well as room for you to spend the night." She also named her father and grandfather, and Eliezer realised that Rebekah was the granddaughter of Abraham's brother.

Then Eliezer bowed down and worshipped God, saying, "Praise be to the Lord, God of my master Abraham, who has not abandoned his kindness and faithfulness to my master."

Rebekah ran home and told her family about what had happened. After her brother, Laban, heard her story and saw the ring and the bracelets on her arms, he went out to find Eliezer.

"Come, you who are blessed by God," he said. "Why are you standing out here? I have prepared the house and a place for the camels."

So Eliezer went to the house. Straw and fodder were brought for the camels, who were settled in the open courtyard. Water was brought for Eliezer and his men to wash their feet. They were given food, but Eliezer said, "I will not eat until I have told you what I have to say."

"Then tell us," Laban said.

"I am Abraham's servant," said Eliezer. "The Lord God has blessed my master, Abraham, and he has become wealthy. He has given him sheep and cattle, silver and gold, camels and donkeys, and many servants. My master's wife, Sarah, has given birth to a son in her old age, and he has given his son everything he owns. Abraham sent me here, to his family, to find a wife for his son."

Then Eliezer told them how, when he came to the well outside the city, he prayed for God to give him a sign to show him who he had chosen to marry Isaac, and how Rebekah had said and done all the things he had asked for.

Laban and Rebekah's father said, "This is truly a sign from the Lord God. If she is willing, let Rebekah become the wife of your master's son, as the Lord God has directed."

Rebekah agreed, and Eliezer bowed down to the ground before God. Then he brought out gold and silver jewellery and clothing and gave them to Rebekah, and he also gave precious gifts to her brother and to her mother. Only after all this did he and his men sit down to eat and drink.

The next morning, Rebekah's brother and her mother asked Eliezer, "Will you let Rebekah remain with us for ten days or so before you go?"

Eliezer said to them, "Please do not delay me, now that the Lord God has made my journey successful."

They replied, "Let's call Rebekah," and asked her, "Will you go with this man today?"

"I will go," she said simply. Rebekah and her attendants got ready, then mounted the camels and travelled to Beersheba in the land of Canaan with Eliezer and his men.

One evening, Isaac was out in the field when he looked up and saw camels approaching.

Rebekah also looked up and saw Isaac. She got down from her camel and asked Eliezer, "Who is that man in the field coming to meet us?"

"He is my master's son, Isaac," Eliezer answered.

She quickly covered herself with her veil, as was the custom. Then Eliezer told Isaac everything that had happened. Isaac and Rebekah were married, and they loved each other.

Jacob

Jacob and Esau

Isaac and Rebekah had been married for twenty years, but had no children. Isaac prayed to God, and God answered his prayer. Rebekah realised that she was pregnant with twins, because they were restless and she could feel them fighting inside her womb. She was troubled and prayed to God, asking, "Lord, why are these two babies fighting each other?"

God answered, "You are carrying two nations within you, and the two peoples will be separated: one people will be stronger than the other, and the older will serve the younger."

Soon Rebekah gave birth to twin boys. The first baby was covered with red hair all over his body, so they named him Esau, which means "hairy one".

When the second baby was born, his hand was grasping Esau's heel. They named him Jacob, which means "heel-catcher".

Esau grew up to be strong and a skilful hunter, and he was Isaac's favourite. Because Esau was the eldest, Isaac saw him as the son from whom the promised descendants would come. But Rebekah loved Jacob, who was content to stay at home, and was quiet, thoughtful and cunning.

One day Esau came home from hunting, very hungry, and found Jacob alone, cooking some stew. He said to Jacob, "Quick, let me have some of that stew! I'm famished!"

Jacob knew that Esau, as the eldest son, would inherit all their father's possessions, so he replied, "First sell me your birthright."

Esau was so hungry, he said, "Look, I am about to die from hunger. What good is the birthright to me?"

But Jacob said, "Swear to me first."

So Esau swore an oath, selling his birthright to Jacob for some stew. And neither brother said anything about it to their parents.

Jacob steals Esau's blessing

Isaac grew old and his eyes grew weaker until, one day, he became blind. Feeling that he might soon die, he called Esau and said, "My son, I am an old man and the day of my death is near. Take your bow and arrows, and hunt some wild game for me. Prepare some tasty food that I like and bring it to me, so that I can give you my blessing before I die."

Rebekah was listening at the door, and as soon as Esau left, she called Jacob and told him what she had heard. Then she said to Jacob, "Now listen carefully. Go and bring two of the best young goats from our flock, and I will prepare some tasty food for your father as he likes it. Then take it to your father so that he will give you his blessing."

But Jacob said, "What if my father touches me? Esau has hairy skin, while mine is smooth. If my father thinks I am tricking him, he will curse rather than bless me."

Rebekah said, "If that happens, let the curse fall upon me. Now go and do what I told you."

So Jacob did as she said. Then she told Jacob to dress in Esau's best clothes, and covered the backs of his hands and his neck with some goatskin. Finally, she gave Jacob the tasty food she had made. Jacob took it to his father.

Isaac asked, "Who is it?"

Jacob replied, "I am Esau, your firstborn son. I have done as you told me. Father, sit up, eat some of my food and give me your blessing."

Isaac was surprised, and asked, "How did you find wild game so quickly, my son?

"God helped me," Jacob replied.

Isaac said, "Come closer, so that I can touch you and know whether you are really Esau."

Jacob moved close, and Isaac felt his hands and arms. But he was still a little puzzled. "Your voice is like Jacob's voice, but your hands are like Esau's. Are you really Esau?"

Jacob simply replied, "I am."

So Isaac asked for the food and Jacob brought it to him, along with some wine.

Isaac then said, "Come here and kiss me."

When Jacob did that, Isaac caught the smell of his clothes and was finally convinced. "The smell of my son Esau is like the smell of a field that the Lord God has blessed."

Then he spoke a blessing: "May God give you dew from heaven and richness from the earth, so that you have plentiful grain and wine. May many nations serve you, and people bow down to you, and may you be lord over your brother. And may those who bless you be blessed."

After blessing Jacob, Isaac sent him away. Only moments later, Esau came into his father's room. He had returned from hunting and prepared some tasty food. He brought it to Isaac, saying, "Father, sit up, eat some of my food, and give me your blessing."

Isaac asked, "Who are you?"

"I am your firstborn son, Esau," he replied.

Isaac trembled with fear. "Who was it, then, that brought food to me? Just before you came, I ate it and blessed him. And he will be blessed, for I cannot take that back."

Esau realised that his father had been tricked, and he burst into a loud and bitter cry. "But Father, bless me too!"

Isaac only answered, "Your brother deceived me and took your blessing."

Esau replied, "It is not for nothing he is called Jacob, the heel-catcher! It is the second time he has tricked me. First, he took my birthright, and now he has taken my blessing. Father, is there really no blessing left for me?"

Isaac said, "I have made your brother lord over you and all your relatives and servants. I have blessed him with grain and wine. What can I give you?"

"Do you only have one blessing? Bless me too, Father!" Esau pleaded.

Then Isaac declared, "You will dwell away from the richness of the earth and away from the dew of heaven. You will live by your sword, and you will serve your brother until you throw off that burden."

Esau was very angry with Jacob and held a grudge against him. He muttered, "When my father has died, and the time of mourning is over, I will kill Jacob."

Some time later, a servant told Rebekah about Esau's oath to kill his brother. She called for Jacob and told him, "After I have spoken to your father, you must flee to my brother, Laban, in Haran, in the Land of the Two Rivers. Stay there until your brother's anger has passed. When he forgets what you have done, I shall send word to you to return."

Then Rebekah went to Isaac and said, "I cannot bear the thought of Jacob marrying one of the women of Canaan."

Isaac called Jacob and told him, "Do not marry a woman from these lands. Go to Haran and ask one of the daughters of Laban, your mother's brother, to be your wife. May God bless you and give you many children. May he give you and your descendants the land, as God promised to Abraham your grandfather."

So Isaac sent Jacob away.

Jacob's ladder to heaven

Jacob left his parents' home in Beersheba and went north through the mountains of Judea. After sunset, he stopped, took a stone to rest his head on and lay down to sleep. He felt troubled about tricking his brother and having to flee.

He dreamed he saw a ladder that rested on the earth and reached right up to heaven. Angels were ascending and descending the ladder, and God stood at the very top.

God said, "I am the Lord, the God of your grandfather Abraham and your father Isaac. I will give you and your descendants the land on which you are lying. Your descendants shall be as countless as the dust of the earth, and they will spread to the west and the east, to the north and the south. All the people on earth will be blessed through you and your descendants. I will watch over you and bring you back to this land. I will not leave you until I have done what I have promised."

When Jacob woke up, he felt a great sense of wonder. He felt that God was in this place and was all-powerful. He even felt God forgave him for

deceiving his brother. Jacob declared, "This place fills me with awe. It is the house of God and the gate to heaven."

Early the next morning, he took the stone on which he had rested his head and set it up as a pillar. In those days all holy places and holy people were anointed with oil, so Jacob poured oil on the pillar. He called the place Bethel, which means "the house of God". Though Jacob did not know it, his grandfather Abraham had also stopped at this place to build an altar, and he had also called it Bethel.

Jacob made a promise to God: "If God will be with me on this journey, if he will give me food and clothes and let me return safely to my father's house, the Lord God will be my God. This stone that I have set up will be God's house, and I will make an offering on my return."

Jacob meets Rachel

After many days of travelling, Jacob came to a well in the countryside. Shepherds with their flocks of sheep were gathered around it, waiting to draw water. A large stone covered the top of the well to stop the water evaporating in the heat.

Jacob asked the shepherds where they were from, and they replied, "Haran."

Realising he was close to the end of his journey, Jacob asked them, "Do you know Laban?"

"Of course we know him," they replied. "Look, his daughter Rachel is making her way here with the sheep."

It was midday, and Jacob wondered why the shepherds did not give water to their sheep and take them back to graze. But the shepherds told him they would have to wait until every shepherd arrived, so that together they could roll the great stone from the mouth of the well.

While they were talking, Rachel reached the well with her father's flock. Jacob saw that Rachel was beautiful, and he felt great joy and love for her. He was suddenly filled with such strength that he rolled the stone from the well by himself. Ignoring the other shepherds, he drew up water for his uncle's sheep. He greeted Rachel and told her that he was the son of Rebekah, her father's sister. Rachel was intrigued by the tale, and she ran immediately and told her father.

As soon as Laban heard the news about Jacob, he hurried out to meet him and invited him back to his home.

After Jacob had stayed at Laban's house for a whole month, Laban said, "You are my relative and part of my family, but you should not work for me for nothing. Tell me what I should pay you."

Laban had two daughters. Rachel was the youngest, and her elder sister was called Leah. Jacob was in love with Rachel, and said to Laban, "I will work for you for seven years if you will let me marry Rachel." Laban agreed.

Jacob worked for seven years, but the time passed so quickly if felt like just a few days because he got to be with Rachel, whom he loved so much. Jacob worked hard and took great care of the flocks, which grew in size as never before, and Laban came to rely on him.

When the seven years were over, Jacob reminded Laban, "My time is completed. Let me now marry Rachel."

Laban called everyone together for a great wedding feast. The bride, covered in veils as was the custom in those times, sat next to Jacob. He would not get to see the face of his wife until the following morning. When they awoke, Jacob discovered that he had married Leah: Laban had tricked him, just as Jacob had tricked Esau.

Jacob went in a fury to Laban, asking, "I served you for seven years in exchange for Rachel's hand in marriage. Why have you deceived me?"

"It is not our custom to marry the younger daughter before the older one," answered Laban. "But after a week, you may also marry my younger daughter in return for another seven years of work."

Jacob agreed, because in those days men often had more than one wife. After a week he married Rachel too, and served Laban for another seven years. But Jacob loved Rachel, not Leah.

Jacob leaves Laban

When God saw that Jacob did not love Leah, he made it possible for her to have children, but Rachel remained without a child. Jacob became a father to ten sons and a daughter before Rachel finally bore a son. She named him Joseph, and Jacob loved him more than any of his other children.

Now he felt it was time to return to Canaan, the land of his birth. He said to Laban, "I have worked for you for fourteen years, now let me go back to my homeland with my wives and children."

But Laban said, "God has blessed me because you are here with me. Please stay, and tell me what you would like to be paid."

Jacob said, "Your flocks have grown in number since I came and served you, and God has blessed you wherever I have been. I shall look after your flock, but for my wages let me own the spotted and striped sheep and goats. You will own all the single-coloured ones, so you will know that any single-coloured animals in my flock have been stolen from you".

Laban agreed, because the wool from single-coloured sheep and goats was much more valuable. But he again tricked Jacob by removing all the spotted and striped animals from the flock, putting them in his sons' care and sending them three days' journey away. Laban left Jacob to care for all the single-coloured sheep and goats, knowing that he would have no animals of his own.

Jacob, however, was also cunning. He took fresh-cut tree branches and peeled back strips of bark so that white stripes and spots appeared. He set these branches into the ground where the flocks came for water. After a time, as if by some kind of magic, the lambs and kids that were born to these flocks became striped and spotted, and also stronger. And now these strong, young sheep belonged to Jacob, while the older, single-coloured animals were Laban's.

Jacob noticed that Laban and his sons were becoming jealous, saying, "Everything Jacob has gained in wealth he has taken from us."

One day, God spoke to Jacob, telling him to go back to the land of his fathers, and promising to be with him.

Jacob sent for Rachel and Leah to come from the fields with his flocks. He told them, "Your father has changed his attitude to me. I have worked for him with all my strength and brought him wealth, but he has changed the wages we agreed and cheated me. God has spoken to me and told me, 'I have seen everything Laban is doing to you. I am the God of Bethel, where you anointed a pillar and made a vow to me. Now leave this land and return home.'"

Rachel and Leah replied, "Do whatever God has told you."

Like most people of the Land of the Two Rivers, Laban had a family shrine where he kept little statues of gods and worshipped them. Without Jacob knowing, Rachel went to the family shrine and stole her father's statues. Laban had left for a few days to shear his sheep, so Jacob loaded up his camels with all his goods, as well as his wives and children, and gathered all his servants to help drive his flock before him.

And so Jacob left Haran to return to the land of Canaan.

Laban pursues Jacob

After three days, Laban returned and was told that Jacob had left. He also discovered that the statues of his gods had disappeared from his shrine. Laban was angry that his daughters and grandchildren had not said farewell to him. Taking his sons with him, he set off in pursuit, but during the night God told him in a dream: "Do nothing to harm Jacob."

After seven days Laban caught up with Jacob, and asked him, "What have you done? You have deceived me and taken away my daughters. You did not even let me kiss my daughters and grandchildren goodbye. Why did you do such a foolish thing? And why did you steal my household gods? But it is not in my power to harm you, because last night the God of your fathers warned me not to in a dream."

Jacob answered, "God told me to leave and I was afraid that you would not let me go and would stop me from taking my wives with me. As for your household gods, I know nothing of them. You can search all my possessions, and if you find them, the person who took them shall die. If there is anything else of yours here, then take it."

Laban set about searching for the statues of his gods. He searched in Jacob's tent, in Leah's and among the servants' things, before going to Rachel's tent. Rachel had hidden the gods inside her camel's saddle, which she was sitting upon. She said, "Allow me to remain sitting while you search." So Laban found nothing.

Jacob was angry now, and asked Laban, "What is my crime? I have done nothing to harm you and taken nothing of yours. I have served you for twenty years – fourteen years for your daughters and six years for the flock – and you have grown rich because your flocks have increased. If the God of my fathers, the God of Abraham and of Isaac, had not been with me, you would have sent me away empty-handed, but God has seen my hardship and my work, and last night he spoke to you."

Jacob suggested they make a pact, so he set up a stone pillar and his people gathered stones around it. Laban said, "Let these stones be a witness, and may God keep watch over you and me when we are away from each other. I will not go past these stones to harm you, and you will not go past them to harm me."

Both men offered a sacrifice to God, and they and all their followers had a meal together. Laban spent the night there, and early the next morning he kissed his daughters and grandchildren goodbye. Jacob and Laban parted in peace.

Jacob wrestles with the angel

Jacob travelled on towards Canaan until he came to the ford of the River Jabbok. He had sent some of his servants ahead with the flocks, so they had already crossed. Late in the evening, he sent his remaining servants across the ford with his wives and children and their possessions. When it was dark, Jacob prepared to ford the river alone. Suddenly a man appeared, who began to fight him. The man was so powerful that Jacob felt he must be an angel of God. Yet Jacob, too, was strong, and they wrestled all night.

At dawn, the man touched Jacob's hip and Jacob felt a great pain in his leg. Then the man said, "I must go now, for day is breaking."

Now Jacob was sure that the man was an angel of God, and replied, "No, I will not let you go until you give me your blessing."

"What is your name?" the angel asked.

"Jacob."

"Your name will no longer be Jacob," the angel said.

Jacob was dumbstruck. He did not want to be left nameless!

But the angel continued, "Your name shall be Israel, because you have struggled and fought with God." Israel means "he who strives and is upright before God".

Jacob suddenly felt new life and strength enter him. He asked the angel's name, but he only replied, "Why do you ask my name?" Then he blessed Jacob and vanished.

Jacob called that place Peniel – meaning "the face of God" – saying, "Here I saw God face to face, and yet I did not die." Then the sun rose, and Jacob (now also named Israel) joined his family across the ford, limping because of his injured hip.

Jacob returns to live in Canaan

Jacob had sent some of his servants and flocks ahead to meet his brother, Esau, and give him gifts, because Jacob was unsure of how his brother would feel about him returning. He had not seen Esau since he had fled after tricking him out of their father's blessing. But Esau travelled a long distance from his home to come and meet him, and when he spotted Jacob he ran to embrace him.

"Come home quickly. When our father Isaac heard you were returning, he rejoiced. He is very old now, but he is longing to hear from you."

Jacob replied, "You hurry on ahead. I have large flocks and family. We will follow at a comfortable pace."

On his way home, Jacob stopped at Shechem, where his grandfather Abraham had built his first altar. There, God spoke to Jacob, telling him to return to Bethel – but first he needed to get rid of any household gods that his followers had brought with them. His servants brought out their household gods, and Rachel revealed those she had stolen from her father.

She had seen for herself, now, how God blessed Jacob without him having any little statues to worship. Jacob buried them under the oak at Shechem and then took his whole company to Bethel.

Once more God spoke to him there: "No longer will you be called Jacob; your name is Israel. The land I promised to Abraham and to Isaac, I will give to you and your descendants."

Israel set up another stone pillar and made an offering on it, as he had promised. Once more he named the place Bethel, the house of God.

On their way south from Bethel, Rachel gave birth to another son, but she died as soon as he was born. Israel buried Rachel and set up a stone pillar to mark her tomb, which still stands outside the village of Bethlehem. Israel named his youngest son Benjamin, which means "son of the south" or "son of the right".

Finally, Israel returned to Hebron, to the oak of Mamre, where Isaac – now a very old man – welcomed his son, his twelve grandsons and his granddaughter.

Joseph

Joseph's dreams

Jacob was now called Israel, and he had twelve sons named Reuben, Simeon, Levi, Judah, Dan, Naphtali, Gad, Asher, Issachar, Zebulun, Joseph and Benjamin, as well as a daughter named Dinah. His favourite child was Joseph, Rachel's firstborn son. As Joseph grew, in his eyes Israel saw the eyes of Rachel; in his voice he heard the voice of Rachel; and in his walk he saw the walk of Rachel, the woman he had loved since he had first set eyes on her. Israel made Joseph a special coat of many colours, which he wore all the time.

When Joseph's brothers saw that their father loved him more than any of them, they hated him. None of them had a good word to say about him.

But Joseph seemed unaware of their feelings, and lived in a world of his own. One day he said to them, "Listen to the dream I had. We were binding sheaves of grain in the field, when suddenly my sheaf stood upright and your sheaves gathered around mine and bowed down to it."

His brothers mocked him, saying, "What? Do you think you are going to rule over us?" And they hated him all the more.

Later he had another dream and told his father and brothers, "This time the sun and moon and eleven stars bowed down to me."

His father rebuked him. "What kind of a dream is that? Is it supposed to mean that your mother (may she rest in peace) and I, and your brothers should bow down to the ground before you?"

Nevertheless, Israel kept the dream in his heart, in case some truth may come from it one day. But Joseph's brothers were still jealous and hated him even more.

Joseph is sold to Egypt

Joseph's brothers had gone to graze their father's flocks near Shechem in the north. When they had been away for quite some time, Israel told Joseph, "Go and see how your brothers and our flocks are getting on, then bring back word to me."

"Very well, I will go," said Joseph.

Joseph took his many-coloured coat and set off from Hebron, going north to where the land was a little greener and there was better grazing. Soon after passing Shechem, he saw his brothers and began to run joyfully towards them.

When they saw him in the distance, they groaned, "Here comes the dreamer. Let's kill him and throw him into one of the empty cisterns." The cisterns were deep holes dug out of the rocks to store water from the winter rains. "We can say that a wild animal attacked and ate him. Then we'll see what comes of his dreams," they said to one another.

But Reuben, the oldest son, felt uneasy about this plan. Although he did not like Joseph, he did not want to kill him, so he said, "Let's not shed blood or take his life. We can throw him into the cistern and just leave him there." That way, Reuben could come back to rescue Joseph and take him home to their father.

When Joseph caught up with his brothers he reached out to embrace them, but instead they grabbed him, tore off his many-coloured coat, tied him up and threw him into the cistern.

Joseph called after them, "What's happening? Where are you going? Please don't leave me here!" But the brothers turned and ran.

Reuben went to check on the sheep and goats while the others sat down to eat a meal. As they were eating, they saw a caravan – a long line of camels tied together. This was the way merchants transported their goods over long distances in those days, because camels can carry great loads over rough tracks and across deserts, and they can go for many days without water. The merchants leading the caravan were going to Egypt, and their camels were loaded with spices, olive oil and myrrh.

One of the brothers said, "If we leave Joseph to die, we will have his blood on our hands, and he is after all our own brother. Let us sell him to the merchants instead."

So when the merchants came by, Joseph's brothers pulled him out of the cistern and sold him for twenty silver coins to the merchants, who carried him off on their caravan of camels to Egypt.

When Reuben returned from checking the flocks, he looked into the cistern and saw Joseph was not there. In great alarm, he ran to his brothers, telling them that Joseph had disappeared. They told him what had happened, and although Reuben was upset at what they had done, he went along with their plan. They killed a goat and dipped Joseph's coloured coat in the blood.

When they returned home, they showed their father the coat and said, "We found this robe. Is it Joseph's?"

Israel immediately recognised it. "It is my son's! Some wild animal must have ripped him to pieces."

Israel tore his clothes in anguish and mourned for his favourite son. His children tried to comfort him, but he swore, "I will continue to mourn for Joseph until the day I die." And Israel would not be comforted.

Joseph's rise and fall in Egypt

Meanwhile, the merchants travelled to Egypt with Joseph. There, Joseph saw many strange things that he had never seen before. After days of journeying across the desert, the land suddenly turned green. There were wheat fields and orange trees, palms with dates hanging from them and ditches of water everywhere. There was a great river with boats sailing on it, called the River Nile. Joseph had never seen such a big river; where he grew up, rushing brooks would spring up for a day or two after it rained and then dry out again. Beyond the river, Joseph saw some smooth white mountains. The merchants spoke in awe when they told him, "They are the pyramids."

Finally, they arrived at the city where Pharaoh, the king of Egypt, lived. Potiphar, the captain of Pharaoh's guard, was looking to buy a servant, and the merchants sold Joseph to him.

Potiphar soon found that Joseph was a willing helper who quickly learned new things, including the Egyptian language. God was always with Joseph, and everything Joseph did turned out well. Before long, Potiphar put him in charge of his whole household. That meant Joseph had to make sure there was always enough food in the house, to plant the right vegetables in the garden at the right time, and to check that Potiphar and his family always had clean clothes, so he had to tell the other servants what needed doing each day.

Potiphar's wife saw how handsome Joseph was, and she began to love him. But her love was selfish and she wanted Joseph all to herself. One day, when Potiphar was away, she tried to persuade Joseph to come and visit her alone. But he refused, saying, "My master has entrusted me with everything, except you, because you are his wife. How could I break his trust by visiting you?"

She would not leave him in peace, and one day when no one was around she caught his cloak and said, "Come with me."

But Joseph slipped off the cloak, leaving it in her hand, and ran from the house. Potiphar's wife was filled with rage. With his cloak in her hand, she called out aloud, "Help!"

When the servants came running, she said, "Look, Joseph, this foreigner, came to harass me, but when I called for help he ran away, leaving his cloak behind."

That evening when Potiphar returned home, she told him the story, adding, "And that is how the servant you bought and trusted has treated me."

Potiphar was very angry. He found Joseph and put him in prison.

But even in prison God was with Joseph, and the prison warden soon noticed how helpful Joseph was. Before long, the warden, a lazy man, put Joseph to work and made him do all his tasks, organising everything that happened in the prison.

Joseph interprets dreams in prison

Some time later, Pharaoh, the great ruler of Egypt, had guests visiting for a meal. The chief baker was to bake the best bread and the chief cupbearer was to serve the best wine. But when Pharaoh tasted the bread, he bit on a small stone that had found its way into the dough. And when he tasted the wine, it was sour. Pharaoh was angry, and summoned the chief baker and chief cupbearer and had them cast into the prison where Joseph was being kept.

After the baker and cupbearer had been imprisoned for a time, they each had a mysterious dream. When Joseph saw them the next morning, he saw they were troubled and asked, "Why do you look so sad today?"

They answered, "We both had strange dreams, but we have no one to interpret them."

Then Joseph said, "Tell me your dreams."

So the chief cupbearer told Joseph his dream: "I saw a vine in front of me, with three branches. As soon as it came into bud it blossomed and its clusters ripened into grapes. Pharaoh's cup was in my hand, and I took the grapes, squeezed them into Pharaoh's cup, and put the cup in his hand. Then he drank from it."

"This is the meaning," Joseph said to him. "The three branches stand for three days. Within three days, Pharaoh will restore you to your position, and you will put Pharaoh's cup in his hand, just as you used to do when you were his cupbearer."

Joseph added, "When all goes well with you, remember me. Mention me to Pharaoh and get me out of this prison. I was carried off from the land of my birth and sold here as a slave, but I have done nothing to deserve being locked away."

"I will do that," said the chief cupbearer, who was happy with Joseph's interpretation.

Then the chief baker told Joseph his dream: "I was carrying three baskets of bread on my head. In the top basket were all kinds of baked cakes for Pharaoh, but the birds were eating them."

"This is the meaning," Joseph said to him. "The three baskets stand for three days. Within three days, Pharaoh will call you out of prison, but he will hang your body on a pole and the birds will eat your flesh."

The baker was alarmed and hoped that Joseph's explanation would not come true.

Three days later it was Pharaoh's birthday and he gave a feast for all his officials. He restored the chief cupbearer to his position, but he had the chief baker hung from a pole, just as Joseph had said when he interpreted their dreams.

However, in his joy, the chief cupbearer did not mention Joseph to Pharaoh. He forgot him.

Pharaoh makes Joseph his second-in-command

Two years later, Pharaoh had a dream. As he was standing by the River Nile, he saw seven cows grazing among the reeds. They were sleek and fat. Then another seven cows came out of the Nile and stood by the bank. They were sickly and thin. The thin cows then ate up the fat cows. After this, Pharaoh woke up.

He fell asleep again and had another dream. This time, seven strong and healthy heads of grain grew from a single stalk. Then seven other heads of grain sprouted, but they were thin and scorched by the desert wind. The thin heads of grain swallowed up the healthy grains.

In the morning, Pharaoh was troubled by his dreams. He called all his wise men and magicians to his court and told them his dreams, asking what they meant. But even after long discussions, none of the wise men or magicians could interpret the dreams. Pharaoh was even more troubled, and all the servants and officials at Pharaoh's palace were worried about him.

Then the chief cupbearer suddenly remembered Joseph, and said to Pharaoh, "My lord, when I was in prison, there was a foreigner who told me the meaning of a dream, and it came to pass exactly as he said it would."

So Pharaoh sent for Joseph. Joseph had to bathe and have his hair cut, and he was given new clothes, for he could not appear before Pharaoh looking as dirty and unkempt as he did in prison. And Joseph knew he must not speak to the great ruler like he might speak to others, saying "you", but must always address Pharaoh indirectly. When he was summoned into Pharaoh's presence, he bowed low.

Pharaoh said to Joseph, "I had a dream, and no one can tell me its meaning, but I have heard that you can interpret dreams."

"I cannot do it by myself," Joseph said, "but God will give Pharaoh the answer. God is warning Pharaoh, so that Pharaoh may be blessed."

Pharaoh then told Joseph his dreams of the seven fat cows and the seven gaunt cows, and of the seven healthy heads of grain and the seven scorched

heads. He added, "I told this dream to the wise men and magicians, but no one was able to tell me its meaning."

Joseph listened carefully. "Pharaoh's two dreams are one and the same," he said. "The seven fat cows and the seven healthy heads of grain are seven years of plenty. And the seven gaunt cows and the seven scorched heads of grain are seven years of famine. It is as I said to Pharaoh: God has shown Pharaoh what to do."

Joseph continued, "The famine will be so severe that no one will remember the years of plenty. The reason that Pharaoh had two dreams was that God has firmly decided on this, and it will soon come to pass. So let Pharaoh appoint a wise councillor to be in charge of the land, to take a fifth of all the harvest of Egypt during the seven years of abundance and store it safely to be used during the years of famine that are to come, so that the people will not starve."

Pharaoh and all his officials thought this was a good plan. Pharaoh said to Joseph, "Since God has made the meaning known only to you, there is no one as wise as you. You shall be in charge of my palace, and all the people shall obey your orders. Only I will be greater than you. I hereby put you in charge of the whole land of Egypt."

Then Pharaoh made Joseph his second-in-command: he put his ring on Joseph's finger, dressed him in robes of fine linen, put a gold chain around his neck, and had him ride in a chariot. Pharaoh said to him, "I am Pharaoh, but without your word no one will lift hand or foot in all of Egypt." Pharaoh also gave Joseph an Egyptian name, Zaphenath-Paneah, which means "the man to whom mysteries are revealed".

Pharaoh arranged for Joseph to marry Asenath, the daughter of the highest priest of the land. Before long, she had a son whom Joseph called Manasseh, which means "making someone forget", because he said that the birth of his son made him forget all his troubles in the years before. Later, Asenath had a second son, whom Joseph named Ephraim, meaning "fruitful", because God had made Joseph's life rewarding in the land of his suffering.

During the seven years of abundance, Joseph travelled up and down Egypt, collecting a fifth of the food that was produced and storing it. There was so much grain stored in each city that no one could keep track of it; it was like grains of sand on a beach.

Then the seven years of abundance came to an end, and there were seven years of famine, just as Joseph had said. When people began to feel the effects of the famine, they turned to Pharaoh for food. Pharaoh told the people, "Go to Joseph and do what he tells you."

Joseph opened the stores and sold grain to the people. And because there was famine in all the surrounding lands too, people came from far away to buy grain from Egypt.

Joseph's brothers go to Egypt

In Canaan, where Israel (as Jacob was now called) lived with Joseph's brothers, there was famine too. When Israel learned that there was grain in Egypt, he said to his sons, "Go there and buy some grain for us, so that we may live and not die."

He gave his ten oldest sons donkeys, money and sacks for grain and sent them off, but he kept Benjamin, Rachel's son, at home, for he feared that harm might come to him.

When the brothers arrived in Egypt, they were sent to Joseph. Joseph recognised them immediately, but pretended to be a stranger. He spoke to them in Egyptian and a translator repeated his words in Hebrew, the language of Abraham and his descendants. "Where do you come from?" he asked.

Not recognising Joseph in the splendid attire and gold chain of Pharaoh, his brothers replied, "We have come from Canaan to buy food."

Joseph remembered his dreams from years ago, when he dreamt that his brothers bowed down to him. Then he said, "You are spies who have come to see where our land is unprotected!"

"No, my lord," they answered. "We are honest men, not spies. We were twelve brothers, all born to one father who lives in Canaan. The youngest brother is still with our father, and one brother is no more."

"It is as I said. You are spies!" Joseph replied. And he had them cast into prison for three days.

On the third day, Joseph summoned his brothers and said, "You must prove to me that you are honest men. One of you must stay here in prison, while the others take grain back to your starving household in Canaan. Then you must bring your youngest brother to me, so that I can see whether your word is true. If you return without him, you will not live to see him or your father again."

Reuben, the oldest brother, said to the others, "Surely we are being punished for what we did to Joseph. We bound him and sold him as a slave."

They did not know that Joseph could understand every word of what they said to each other. Joseph was overcome with the memory of everything he had been through, and he went outside to weep. He had learned from his trials, and wanted his brothers to be tested and learn from their trials too. He returned and had Simeon, the second oldest of the brothers, taken away and bound. When the brothers paid for their grain, Joseph gave secret orders that their sacks be filled with grain, but that their money be put back into the sacks too. The sacks were loaded onto their donkeys and then Joseph sent them on their way.

When the brothers stopped for the night, one of them opened his sack to feed the donkeys, and saw the money sitting there.

"My silver has been returned," he said in fear. "What has God done to us? Now we will be accused of theft!"

When they arrived home in the land of Canaan, they told their father everything that had happened, and about the strict overseer in Egypt: "The man who is lord over all of Egypt spoke harshly to us and accused us of being spies. But we told him we were honest men, and we were twelve brothers, the youngest at home and one who is no more. Then he said that we had to prove we were honest. He kept Simeon and told the rest of us to go and fetch our youngest brother. If we bring Benjamin to him, he will release Simeon."

When they were emptying their sacks, they found silver in each. Then the brothers and their father were frightened.

"What have you done?" Israel cried. "First I lost Joseph, then Simeon, and now you want to take Benjamin. Everything is against me!"

Reuben promised his father, "Entrust Benjamin to my care and I will bring him back safely. If I fail, take both of my own sons and kill them."

But Israel would not hear of it. "My son will not go with you. Joseph, the son of my beloved Rachel, is dead. If anything befalls Benjamin, I shall not be able to live in peace and will die in sorrow."

The second journey to Egypt

The famine in Canaan was still severe, and when all the grain that the brothers had brought from Egypt was finished, Israel told his sons, "Go back and buy us some more food."

But the brothers said, "The man warned us solemnly that we would not live unless our youngest brother was with us. If we can take Benjamin, we will go to buy food, but if we cannot take him, we will not go to Egypt."

"Why did you have to tell this man that you had another brother?" asked Israel.

"The man questioned us about our family, and we simply answered," they replied. "How were we to know that he would ask us to bring him to Egypt?"

Judah, the fourth son, said, "Send Benjamin along with us, so that we and you and our children may live and not die. And if we do not bring Benjamin back safely with us, then I will bear the blame for it all my life."

At last Israel said, "If it must be, then take Benjamin. Put some of the best products of our land into your bags and give them to this man as a gift – some olive oil and some honey, spices and myrrh, pistachio nuts and almonds. Take double the amount of silver with you, for you must return the silver that was put back into your sacks. Perhaps it was a mistake. May God Almighty grant you mercy before the man so that he will let Simeon and Benjamin come back with you. As for me, if I am to lose my children, oh, then so be it."

The brothers hurried to Egypt with the gifts and money and Benjamin, and went to see Joseph. When Joseph saw Benjamin with his brothers, he told his steward to take them to his house: "Prepare a great feast. They are to eat with me at midday."

The brothers were afraid when they were taken there, thinking it was because of the silver that had been put back into their sacks the first time. "He wants to seize us and make us slaves," they worried.

They said to Joseph, "We beg your pardon, lord. We came here the first time to buy food, but when we stopped for the night on our journey home and opened our sacks, we each found the money we had paid you. So we have brought it back to you, as well as money to buy more food."

All this was translated into Egyptian by the interpreter, and Joseph's answers were then translated into Hebrew, so Joseph's brothers still took him for an Egyptian.

Joseph answered, "It is all in order. Do not be afraid, for I received the payment. It must have been your God, the God of your father, who put the silver back in your sacks."

Then he released Simeon, and the steward took all the brothers into Joseph's house to eat. There, they presented Joseph with the gifts they had brought. Joseph asked how they all were and how their aged father was.

They replied, "Your servant our father is still alive and well." And again they bowed down before him.

Joseph looked about and saw his brother Benjamin, his own mother's son, and said, "And this must be your youngest brother, the one you told me about."

Joseph ordered the food to be served. He sat at one table, his brothers at another, and at a third table sat the other Egyptians of Joseph's household. (Egyptians would not eat at the same table as foreigners.) The brothers were astonished that they had been seated before Joseph in order of age, because how could anyone tell their ages so exactly, seeing as they were all grown men?

When the food was served, Benjamin's portions were five times bigger than anyone else's.

The silver cup in the sack

When they had finished eating, Joseph quietly gave instructions to his steward: "Fill the men's sacks with grain and as much food as they can carry. Then put each man's silver in the top of his sack, and put my silver cup in the top of the sack of the youngest one."

The following morning at dawn, the eleven brothers set out for home again with their donkeys, greatly relieved that it had all gone so well. But they had only just left the city when Joseph's steward, riding a fast horse, caught up with them, calling (as Joseph had instructed him), "Stop at once! Why have you repaid good with evil? You have stolen my master's silver cup!"

They were surprised and asked, "Why does my lord say this? We brought back the silver we found in our sacks the first time we came. Why would we steal anything now? If any of us has done such a thing, let him be put to death and the rest of us be taken as slaves."

"Very well," said the steward. "Whoever is found to have the cup will become my slave. But the others will be free to leave."

The steward unloaded all the donkeys and started searching, beginning with the oldest and working his way through in order of age, until he found the cup in Benjamin's sack.

The brothers were greatly troubled and tore their clothes in anguish. They reloaded their donkeys and returned to the city. Joseph was still at his house when the brothers arrived there, throwing themselves down on the ground before him.

Looking fiercely at them, Joseph said, "What is it that you have done? Don't you know that a man like me can find out all things?"

Judah spoke carefully, "What can we say, my lord? How can we prove our innocence? God has shown our guilt."

Judah knew, of course, that they were not guilty of the theft of the cup, but deep in his heart he knew they were guilty of what they had done to Joseph many years ago, and that somehow this was connected. "We are now your slaves – all of us, not only the one in whose sack the cup was found," Judah declared.

But Joseph replied, "I will not do such a thing. Only the man who was found to have the cup will become my slave. The rest of you can go back to your father in peace."

Now Judah said, "My lord, you said that we must bring the youngest son, though we told you that the boy cannot leave our father, or our father will die of sorrow. But you insisted that we must bring him. If we now return without him, our father will die in deep sorrow. I assured him that I would bring back the boy safely, and promised that if I did not do so, I would bear the blame all my life. I cannot go back to my father without him, so I ask you, please, let me remain as your slave and let the youngest return with his brothers."

Joseph makes himself known

On hearing Judah's words, Joseph was overcome with emotion. He ordered all his Egyptian attendants to leave the room so that he could be alone with his brothers. He cried out in Hebrew, "I am Joseph! Is my father still living?"

His brothers were so shocked that they could not speak. Joseph called them closer and explained, "I am your brother Joseph, the one you sold to Egypt. But do not be distressed or blame yourselves for what you did, for God sent me here to save lives. If I had not come here, you and many other people would have starved. The famine that has swept across all the lands for two years will continue for another five."

His brothers were still unable to speak, for there were such a lot of new things to take in. But Joseph went on, "Now, hurry back to my father and tell him your son Joseph says: 'God has made me lord of all Egypt. Come to me, and don't delay, because five years of famine are still to come. Otherwise, you and all your household and servants will become destitute. You shall all live near me.' Tell my father about the honour given to me in Egypt and about everything you have seen. And bring him here quickly."

After Joseph had spoken, he threw his arms around Benjamin, kissed all his brothers, and wept with joy. Only then did his brothers recover from their shock and find themselves able to speak.

Even though Joseph had sent all his Egyptian attendants away, they had heard the cries and commotion and soon found out what happened. Word spread fast through the palace, and when Pharaoh heard that Joseph's brothers had come, he and all his officials were pleased. Pharaoh sent word to Joseph: "Tell your brothers to bring your father and all their families to Egypt. I will give them the best of my land. They can leave their belongings, for I will give them everything they need here."

So Joseph gave his brothers carts, provisions and new clothing, and to Benjamin he gave five sets of clothing and three hundred silver coins. He sent his brothers away, saying, "Do not quarrel on the way!"

When they arrived home, they told their father, "Joseph is still alive! And he is ruler over all of Egypt!"

Israel was stunned and did not believe them. His spirits revived only when they told him everything Joseph had said and showed him the carts he had sent. Then, Israel was like a new man. With a firm voice, he said, "My son Joseph is alive. I will go to see him before I die."

The deaths of Israel and Joseph

Israel then set out with all his sons, grandsons, servants and possessions. When they reached Beersheba, where his father Isaac had spent most of his life, he offered sacrifices to God. And in the night God called to Israel and said to him in a vision, "Do not be afraid to go to Egypt, for I will make you a great nation there, and I will bring you back again. And your son Joseph will close your eyes when you die."

Now Israel was joyful, for not only would he see his son Joseph, but he also knew that he was doing the right thing and that God would be with his people in Egypt.

When Israel arrived, Joseph met him and threw his arms around his father. They both wept with joy for a long time.

There were seventy people in Israel's family, and Pharaoh gave them the best land to settle on, as well as food for the remaining years of the famine.

Israel lived in Egypt for seventeen years, and when he felt the time of his death was close, he called Joseph and made him promise to bury him at Hebron, where Abraham and Isaac were buried. Then he asked Joseph to bring his sons Manasseh and Ephraim so he could bless them. Israel's eyes were failing and he could hardly see. Joseph led his firstborn son, Manasseh, to Israel's right hand, and Ephraim to his left hand. But Israel reached his right hand to Ephraim and crossed his left hand to Manasseh.

When Joseph saw his father's right hand on Ephraim's head, he took the hand and moved it to Manasseh's head, saying, "This is my firstborn, put your right hand on his head."

But his father replied, "I know, my son. But his younger brother will be greater than he." And Israel blessed the younger son as the firstborn, just as he had received Isaac's blessing as the younger brother of Esau.

Then Israel blessed each of his own twelve sons. After he died, his sons took him to the burial place of his fathers in Hebron.

Joseph lived to see his grandchildren and great-grandchildren. When he felt his time was near, he called his brothers and said, "I am about to die. But God will come to your aid and lead you out of Egypt to Canaan, to the land that he promised to Abraham, Isaac and Jacob." Joseph made them promise that they would bury him in Canaan.

When he died, Joseph's body was embalmed in the manner of the Egyptians and sealed in a coffin. But the descendants of Joseph and his brothers, the children of Israel, had to wait four hundred years before they could carry out their promise to Joseph and return to the land God had promised them.

Moses

Moses Leads the Israelites

The birth of Moses

As long as Joseph was remembered, the Egyptians honoured the children of Israel, who were known as Israelites. The Egyptians also called them Hebrews because they spoke the Hebrew language. But in time Joseph was forgotten. When a new Pharaoh came to the throne, he said to his people, "There are too many Hebrews in our land. If a war breaks out they may join our enemies and fight against us."

Pharoah commanded that the Hebrews be used as slaves for building work – digging foundations, making bricks and carrying heavy loads. But the more they laboured, the more God gave them strength; and the more they were oppressed, the more they grew in number.

Then Pharaoh summoned the Hebrew midwives and commanded them, "When you are helping a Hebrew woman during childbirth, if the baby is a boy, kill him; but if it is a girl, let her live."

The midwives, however, feared God, and secretly agreed not to carry out Pharaoh's terrible orders. When Pharaoh noticed, he called the midwives,

asking them angrily why they had not done what he commanded. They answered, "The Hebrew women are not like Egyptian women; they give birth before the midwife arrives."

So Pharaoh gave an order to all his soldiers: "You must throw every Hebrew boy that is born into the Nile, but let every girl live."

One day, a woman descended from Joseph's brother Levi, who already had a daughter and a son, gave birth to another son. She saw that he was a fine child, so she hid him for three months. When she could no longer hide him, she took a papyrus basket, coated it with tar, put her son inside and hid him among the reeds along the banks of the Nile. His sister, Miriam, watched over him from a distance, to see what would happen.

Shortly afterwards, Pharaoh's daughter went down to the Nile to bathe. She saw the basket among the reeds and sent her servant girl to get it. The princess opened the basket and saw the baby, who was crying. Like the midwives, she feared God and, feeling sorry for the baby, she said to her servant, "This is one of the Hebrew babies."

Then Miriam approached the princess and asked, "Shall I go and fetch one of the Hebrew women to feed and nurse the baby for you?"

"Yes, go," replied the princess.

Miriam went to fetch her mother and brought her to Pharaoh's daughter.

"Take this baby and nurse him for me," the princess said, "and I will pay you. In time, bring him to me. I name this child Moses, for I pulled him out of the water." (The Hebrew word for "pulling out" is "mashah", and Moses was called Mosheh in Hebrew.)

So the woman took her own son and nursed him, and he grew up with his sister, Miriam, and his brother, Aaron. When Moses was older, his mother took him to Pharaoh's daughter, as she had been asked, and the princess adopted him as her son. Moses grew up in Pharaoh's court, learning royal customs and the Egyptian language.

Moses flees to Midian

When Moses was grown up, one day he went out to where his own people were toiling with heavy work. He saw one of the Egyptian overseers beating a Hebrew man. It was clear that the old man was not strong enough to do the work, and Moses was angry with the overseer for being so unjust. He told the overseer to stop, but he took no notice. Looking around to check no one was watching, Moses attacked the overseer, beating him so hard that he died. Moses was alarmed at what he had done, and quickly hid the overseer's body in the sand.

The next day Moses saw two Hebrew men fighting each other. He felt furious. Why were they fighting when they should be united? He went up to them and asked the one in the wrong, "Why are you hitting your fellow Hebrew?"

The man only replied, "Who made you a judge over us? Or are you thinking of killing me, like you killed the Egyptian?"

Moses felt afraid, because he realised that other people knew his secret. Before returning to the palace, he was warned that Pharaoh had heard of his deed and wanted to kill him. So Moses fled eastwards to Midian, in the Sinai Desert.

After walking through the desert for many days, Moses rested by a well. Seven young women came along to draw water for their sheep, but then some shepherds arrived and drove the women away so that they could water their flocks first. Moses was angered by the injustice, and said to the shepherds, "Why don't you let the women finish watering their flocks? Weren't they here first?"

Wary of the outspoken stranger, the shepherds muttered among themselves, "Who is this man, to speak to us like that?" But they withdrew, letting the women finish. As Moses helped the women water the sheep, his eyes were drawn to one of the young women, who returned his gaze and smiled.

The seven young women were the daughters of Jethro, the priest of

Midian. When they returned home, their father was surprised and asked them, "Why have you returned so early today?"

"An Egyptian helped us when the shepherds tried to stop us using the well, and he even drew water for us," they answered.

"Where is he?" Jethro asked. "Why did you leave him? Invite him to have something to eat."

Zipporah, the daughter who had smiled at Moses, ran back to the well and invited him to her father's house. Moses gladly followed, and Jethro asked him to stay.

In time, Zipporah and Moses were married, and Zipporah gave birth to two sons.

Meanwhile, back in Egypt, the Pharaoh died and his son, the new Pharaoh, treated the enslaved Hebrews even more harshly. They cried out to God to help them. And God heard their cries.

The burning bush

One day, Moses was in the wilderness at Mount Horeb, tending the flock of his father-in-law, Jethro, when a nearby bush suddenly burst into flames. When Moses looked closer at this strange sight, he noticed that the flames were not dying down and that the bush itself was not burning. Then he heard a voice from the bush calling, "Moses, Moses."

"Here I am," Moses replied.

"Do not come any closer," the voice said. "Take off your sandals, for the ground on which you stand is holy."

Moses removed his sandals, then asked who was speaking to him.

"I am the God of your father, the God of Abraham, the God of Isaac and the God of Jacob," the voice replied.

Moses was filled with fear and hid his face in his cloak, for he knew that anyone who saw the face of God would die.

God said, "I have seen the misery of my people in Egypt and I have heard their cries for help. I have come to rescue them from the Egyptians and bring them to the land I promised to them, a lush land flowing with milk and honey. I am sending you to Pharaoh to bring my people out of Egypt."

Moses was afraid to return to Egypt, because Pharaoh's father had wanted to kill him for what he had done to the Egyptian overseer. He asked, "Who am I that I should go to Pharaoh and bring the children of Israel out of Egypt?" (Israel was also known as Jacob.)

God replied, "I will be with you. And this will be a sign to you: when you have brought your people out of Egypt, you will worship God on this holy Mount Horeb, the mountain of God."

Moses was still unwilling, and said, "What if I go to the Israelites and say, 'The God of your fathers has sent me to you,' and they ask, 'What is his name?' What shall I tell them?"

With a mighty voice, God spoke: "I am the I AM."

He continued, "Tell the Israelites, 'The God of the I AM has sent me to you. The Lord, the God of your fathers, the God of Abraham, the God of Isaac, the God of Jacob has sent me to you."

The mighty words "I am" echoed in Moses' soul, but still he was unwilling to go to Egypt.

God spoke again: "Go, assemble all the leaders of the Israelites and tell them, 'The God of your fathers has heard you, and he has promised to bring you out of your misery in Egypt into the land of Canaan, a land flowing with milk and honey.' The leaders will listen to you. Then go with them to Pharaoh and say, 'Let us take a three-day journey into the desert to offer sacrifices to the Lord our God.'

"But Pharaoh will not let you go unless he is forced to, so I will stretch out my hand and strike the Egyptians with all kinds of strange disasters. After that they will let you go."

Moses was still troubled and in doubt, and said, "What if they don't believe me and say, 'The Lord God did not appear to you'?"

Then God said to him, "What is in your hand?"

"A staff," Moses replied, puzzled.

"Throw the staff on the ground."

Moses did as he was told: his staff became a snake, and he ran from it.

God instructed, "Reach out your hand and take the snake by the tail."

When Moses reached out and took the snake, it turned back into a staff in his hand.

"Do this and they will believe that the God of their fathers appeared to you," said God. "Now put your hand into your cloak."

Moses did so, and when he took it out and looked at it, his skin was white and dead. He had the dreaded disease leprosy.

Then God said, "Now put your hand back in your cloak."

Moses did as he was told, and when he took it out again, his hand was healthy and restored.

God said, "If they do not believe you after the first sign, they may believe the second. But if they do not believe those two signs, take some water from the River Nile and pour it on the ground. The water will become blood."

Moses was still reluctant, and argued, "Pardon your servant, Lord. I have never been good at speaking before many people. I am slow of speech and tongue."

God said to him, "Who gave human beings mouths and who made them speak? Is it not I, the Lord? Now go. I will help you speak and teach you what to say."

But Moses pleaded, "Pardon your servant, Lord. Please send someone else."

Then God was angry with Moses, but said, "What about your brother Aaron? I know he can speak well. He is already on his way to meet you, and will rejoice to see you. You shall speak to him and put words in his mouth. He will speak to the people for you, and it will be as if he is your mouth, and you are God to him. But take your staff in your hand so you can perform the signs with it."

Moses returns to Egypt

Moses went to his father-in-law and asked to go to Egypt to see if his people were still alive. Jethro said, "Go, and I wish you well."

Moses knew that he was no longer in any danger, for God told him, "Everyone who wanted to kill you in Egypt has died. When you return, perform before Pharaoh all the wonders I have given you power to do. But I will harden Pharaoh's heart so that he will not let the people go."

Carrying his staff, Moses set off for Egypt. When he came to Horeb, the mountain of God, he met his brother Aaron, and Moses explained to him everything God had told him.

In Egypt, Moses performed the signs before his people – his staff turned into a serpent and became a staff again, his hand became white with leprosy and was healed again, and the water of the Nile that he poured on the ground turned into blood. Then the children of Israel did believe that God had sent Moses to lead them out of their misery.

Moses and Aaron went to Pharaoh and said, "This is what our Lord, the God of Israel, says: 'Let my people go to the wilderness for three days to offer sacrifices to their Lord God.'"

But Pharaoh said, "Who is this Lord and why should I obey him? I will not let the people of Israel go. Why are you taking the people away from their work? I order them to get back to it!"

That same day, Pharaoh ordered the overseers to no longer give the Hebrews straw to put into the clay bricks they were making. Instead, the Hebrews were to gather their own straw – but still make the same number of bricks every day. They would just have to work harder.

The Israelites struggled to make as many bricks as before, and sent some of their leaders to appeal to Pharaoh. "Why are you treating us like this?" they asked. "We are being beaten, but it is your own people who have not given us straw to make the bricks."

Pharaoh was angry. "You are just lazy! That is why you want to go off and worship in the desert. Now get back to work. You will not be given straw, but you must make the same number of bricks every day."

The leaders left Pharaoh and went to Moses and Aaron, saying, "It is your fault! You have made Pharaoh treat us even more harshly." The Israelites no longer believed that Moses would lead them out of Egypt.

Moses turned to God, asking, "Why, Lord, have you brought trouble on our people? Ever since I went to Pharaoh to speak in your name, there has only been more misery for them. You have not rescued them."

God said to Moses, "Go and tell Pharaoh everything I am about to tell you."

But Moses said, "Lord, why would Pharaoh listen to me when my own people no longer listen to me?"

God said to Moses, "I will make you like God to Pharaoh, and your brother Aaron will be your prophet and speak the word of God. Say everything I command you to say. Your brother will tell Pharaoh to let the Israelites out of his country. I will harden Pharaoh's heart and he will not listen to you, but then I will stretch out my hand against Egypt and bring the Israelites out of the land. Then the Egyptians will know that I am the Lord God."

God continued, "When Pharaoh orders you to perform a miracle, tell Aaron, 'Take your staff and throw it down.' Then I will show Pharaoh a miracle."

Moses and Aaron went to Pharaoh to ask him to let the Israelites go to the desert, but Pharaoh would not listen. Then Aaron did what God had commanded: he threw his staff down in front of Pharaoh and it became a snake.

Pharaoh summoned his wise men and magicians, and they performed the same feat with their magic: each one threw down his staff and it became a snake. But Aaron's staff swallowed up all their staffs.

The ten plagues of Egypt

God commanded Moses to go with Aaron and meet Pharaoh at the River Nile the next morning when he went to bathe, and God told them what to say and do there.

When they met Pharaoh at the river, Aaron raised his staff and struck the water, which turned into blood. The Egyptians could no longer drink the water and all the fish in the river died, making a terrible smell. Pharaoh summoned his magicians, and they did the same thing with their magic. For seven days, all the water in Egypt was turned to blood, and no one could drink.

Then Moses and Aaron went again to Pharaoh to ask him to let the Israelites go, threatening to send a plague on the land if he refused. But Pharaoh would not listen, so Aaron stretched his staff over the Nile for the second time. Frogs leapt out and covered the whole of Egypt. They sprang into the palace, hopping into every room, into the ovens and troughs, even into Pharaoh's bedroom and onto his bed, and into the houses of all his officials and people. Pharaoh's magicians did the same thing with their magic.

Then Pharaoh summoned Moses and Aaron and said, "Pray to the Lord your God to take the frogs away from me and my people, and I will let your people go to offer sacrifices to their Lord."

Moses prayed to God about the frogs, and the frogs died in the houses, in the courtyards and in the fields. They were piled up in heaps and the land stank of them. But when Pharaoh saw that he was rid of the plague, his heart hardened against the Israelites again and he would not let them go.

Then Aaron stretched out his staff for the third time and struck the dust of the ground. The dust turned into gnats, tiny biting flies, that swarmed everywhere and settled on animals and people, crawling into their eyes and mouths and noses. When Pharaoh's magicians tried to do the same, they could not. They told him, "This is a sign of God." But Pharaoh's heart was hard and he would not listen.

Moses went again to Pharaoh, and Aaron spoke as God had commanded: "Let my people go to worship. If you do not let them go, the Lord will send swarms of flies to you and your officials and your people. Every Egyptian house will be full of flies and the ground will be covered with them, but the houses and fields of the Israelites will be clear."

The next morning, when Aaron stretched out his staff for the fourth time, dense swarms of flies appeared in Pharaoh's palace and in all the Egyptian houses, and the land was ruined. Yet there were no flies in the houses and fields of the Israelites. Then Pharaoh said, "I will let you go to offer sacrifices to the Lord if you rid me of these flies."

Moses replied, "I will pray to the Lord as soon as I leave you, and tomorrow the flies will leave you and the land. But Pharaoh must not act deceitfully again."

Moses left Pharaoh and prayed, and God did what Moses had asked. But once more, Pharaoh's heart was hardened and he would not let the Israelites go.

A fifth time Moses pleaded with Pharaoh. This time, without Aaron doing anything, God sent a plague on all the Egyptians' livestock. Their horses, donkeys, camels, sheep, goats and cows all died, while the Israelites' animals were spared. But Pharaoh's heart remained unyielding.

Then Moses took a handful of soot from a furnace and tossed it in the air in the presence of Pharaoh. The soot became the sixth plague: a fine dust that spread over the whole land of Egypt, causing people and animals to erupt with festering boils. Pharaoh's magicians could not confront Moses, because of the boils covering their skin. But Pharaoh still would not listen.

For the seventh time, Moses spoke with Pharaoh. Moses stretched out his hand, and God sent such a thunder and hailstorm as had never before been seen in the land of Egypt. Hail fell and lightning flashed to the ground, striking everything down – people, animals and crops. Every tree was stripped bare. But the Israelites and their fields were spared.

Pharaoh called Moses and said, "The Lord your God is right. I will let your people go."

Yet when the thunder and hail stopped, Pharaoh broke his word again.

Moses and Aaron went to Pharaoh for an eighth time. Moses stretched out his staff and God made an east wind blow across the land all day and all night. In the morning, the wind brought great swarms of locusts that settled on every field and devoured all the plants until the land was black. This time, all of Pharaoh's officials pleaded with him to do as Moses asked, for their country was in ruins. Pharaoh promised to let the Israelites go, but when God changed the winds and all the locusts were blown away, again he refused.

Moses stretched out his hand to the sky for a ninth time and total darkness fell over all of Egypt for three days. No one could see or move about, yet there was still light where the Israelites lived.

Pharaoh summoned Moses and said, "Go, worship your Lord. Your families may go with you, but your flocks and herds must stay behind."

Moses replied, "You must allow us to take our cattle and flocks of sheep, for we will need some of them to sacrifice to the Lord."

Pharaoh's heart was hardened again and he would not let the Israelites go. In a rage, he said to Moses, "Get out of my sight! Make sure you never appear before me again! The day you next see my face you will die."

Moses replied, "Just as you say, I will never appear before you again. But this is what the Lord God says: 'Around midnight I will go through the land of Egypt. Every firstborn son in Egypt will die, from the firstborn son of Pharaoh to the firstborn son of the lowliest slave, and all the firstborn of the cattle shall die as well."

Then Moses, hot with anger, left Pharaoh while all his officials were begging him to change his mind. The Egyptian officials and people held Moses in high regard, for they had seen what great power he had. But Pharaoh still would not let the Israelites go.

The Passover

God spoke to Moses and Aaron: "This month shall become the first month of the year for you. On the fourteenth day of this month, all the people of Israel must kill a lamb without blemish or defect, and paint some of the blood on each side and the top of the doorframe of their houses. They must eat the lamb the same evening and burn any leftovers. After they have eaten, they must be ready to leave, with their cloaks tucked into their belts, their sandals on their feet and their staffs in their hands. They must take dough without yeast for making bread, and they must eat in haste, for it is the Lord's Passover.

"That same night I will pass through Egypt and strike down every firstborn of both people and animals, but when I see blood on the doors, I will pass over your houses and not strike down anyone inside.

"From this day on, every year you are to commemorate this day: for seven days from the fourteenth day of this month, you will not eat bread made with yeast or keep yeast in your house. For generations to come, celebrate the Festival of Unleavened Bread, because it is the day that I brought you out of Egypt."

Moses summoned all the Israelites and told them what God had said, and the people did what Moses asked of them.

At midnight, God struck down all the firstborn of Egypt, from the Pharaoh's firstborn to the firstborn slaves and prisoners, and all the firstborn animals as well.

The escape from Egypt

Pharaoh heard loud wailing and moaning from his people, for there was not a house in Egypt in which someone had not died. He summoned Moses and Aaron and said, "Go! Leave this land and worship your Lord God as you have asked. Take your flocks and herds. But also bless me."

The Egyptian people gave them silver, gold and clothing, because they held Moses and his people in high regard. The Egyptians urged them to hurry and leave their country, saying, "Go quickly, otherwise we will all die!"

So the Israelites left and did as Moses commanded, taking their dough without yeast, and their flocks and herds.

Moses took the bones of Joseph with him, for Joseph had made the Israelites promise to bury him in the land that God had promised to them. For four hundred years – the time they had lived in Egypt – the Israelites remembered their promise to Joseph.

God did not lead them out along the shorter road by the coast, but led them around by the desert road towards the Sea of Reeds. By day, God went ahead of them in a pillar of cloud; by night, in a pillar of fire. The Israelites soon grew tired of marching through the arid desert, as they were used to the lush and fertile fields of Egypt. But they trudged on wearily.

God said to Moses, "Camp here by the sea. Pharaoh will think that the Israelites are wandering around the land in confusion. I will harden Pharaoh's heart and he will pursue you, but I will show Pharaoh and the Egyptians that I am the Lord."

When Pharaoh was told that the Israelites had left, he and his officials had second thoughts. "What have we done?" they asked themselves. "By letting the Israelites go, we have lost all our workers!"

Pharaoh summoned his horses and chariots, his horsemen and troops, and they set off in pursuit of the Israelites. When Pharoah's army caught up with them, the Israelites were terrified. They called to Moses, "What have you done to us? It would have been better for us to serve the Egyptians than die here in the desert."

Moses answered, "Do not be afraid. Stand firm, and the Lord will fight for you."

And God said to Moses, "Raise your staff and stretch out your hand over the sea to divide the waters, so that the Israelites can pass through."

Then the pillar of cloud moved between the Israelites and the Egyptian army, bringing darkness over the Egyptians so they could no longer see. Yet in front of the cloud, where the Israelites were, it was still light. Moses stretched out his hand over the sea and God drove the sea back with a strong wind to make a passage of dry land.

The Israelites, with their families and herds of sheep and cattle, passed through as God held back the waters on either side. When the Egyptian army gave chase, the Lord threw the army into confusion, jamming the wheels of their chariots. The Egyptians cried, "Let us stop pursuing the Israelites. Their God is fighting for them against Egypt."

At daybreak, the Israelites reached the other side of the sea. Then God said to Moses, "Stretch out your hand, so the waters will flow back over the Egyptians and their chariots and horsemen.

Moses stretched out his hand and the waters rushed back, sweeping the troops and chariots and horses away. Not one of the Egyptians survived.

When the Israelites, on the far shore of the Sea of Reeds, saw the mighty hand of God working against the Egyptians, they put their trust in him and in his servant Moses, and celebrated with a great feast of singing and dancing.

The Years in the Desert

The Israelites wander in the desert

Moses led the Israelites from the Sea of Reeds into the desert. It was hot by day and cold by night. Every day they followed the pillar of cloud, and every night when they rested it turned into a pillar of fire.

For three days they walked across the barren, stony ground without finding water. The women and children cried out in thirst, and the men complained to Moses. Finally, they came to an oasis with green palm trees and bushes growing around it.

When one of the men tried some water from the small pool at the oasis, he found it was so bitter that he could not drink it. Then the people clamoured against Moses, asking, "What shall we drink?"

Moses prayed to God, who showed him a piece of a wooden branch lying on the ground and said, "Throw it in the water." After Moses threw the branch, another man tried the water and found it was fresh and fit to drink. They named the oasis Marah, which means "bitter".

Following the pillar of cloud, the Israelites travelled further into the desert. There were only a few small, thorny bushes growing there, and they could find no food. They began to say to each other, "If only we had stayed and died in Egypt. There we had pots of meat and all the food we wanted! Moses has brought us out into the desert to starve."

Then God spoke to Moses: "I have heard the people grumbling. Tell them, 'At twilight you will eat meat, and in the morning you will be filled with bread.'"

That evening a great flock of small fat birds called quail covered the camp.

Because they were easy to catch, all the families could eat.

In the morning, the ground was covered in dew. As the sun rose and the dew disappeared, thin white flakes like frost were left. When the people saw this, they asked, "What is this?", for they did not know. (In their language, Hebrew, it sounded like "Man ha?")

Moses explained, "It is bread from the Lord God. He has commanded everyone to gather as much as they need, but not to keep any of it for tomorrow."

The Israelites called this strange bread manna. However, a few people ignored Moses and kept some of the bread for the next day. But in the morning, it was full of maggots and stank. Moses was angry with them. After that, people only gathered as much as they needed, and when the sun grew hot, it melted away.

Moses said to them, "On Friday, the sixth day of the week, you may also gather enough for the Sabbath, the seventh day. On the Sabbath, you must rest, for the seventh day is holy to the Lord, and you are not to go out gathering bread or do any work like cooking."

Nevertheless, some of the people went out on the seventh day, but they found no bread. Then God asked Moses, "How long will it be before the people keep my commands? I, the Lord, have given you the Sabbath, and that is why on the sixth day I give you bread for two days. On the seventh day, you are to rest and not go out."

The Israelites travelled on, following the pillar of cloud. Once they camped in a place where there was no water to drink, and they complained to Moses.

Moses replied, "Why do you quarrel with me? We are following the Lord."

But the people grumbled again that Moses had taken them out of Egypt only to lead them into this desert where they would all die of thirst.

Moses prayed and God spoke to him: "Go out in front of the people, taking the staff that you used to strike the River Nile. I will stand before you, and you must hit the rock below me." When Moses saw the pillar of cloud above a rock, he struck the rock with his staff, and water flowed out for all the people to drink.

Moses called the place Massah (which means "proof") and Meribah (which means "quarrel"), because there God gave proof of his guidance when the people quarrelled.

Jethro visits Moses

Jethro, Moses' father-in-law, had heard about everything that Moses had done for the Israelites and how God had brought them out of Egypt. The Israelites were now camped near Mount Horeb, the mountain of God, so Jethro sent word to Moses that he was coming with Moses' wife, Zipporah, and their two sons.

Moses went out to meet Jethro and bowed low before him, and he joyfully embraced Zipporah and his two sons, who had grown into tall boys. Moses brought them to his tent, where Jethro made offerings to God. Together with Aaron, they all ate bread.

Moses told Jethro everything that had happened since he left them. Jethro was delighted to hear all the things that God had done to rescue the Israelites from the Egyptians who were oppressing them. "Praise be the Lord!" he cried. "Now I know that the Lord God is greater than all other gods, for he has rescued his people from the proud Egyptians."

The next day, as he did every day, Moses took his seat before the people, who brought all their disputes and arguments for him to judge. Jethro watched, and in the evening he told Moses, "What you are doing is not good. You will wear yourself out with all that work. Listen to me.

"Teach the people God's decrees and show them how they should behave. Select capable men who are trustworthy and who revere God. Let them serve as judges over a thousand, over a hundred, over fifty or over ten people. They can decide the simple cases, so they need only bring the difficult cases to you. That way your load will be lighter, and you will still have the strength to lead your people."

Moses listened to his father-in-law and saw that his advice was wise. He chose capable men and made them leaders and officials over the thousands, hundreds, fifties and tens.

Content that Moses was managing his people wisely, Jethro said farewell to Moses, Zipporah and the two boys, and returned home.

The Ten Commandments

Three months after the Israelites left Egypt, they camped at the foot of a mountain in the Sinai Desert. Moses climbed the mountain and God called to him, "This is what you are to say to the descendants of Israel: if they obey me fully and keep to my laws, then they will be my treasured people. They will be a holy people and a kingdom of priests."

When Moses descended, he summoned the elders of the people and told them what God had commanded him. The elders responded: "We will do everything the Lord has said."

Moses went up the mountain again to share their answer with God, who said, "I am going to come down to you in a dense cloud so the people will hear me speak with you. Go to the people and tell them to purify themselves with prayer, to wash their clothes and be ready. But they may not approach the mountain on pain of death."

Moses descended and told the people to prepare themselves.

On the morning of the third day, there was thunder and lightning, and a thick cloud gathered over the mountain. Then, the people heard the sound of a trumpet. Everyone in the camp trembled. Moses led the people out to the foot of the mountain, and they heard the voice of the Lord calling Moses to the top of the mountain.

At the top of the mountain God said to him, "Warn the people not to come up the mountain and force their way to see the Lord."

Moses replied, "The people will not come up, because you yourself warned them not to approach the mountain. They know it is holy."

But God replied, "Go down and bring Aaron up with you. But no one else must come."

So Moses went down to the people and told them what God had said. Then all the people heard the voice of God:

I am the Lord your God. You shall have no other God but me.
You shall not make an image of any living thing in heaven or on earth, and you shall not bow down and worship them.
You shall not misuse the name of the Lord your God.

Remember the Sabbath day by keeping it holy: you shall work six days, and on the seventh you shall rest, for in six days the Lord created heaven and earth and on the seventh he rested.
Honour your father and your mother.
You shall not murder.
You shall keep marriage sacred and not break it.
You shall not steal.
You shall not say false things against your neighbour.
You shall not desire and crave for your neighbour's house, wife, servants, possessions or animals.

Again, the people saw thunder and lightning and heard the sound of a trumpet, and they trembled with fear. They kept their distance and said to Moses, "Speak to us yourself and we will listen, but do not have God speak to us or we will die."

Moses replied, "Do not be afraid. God has come to test you."

The people remained at a distance while Moses climbed the mountain again and approached the thick cloud where God was. Then God gave him many more instructions and commands for the people.

On hearing these commands from Moses, the people said with one voice: "All the words which the Lord has spoken we will keep."

Moses receives the tablets of the law

Moses wrote down the Ten Commandments that God had spoken. In the morning he built an altar at the foot of the mountain and set up twelve stone pillars, one for each of the twelve tribes of Israel: the descendants of Israel's twelve sons. And on the altar, the people made a burnt offering to God.

God commanded Moses to climb the mountain again, along with seventy leaders, Aaron, and Joshua, the son of Nun of the tribe of Ephraim, though they were only allowed to go partway. There they saw the God of Israel in all his glory and they were allowed to live. They were also allowed to eat and drink in his presence.

Then God said to Moses, "Come with me to the top of the mountain, stay with me, and I will give you tablets of stone with the law and my commandments written on them."

Moses said to the leaders, "Wait for me until I come back. Aaron will lead you while I am away."

Moses was allowed to take Joshua, and together they went up the mountain. For six days, the cloud covered the mountain, and on the seventh day God called Moses from within the cloud. He entered the cloud and stayed there for forty days and forty nights.

God gave Moses exact instructions for making a holy tent in which to keep the stone tablets with the commandments. When the Lord finished speaking, he gave Moses two tablets of stone, with the law and commandments written on them, inscribed by the finger of God.

The golden calf

While Moses was on top of Mount Sinai with God, the Israelites started to lose their faith in him and his Lord. They forgot the commandments to have no other gods, and that they were not to make images of living creatures and worship them. It had been weeks since they had seen the man who led them out of Egypt, and they angrily complained to Aaron, "We do not know what has happened to Moses. Who is supposed to lead us now? Make us a new god that we can worship."

Aaron, fearing the anger of the mob, answered, "Take off the gold jewellery your wives and daughters are wearing and bring them to me."

So they brought all the gold to Aaron. He took it, melted it and cast it in the shape of a calf. Then the people said, "This is the God of Israel who brought us out of Egypt."

Aaron built an altar in front of the calf and announced, "Tomorrow there will be a festival to the Lord."

The next day, the people rose early and sacrificed burnt offerings, and then they sat down to eat and drink and make merry.

Then God said to Moses on the mountain, "Go down, because the people have already turned away from my commandments and made themselves an idol in the shape of a calf. They have bowed down before it and made sacrifices to it, saying, 'This is the God of Israel.' Leave me alone, so that I can destroy them in my anger. I will make a new nation out of you and your descendants."

But Moses pleaded with the Lord, "Do not let your anger burn against the people you brought out of Egypt. Do not give the Egyptians cause to say, 'See, their god brought them out of Egypt into the desert to kill them there.' Remember the promise you made to your servants Abraham, Isaac and Jacob: 'I will make your descendants as numerous as the stars in the sky, and I will give your descendants this land.'"

God relented and did not create the disaster he had threatened.

Moses went down the mountain with the two stone tablets of the law in his hands. Joshua was with Moses when he heard the noise of the people shouting and said, "There is the sound of war in the camp."

But Moses replied, "It is not the sound of war that I hear, but the sound of singing."

When they approached the camp and Moses saw the calf and the dancing, he was furious. He threw down the tablets, breaking them to pieces. He took the calf Aaron had made and burned it in the fire, then ground it to powder and scattered it on water, which he made the Israelites drink.

Moses saw that the people were running wild and that Aaron had let them become a laughing stock to their enemies. He asked Aaron, "What did these people do to you that led you to go against God's commands?"

"Do not be angry with me," Aaron answered. "The people implored me to make gods, because they did not know what had happened to you. And I was afraid they would kill me."

Moses called out to the people, "Whoever believes in the Lord, come here to me."

All the descendants of Levi came to Moses. He told them, "The Lord, the God of Israel, has given you a task to test you and show that you are worthy of serving the Lord as priests. Go into the camp and kill all the leaders of this revelry."

The Levites did as Moses asked, and showed that they loved God more than their people. Moses declared, "The Lord has set you apart, and he has blessed you today."

The next day Moses told the people, "You have committed a great sin. I will now go up to the Lord. Perhaps I can persuade him to forgive your sin. Otherwise, you will all die."

He climbed back up the mountain and pleaded, "The people have committed a great sin and made themselves a god of gold. But, Lord, please forgive their sin."

God replied, "Go, lead the people to the place I spoke of. My angel will go before you."

Then God continued, "Chisel out two stone tablets like the first ones, which you broke, and I will write the law and commandments on them again. Be ready in the morning to come to the top of the mountain."

Moses chiselled two stone tablets like the first ones, and went up the mountain early in the morning. God came down in a cloud and passed in front of Moses, who bowed to the ground at once.

Again, Moses remained on the mountain with God for forty days and forty nights, without eating bread or drinking water. God repeated all the commandments he had given Moses before, then wrote the words of the Ten Commandments on the stone tablets Moses had brought.

After Moses at last came down from the mountain, his face was radiant because he had spoken with the Lord. Aaron and the Israelites were afraid to come near him, but Moses called to them and gave them all the commandments. When he had finished speaking he put a veil over his face, which from that day on he always wore, only removing it when he spoke with God.

The holy tent for God

Moses called together the Israelites and told them to make a holy tent for God. They were all to bring an offering to the Lord – gold and silver, blue, purple and scarlet cloth, leather, wood and olive oil – and were all to help make the tent.

Two men were chosen to oversee the construction of this sanctuary. They made an ark out of hard wood – a miniature of Noah's ark – to hold the tablets of the law. They named it the Ark of the Covenant (which means "agreement" or "contract") and placed it inside the tent, with a curtain hiding it from sight. They made a wooden table for the bread that would always be there to show the presence of the Lord, a pure gold lampstand with six branches, and a small altar for burning incense. Outside the tent they built a large altar for burnt offerings and a bronze basin for purifying, and they made a great courtyard with curtains around it. They sewed fine garments for the priests.

Finally, when everything was ready, Moses sprinkled oil on the tent and on everything inside to consecrate it and make it holy. Then Aaron and his sons, who were from the tribe of Levi, dressed in the sacred garments and Moses anointed them with oil on their heads, making them priests. He repeated words that God had said to him: "These men are anointed to the priesthood that will continue throughout their generations."

When Moses had finished his work, the pillar of cloud covered the tent and the glory of the Lord filled the holy innermost part of the tent. No one except the priests were allowed inside the tent, so the people gathered in front of it.

Whenever the pillar of cloud lifted from the tent, the Israelites would continue their journey, but if it did not lift they remained where they were, still in the desert between Egypt and Canaan, the land that God had promised to Abraham and his descendants.

Scouts are sent to Canaan

God told Moses to choose twelve men to go ahead to Canaan to explore the promised land, so Moses called one from each tribe, including his faithful followers Joshua of the tribe of Ephraim and Caleb of the tribe of Judah.

Moses told them, "See what the land is like. Are the people who live there few or many? Are they strong or weak? What kind of towns do they live in? Are they fortified and have walls or are they unprotected? Is the land fertile or poor? Are there trees or not? Bring back some of the fruits of the land."

They went through the Negev desert into the hill country of Judea, observing everything carefully. In a valley they found a cluster of grapes so large that two men carried it on a pole between them. They also took some pomegranates and figs.

After forty days they returned from exploring the land. Joshua and Caleb reported to Moses and the people, "We found that the land flows with milk and honey. Here are its fruits."

The people were amazed, for they had never seen such a large cluster of grapes. The other scouts continued, "But the people who live there are powerful, and the cities are large and fortified. Some of the people are like giants, and we seemed like grasshoppers to them."

That alarmed the people, who wept and complained to Moses and Aaron, "Why is the Lord leading us through this desert only to let us die when we fight these giants? It would be better for us to return to Egypt. Let us choose a leader to guide us back there."

But Joshua and Caleb stood up and said, "The land we passed through is exceedingly good. If the Lord is with us, he will lead us to this land and give it to us."

But the people were so angry that they talked of killing Moses, Aaron, Joshua and Caleb by throwing stones. Suddenly they saw the pillar of cloud before the holy tent, and they heard the voice of God speaking to Moses.

"How long will these people despise me?" God asked him. "How long will they refuse to believe me, in spite of all the signs and miracles I have performed? I will strike them all down with a plague!"

Moses again pleaded with God, "The Egyptians know that the Lord is with these people, but when they hear that the people have all died, they will say, 'See, their god brought them out of Egypt into the desert to kill them there.' And they will know that the Lord is not all-powerful."

Then God replied, "I will forgive them as you asked. But not one of the people who have seen my glory and the miracles I performed will see the land I promised. Your children will wander in the desert until the last of you have died. I will only bring Joshua and Caleb, who followed me wholeheartedly, into the land I promised to your ancestors."

When God had spoken, the scouts who had spread the alarming reports about the land were struck down dead. Only Joshua and Caleb survived.

When the people heard God's words, they mourned bitterly. Early the next morning some of them said, "Now we are ready to go up to the land the Lord has promised."

Moses said, "Why are you disobeying the Lord's command? This will not succeed! Do not go, because the Lord is not with you."

But in their haste some of the Israelites did not listen and went up to the hill country of Canaan. Moses stayed at the camp, with the Ark of the Covenant in the holy tent, which was still covered by God's pillar of cloud.

When the Israelites arrived in Canaan, the Canaanites attacked them and beat them away. In disarray, they returned to Moses in the desert.

When the pillar of the cloud lifted, the people moved on, following it until they came to Kadesh. There, Miriam, Moses' sister, died and was buried.

When the thirty days of her mourning had passed, the Israelites went eastwards, down into the Arabah valley and up into the mountains beyond. There God told Moses, "Take Aaron and his son Eleazar up Mount Hor. Take Aaron's garments and put them on his son, for Aaron will die there."

Moses did as he was told, and Aaron died at the top of the mountain. When Moses and Eleazar descended and the people heard that Aaron had died, they mourned him for thirty days.

Balaam and his donkey

The Israelites moved northwards and camped on the plains of Moab, opposite Jericho. When the king of Moab saw the great number of people coming into his land he was terrified, because he knew he did not have enough men to fight them. But he thought of another way. He sent messengers to summon a prophet from the east called Balaam, who heard and spoke the word of God.

The messengers told the prophet, "A group of people has left Egypt and settled on our land. Our king asks you to come and put a curse on them to drive them away. He will reward you well."

"Spend the night here," replied Balaam. "I will pray to the Lord and tell you what answer he gives me."

Balaam went aside to pray, and God answered, "Do not go. You must not put a curse on these people, because they are blessed."

The next morning Balaam said the Lord had forbidden him to go. The messengers returned to the king, who then sent a greater number of more distinguished messengers. They told Balaam, "Do not let anything keep you from coming with us, because the king will reward you handsomely and do whatever you say."

Balaam answered, "Even if your king gave me all the gold and silver in his palace, I could not do anything except what the Lord my God commands. Spend the night here, and in the morning I will tell you what the Lord says."

That night God spoke to Balaam: "Go with these men, but do only what I tell you."

The next morning Balaam got up, saddled his donkey, took two of his servants and rode with the messengers to Moab. But even though he had told Balaam to go with the men, God was angry that he had gone with them, and he sent an angel to stand in the road. Balaam and the messengers could not see the angel, but the donkey could, and when it spotted the angel with a sword in his hand, it turned off the road into a field. Balaam beat the donkey to drive it back towards the road.

Then the angel stood in a narrow path with a wall on each side. When the donkey saw the angel it pressed close to the wall, crushing Balaam's foot. So he beat the donkey again.

Then the angel went ahead and stood in a narrow place where there was no room to turn aside. When the donkey saw the angel, it lay down under Balaam. He was so angry he beat it hard with his staff.

God opened the donkey's mouth, and it spoke to Balaam, "What have I done to you that you should beat me three times? Am I not your own donkey which has always carried you? Have I ever done anything like this before?"

Then God opened Balaam's eyes, and he saw the angel standing in the road with his sword drawn. He bowed low before the angel, who said, "I have come here to oppose you, because your journey displeases the Lord. The donkey saw me three times and turned away."

Balaam said to the angel of the Lord, "I have done wrong. I did not see you standing on the road. If you are displeased, I will go back."

But the angel said, "Go with these men, but only speak what I tell you."

When they came to Moab, the king came out to meet Balaam and said, "Why did you not come earlier? Was my reward not enough?"

Balaam replied, "I am here now. Yet I cannot do whatever you ask or what I please. I must speak the words God puts in my mouth."

The next morning the king took Balaam to a hill. From there he could see the Israelite camp. Balaam said, "Build me seven altars here, and prepare seven bulls and seven rams for sacrifice."

The king did as Balaam asked. Balaam spoke with God, and the spirit of God came over him. He stretched out his hand in blessing over the people of Israel, saying, "May those who bless you be blessed, and those who curse you be cursed."

When the king heard these words, he was furious with Balaam. "I summoned you to curse my enemies, but you have blessed them! Go now. You will leave without a reward."

But Balaam replied, "I told your messengers that even if you offered me all the gold and silver in your palace, I could only do what the Lord commands me. Now, before I go back, I will tell you what I see. In the distant future, a star will be born among these people, who will shine over all the people of the earth."

Then Balaam took his donkey and returned home.

The death of Moses

God said to Moses, "Go up the mountain and see the land I have promised the Israelites. After you have seen it, you will die, as your brother Aaron did."

Moses replied, "May the Lord my God appoint someone as leader over these people, so that they will not be like sheep without a shepherd."

God replied, "Take Joshua, son of Nun, and lay your hands on him before all the Israelites to proclaim him as their next leader, so that they will obey him."

Moses did as the Lord commanded him. Then he climbed the barren and stony Mount Nebo above the lush and fertile plains of Moab, opposite the city of Jericho. There, God showed him the whole promised land across the deep valley of the River Jordan.

God said, "This is the land I promised to Abraham, Isaac and Jacob. I have let you see it, but you will not cross over into it."

Then Moses died, there on Mount Nebo.

Moses was one hundred and twenty years old when he died. The Israelites mourned Moses for thirty days. Since that time there has been no prophet like Moses, who spoke with God face to face.

Joshua was filled with the spirit of wisdom because Moses had laid his hands on him. The Israelites listened to him and did what the Lord commanded.

Conquest of the Promised Land

Joshua

Joshua sends spies to Jericho

After the death of Moses, God said to Joshua, "Get ready to cross the River Jordan into the land I am about to give to you and all the Israelites. Be strong and courageous, but be careful to obey all the laws that Moses gave you, and listen carefully to my instructions." Then God told Joshua in detail what to do when they crossed the river.

Joshua instructed the leaders of the tribes, "Go through the camp and tell everyone to get ready. Three days from now we will cross the River Jordan and take possession of the land the Lord has promised us."

Secretly, Joshua sent two men to spy out the land, especially the defences of Jericho, the city just beyond the river. The spies went to a house at the edge of Jericho which formed part of the city wall. It was the house of a woman called Rahab.

But the king of Jericho heard that two strangers had entered the city, and sent soldiers to Rahab's house with a message: "Bring out the men who came to you, because they have come to spy out the land."

Rahab did not like the king of Jericho, because he was always asking for money from house-owners. She hid the men on the flat roof of her house, under some flax she had laid out to dry there. Jericho is low down in the valley of the Jordan, where it is nearly always hot and rarely rains, so people often used the roofs of their houses as a place for guests to sleep or for storing things.

When the soldiers arrived and asked for the men, Rahab said, "Yes, they came here, but they left again before dusk, when the city gates are closed. I don't know which way they went, but if you are quick you may catch up with them."

The soldiers set out in pursuit of the spies on the road that led to the fords across the River Jordan.

Rahab then went up to the roof and said to the two men, "I know that the Lord has given you this land, and everyone here is quaking from great fear of the Israelites. They have heard how the Lord dried up the waters of the sea when you left Egypt. Now swear to me that you will show kindness to my family, because I have shown kindness to you."

She guided them down from the roof to a window that was part of the city wall, and let them down on a red rope.

"If you do not tell anyone what we are doing, we will treat you kindly when the Lord has given us the land," they replied. "But when the Israelites come, make sure all your family is gathered in your house and does not go out, and keep the red rope hanging from this window."

"Agreed," she answered. "Now go to the hills away from the River Jordan, so the soldiers will not find you. Hide yourselves for three days, and then go on your way."

So they departed, hiding in the hills of the Judean Desert as Rahab had told them to, until the soldiers had stopped searching for them. Then they crossed the ford of the Jordan and returned to Joshua.

They told him everything that had happened, saying, "The Lord has surely given us the whole land, for all the people fear us."

The Israelites cross the River Jordan

The next day, early in the morning, Joshua and the Israelites went to the River Jordan and set up camp on its banks. After Joshua had passed on God's instructions to the priests, he told the Israelites, "Purify yourselves, bathe in the river and then pray. Tomorrow the Lord of all the earth will do great wonders. Follow the ark containing the tablets of the law, but do not come too close."

The following morning, the people broke up camp and started to cross the Jordan. The priests followed their instructions: carrying the Ark of the Covenant, they went ahead of the people until they came to the river, which was in full flood. As soon as their feet touched the water, the river stopped flowing, creating a great wall of water a distance away. The priests stopped in the middle of the Jordan, and all the Israelites passed by on dry ground.

When they had finished crossing, Joshua carried out God's commands. He chose twelve men, one from each tribe, and told them to take twelve stones from the middle of the Jordan and carry them across. Then Joshua commanded the priests standing in the middle of the river, carrying the ark, to come across. No sooner had they set foot on the riverbank than the waters of the Jordan returned and ran at full flood as before.

That evening when the Israelites set up camp, Joshua set up the twelve stones from the Jordan. He called the place Gilgal, which means "circle" or "wheel".

While the people were camped at Gilgal, it was the time of Passover. They celebrated the festival, remembering the night their parents had prepared to leave Egypt quickly by eating unleavened bread. From that day on, the Lord did not send daily manna, as he had in the desert.

Joshua was walking near the camp when he looked up and saw a man standing in front of him, a drawn sword in hand. "Are you a friend or an enemy?" Joshua asked.

The man replied, "I have come to lead the army of the Lord."

Joshua bowed to the ground in reverence.

The leader of the Lord's army said, "Take off your sandals, for the place where you are standing is holy."

Joshua did so. When he looked up, he saw no one, but he knew that the angel of the Lord was with him.

The fall of Jericho

The king of Jericho had the gates of the city barred. No one went in or out of the city, because the people were afraid of the Israelites.

God said to Joshua, "I will deliver the city of Jericho to you. For six days, march once around the city with all your armed men. Have seven priests carry trumpets of ram's horns in front of the ark. On the seventh day, march around the city seven times with the priests blowing their trumpets. When you hear the sound of the trumpets, command all the men in the army to give a loud shout. Then the walls of the city will collapse."

Joshua did as God commanded. Every day the inhabitants of the city became more fearful, but each time the army returned to its camp. At daybreak on the seventh day the army again marched around the city, but instead of once they circled it seven times. Joshua commanded his army to shout when the trumpets sounded the seventh time and told them, "The Lord has given you this city. Do not take anything from their temples or their sacred objects. Take the gold, silver and bronze for the Lord's treasury, for they are sacred to God. But make sure the house of Rahab and all who are in it are spared, for she helped us by hiding our spies."

When the priests sounded the trumpets, all the men shouted. Jericho's walls collapsed and the army rushed in. Joshua told the two spies, "Go to Rahab's house and bring out all who are in the house."

The two men brought Rahab and her family out safely to the camp of the Israelites. Then the army killed all the people of Jericho and burned the whole city. The gold, silver and bronze were put into the treasury inside the tent of God, with the ark.

Joshua's fame spread throughout the land, and all its inhabitants were in great fear.

The conquest of Judea

Joshua sent men up into the mountains of Judea and told them to spy out the region.

To conquer Ai, one of the cities of Judea, Joshua marched up into the hills with his army. At night he ordered half the army to hide to the west of the city. He said, "Wait until the men of Ai come out to fight the rest of us in the east. We will lure them out of the city and they will pursue us, leaving the city undefended."

In the morning, the king of Ai saw the Israelites to the east of his city. As soon as the men of Ai had set out to attack them, the half of Joshua's army that had been hiding rushed forward and quickly captured the city.

To celebrate the victory, Joshua built an altar to the God of Israel, and read out all the laws that the Lord had given to Moses.

One after another the towns and cities of Judea were conquered by Joshua and the Israelites. However, the people of Gibeon, a city in the Judean hills not far from Ai, had a cunning idea. They sent out some of their men wearing worn-out sandals and old clothes. Their donkeys were loaded with cracked wineskins and frayed sacks of dry, mouldy bread.

These men went to Joshua and the Israelites at their camp in Gilgal and said, "We have come from a faraway country to make a treaty with you."

The Israelites replied, "Who are you and where do you come from? How can we know that you don't live near us?"

"We have come from a very distant country because of the fame of the Lord your God. We have heard how he parted the sea to let you leave Egypt, and how you have conquered all the kings that have stood in your way. The rulers in our country told us, 'Take provisions for your journey, and make a treaty with them.' See, this bread was fresh and warm when we left, but look how stale and mouldy it has become. And our wineskins, sandals and clothes were new, but look at them now."

The Israelites inspected their clothes and provisions, but did not think to ask God for guidance. Then Joshua made a peace treaty with them, and all the leaders made an oath before God not to harm these people.

Three days later the Israelites heard that the men with whom they had made a treaty were actually from nearby Gibeon, so they set out for the city. But they did not attack it, for they had sworn an oath.

Joshua summoned the Gibeonites and asked, "Why did you deceive us, saying you were from a distant land, when you are neighbours only a day's journey away? We have sworn an oath, so we shall let you live, but you will become our servants and cut wood and fetch water for our temple when we build it."

The Gibeonites gladly accepted this, as they had feared they would be killed. Joshua then returned to Gilgal with most of his army.

The sun stands still

Some time later, five neighbouring kings decided to attack Gibeon together. The Gibeonites quickly sent word to Joshua, asking him to come to their aid. God said to Joshua, "Do not be afraid, I will make sure you conquer them."

Joshua, with his entire army, marched up from Gilgal to Gibeon overnight, taking the kings by surprise and defeating them completely. The Israelites pursued the remnants of their armies into the valley of Ayalon and God let down a storm of great hailstones.

By that time evening was drawing in. They would not be able to fight in darkness, so Joshua called out to the Lord, "Sun over Gibeon, stand still, and moon over the valley of Ayalon." The sun and the moon stood still in the middle of the sky and did not set for a whole day. There has never been a day like it before or since.

The Israelites pursued the fleeing armies and captured all their cities. They went on to conquer the whole land, defeating thirty-three kings in all.

Finally, as God had instructed Moses, Joshua divided the land among eleven of the tribes of Israel. Members of the twelfth priestly tribe of Levi were sent to be priests in the cities throughout the land. From that time on, people began to call it the land of Israel, or simply Israel.

The death of Joshua

Many years later, Joshua assembled all the tribes of Israel at Shechem, the centre of their land and the place where, about seven hundred years earlier, Abraham had first built an altar to God. Joshua reminded the people how God had led Abraham to this place and promised him the land, how Moses had led them out of Egypt, and how God had been with them when they conquered the land. Then he said, "Now serve the Lord with all faithfulness, and keep to his commandments."

The people all replied, "We will serve the Lord our God and obey him."

After this, Joshua died at the age of one hundred and ten, and he was buried in the land God had promised. And Joseph's bones, which the Israelites had carried from Egypt, were buried at Shechem.

The Leader-Judges

Deborah

After Joshua died, the Israelites lost their conquering spirit and many lived alongside the neighbouring Canaanite tribes. Some Israelites married the Canaanites' daughters, and some Canaanites married the Israelites' daughters. In time, they ignored the commands of the Lord and some began to worship the Canaanite gods. In one place in the north, they even became slaves to a Canaanite king, Jabin.

At that time the Israelites were led by a woman prophet, Deborah, who still heard and spoke the word of God. She held court under a palm tree in the hill country of Judea, and people would come to her with their disputes. For that reason, leaders at this time were also called judges. Deborah called Barak, a commander of the army, saying, "The Lord, the God of Israel, orders you to take ten thousand men and lead them up Mount Tabor. From there, they will attack Jabin's army of chariots."

Barak answered Deborah, "If you come with me, I will go."

"I will come," said Deborah. "But because you did not go alone, the honour of victory over Jabin's army will not be yours, but a woman's."

Barak summoned his army and travelled to Mount Tabor, which rises out of the wide fertile valley of Jezreel. When Jabin heard they were coming, he gathered his army and nine hundred chariots in the valley.

Then Deborah said to Barak, "Go! This day, the Lord will give Jabin's army to you."

Barak's men swept down from Mount Tabor and put terror into Jabin's army, who were defeated and killed. Even their commander was killed by a woman when he sought shelter in her tent.

The Israelites were now free from being slaves of the Canaanites, and the battle is remembered in the Song of Deborah.

God speaks to Gideon

As time went on, some Israelites continued to worship other gods. The Midianite tribe became powerful and oppressed the Israelites, raiding their land wherever they planted crops and killing all their cattle. The Israelites cried out to God to help them against the Midianites.

The angel of the Lord appeared before Gideon, a young man who was threshing wheat to keep it safe from the Midianites. The angel sat down under an oak tree and said, "The Lord is with you, mighty warrior."

"Pardon me, sir," replied Gideon, who thought this was a very odd thing for a stranger to say to him, "but if the Lord is with us, why has he let us be oppressed by the Midianites?"

"Go with the strength you have," the angel replied. "I am sending you to free Israel from the Midianites' hands."

"How can I save Israel?" Gideon asked. "I am from the weakest clan of the smallest tribe, and I am the youngest son in my family."

"I will be with you," the angel answered, "and I will strike down the Midianites, leaving none of them alive."

Gideon was not convinced, but he said, "If I am to do this, give me a sign that you have been sent by the Lord. Do not leave until I return."

Gideon left to prepare a young goat, some flour to make bread, and some broth in a pot. When he returned, he offered them to the stranger under the oak.

The angel said, "Take the meat and the bread, place them on this rock and pour the broth over them."

Gideon did so, and the angel touched the offering with the tip of his staff. Fire flared from the rock, consuming the meat and the bread, and the angel of the Lord disappeared.

Then Gideon realised that the stranger had been the angel of the Lord. In great fear he exclaimed, "Alas, my Lord, I have seen the angel of God face to face!"

But God said, "Do not be afraid, you are not going to die."

Gideon built a small altar to God there. That night God said to him, "Tear down your father's altar to the foreign god, Baal, and with its stones build a proper altar to your Lord, the God of Israel on this hill. Take the seven-year-old bull from your father's herd and burn it as an offering."

Gideon took some of his servants and carried out God's commands, but they did so at night, because Gideon was afraid of what his family and neighbours would say. Yet in the morning, when the people saw that Baal's altar had been destroyed, they soon found out that Gideon was responsible. A crowd went to Gideon's father, demanding, "Bring out your son. He must die because he has broken Baal's altar."

But Gideon's father replied, "Are you pleading for Baal? If Baal is really a god, he can defend himself if someone breaks down his altar."

Then Gideon blew a trumpet, summoning all his clan to follow him, and he sent messengers to rally all the neighbouring tribes. But Gideon was still a little doubtful, and prayed to the Lord, "Look at the wool fleece I have put on the threshing floor. If there is dew on it in the morning but the surrounding ground is dry, then I will know you really will free Israel by my hand."

When Gideon rose early the next day, the dew on the fleece filled a bowl when he wrung it out, but the ground around it was dry. However, Gideon was still not convinced that he was the right man for this task, and he prayed again to God, "Do not be angry with me, Lord. Grant me one more request. This time, make the fleece dry and the ground covered with dew."

God could see, though Gideon was filled with doubt, that he was not afraid of standing up to the voice of the Lord. And so God did as Gideon asked, and the next morning the fleece was dry and the ground was covered in dew.

This time, Gideon was finally convinced, and he put his trust in God.

Gideon defeats the Midianites

Early in the morning, Gideon and all his men were camped at a spring. God told Gideon, "You have too many men. If I deliver the Midianites into their hands, the Israelites will say, 'It was by our own strength that we defeated them.' So tell your men that anyone who is afraid can turn back now." Gideon did so, and 22,000 men turned back, leaving 10,000 men behind.

But God said, "There are still too many men. Take them to the water to drink. If they take the time to lap the water from cupped hands, keep them, but if they hastily kneel, putting their head in the water to drink, let them go home."

Gideon took the men to the water and only three hundred drank from cupped hands. The rest he sent home.

That night, as they camped above the Midianites, who were in the valley below, God said to Gideon, "If you are afraid, take your servant and go into the Midianites' camp to hear what they are saying. Then you will no longer be afraid."

Gideon and his servant crept into the Midianites' vast camp that night. There were so many men and so many camels that no one could count them. Gideon and his servant tiptoed up to a tent and heard a man telling his friend about a dream he had had.

The man said, "And then a round loaf of barley bread came tumbling into our camp. It struck one tent so hard that it overturned and collapsed."

His friend replied, "This loaf of barley bread must be a symbol of the sword of Gideon the Israelite. The God of the Israelites has given the Midianites and the whole camp into his hands."

When Gideon heard this, he bowed down in grateful prayer. Then he returned to the Israelite camp and called out, "Get up!" He divided his three hundred men into three companies, and gave each man a trumpet and a jar containing a flare. "Follow my lead," he commanded them. "When I get to the edge of the camp, do exactly as I do."

The three companies reached the edge of the Midianites' camp, completely surrounding it, just after midnight. Gideon blew his trumpet and broke his jar. All around the camp, the Israelites blew their trumpets and broke their jars. Holding the flares up, they shouted, "A sword for the Lord and for Gideon!"

The Midianites woke with a fright and tried to flee. When they heard the trumpets again, they were in such a panic that they turned on each other in the dark, slashing out with their swords, killing each other. Those who survived fled far away.

Gideon conquered the Midianites, and the Israelites lived in peace again for the rest of his lifetime.

Samson's riddle

In later years, a seafaring people called the Philistines settled on the coast of Israel. They became powerful and ruled over the Israelites who lived on the coast for forty years. During that time, an angel of the Lord appeared to a couple who had no children, telling them they were going to have a child who would be dedicated to God and would deliver the Israelites from the Philistines. The angel instructed them to never cut their son's hair.

When the child was born they named him Samson, and as he grew up the spirit of the Lord was with him.

One day, when Samson was a young man, he saw a beautiful young Philistine woman in the nearby town and fell in love with her. He asked his father and mother to arrange a marriage for him, as was their custom. They pleaded with him to find an Israelite woman to be his wife, but Samson would not listen.

They went down to the town and Samson followed some way behind. As he was passing a vineyard, a young lion suddenly came roaring towards him. The spirit of the Lord filled Samson, and he tore the lion apart with his bare hands. He told no one what he had done, and continued walking to the town to meet the woman.

His parents managed to arrange a marriage with the parents of the young woman. Some time later, when Samson went back to marry her, he turned aside at the vineyard to look at the lion's carcass. He saw that a swarm of wild bees was using it as their hive. He scooped out some of the honey and ate it, but he did not tell anyone where he had found the honey.

Samson held a great feast for a week, which was how they celebrated marriages in those days. The host would often set a puzzle for his guests as part of the fun. Thirty Philistine men had been chosen as Samson's companions and he said to them, "Let me tell you a riddle. If you can give me the answer within the seven days of the feast, I will give you thirty linen garments and thirty cloaks. If you can't tell me the answer, you must give me thirty linen garments and thirty cloaks."

This seemed a good bargain to the men, as they would only have to find one garment and cloak each if they lost, but Samson would have to find thirty. So they said, "Tell us your riddle then."

"Out of the eater came something to eat; out of the strong came something sweet," said Samson.

For three days they could not find the answer. On the fourth day, they demanded of Samson's wife, "Persuade your husband to explain the riddle for us, or we will burn you and your parents to death."

She threw herself at Samson, sobbing and asking him to tell her the riddle's answer. But he replied, "I haven't even told my father and mother, so why should I explain it to you?"

But she cried every night until, on the seventh night, Samson relented, for he could not bear to see her so unhappy. He told her the answer and she in turn explained it to her people. Before sunset of the last day of feasting, the Philistines came to him and said, "What is sweeter than honey, and what is stronger than a lion?"

Samson immediately saw that his wife had told them the answer, because no one could have guessed it. In fury he said to them, "You would not have solved my riddle if you had not cheated."

They understood that he meant they forced his wife to give them the answer. Then the spirit of the Lord filled Samson, and in his fury he went to the nearby coastal city, struck down thirty men, stripped them of their clothes, and went back to give them to those who had explained his riddle. Then he stomped back to his parents' house, burning with anger.

Some time later, he went down to visit his wife. But her father would not let him enter the house, saying, "When you left in anger, I was so sure you hated her that I gave her as a wife to one of the thirty companions."

Samson was dismayed and said fiercely, "This time I have every right to be angry and harm the Philistines."

He went out and caught three hundred foxes and tied them tail to tail in pairs. Then he fastened a flare to every pair of tails, lit the flares and chased the foxes into the Philistines' fields of standing grain. The grain caught fire, which spread to the surrounding vineyards and olive groves. When the Philistines found out that Samson was responsible, they killed his wife and her family. Samson was furious and attacked many of the Philistines.

He went to live in a cave in the hills of Judea. When the Philistines came up into Judea, the Israelites, fearing they wanted to fight them, asked why they had come. The Philistines answered, "We have come to take Samson prisoner and do to him as he did to us."

The Israelites went to Samson's cave and asked, "Don't you realise that the Philistines are rulers over us? We have come to tie you up and hand you over to them."

So they bound him with ropes and led him to the Philistines. Then the spirit of the Lord filled Samson again, and the ropes and bindings dropped from his hands like charred threads. He found the jawbone of a donkey and used it to strike down a thousand men. Then he said, "With a donkey's jawbone I have made donkeys of them."

From that day on, Samson became leader of the Israelites.

Samson and Delilah

One day Samson went to the Philistine city of Gaza and spent the night. Word spread that Samson was there, so the Philistines lay in wait for him at the city gates, saying, "At dawn we'll kill him."

But Samson woke in the middle of the night and got up. He took hold of the city gates, tore them loose and carried them on his shoulders into the hill country of Hebron, two days' walk away. The Philistines were amazed at Samson's great strength, and feared him.

Some time later, Samson fell in love with a Philistine woman called Delilah. The rulers of the Philistines went to her and said, "See if you can get Samson

to tell you where his strength comes from, and how we may overcome him. If you find out, each of us will give you a hundred shekels of silver."

Delilah asked Samson about his secret, and he replied, "If anyone ties me with fresh bow-strings, I will become weak."

While Samson was asleep, Delilah tied him with fresh bow-strings, called the Philistines and woke Samson. But he snapped the strings like threads. Three more times Delilah tried to find out Samson's secret, but each time she found that he had made a fool of her. Then she asked, "How can you say 'I love you' to me if you do not tell me the secret of your great strength?"

She nagged and prodded him day after day, until he was sick of hearing her voice, so he told her, "No razor has ever been used on my head because I was born dedicated to God. If my head were shaved, my strength would leave me."

Delilah went to tell the Philistine rulers, and they returned with silver in their hands. After Samson fell asleep in Delilah's lap, she called for someone to shave his hair. Then she called the Philistines and woke Samson. Samson thought he would break free as before, but he found the Lord had left him and all his strength was gone. The Philistines seized him, gouged out his eyes and took him to the city of Gaza.

The rulers called all the people together for a great celebration and sacrifice to their god Dagon, saying, "Our god has delivered Samson into our hands."

The temple of Dagon was so crowded that three thousand people had to stand on the roof. Everyone was in high spirits, and they started to call, "Bring out Samson to entertain us."

The hair on Samson's head had grown again, but he was now blind. He said to the servant who brought him out, "Put me where I can feel the pillars of the temple, so that I can lean against them."

Then he prayed to the Lord, "Please, God of Israel, strengthen me once more and let me get revenge on the Philistines for taking my eyes."

He reached out to the two central pillars of the temple and pushed them with all his might. The pillars, and then the entire temple crashed down on Samson and all the people inside it. Thus, Samson killed many more when he died than while he had lived.

Ruth comes to Bethlehem

In the days when the leader-judges ruled, there was famine in Judea. A man from Bethlehem, together with his wife and two sons, went to live for a while across the River Jordan in Moab. While they were living there, the sons married Moabite women. The man from Bethlehem died, and some years later his two sons also died, leaving their mother, Naomi, and their Moabite wives, Orpah and Ruth, as widows.

Naomi heard that the famine in Judea was over, so she set out with her two daughters-in-law to return home. On the way back, she said to the two women, "Go back to your mothers' homes. May the Lord show kindness to you, as you have shown kindness to my sons and to me."

She kissed them goodbye. Orpah kissed her farewell and returned to her home, but Ruth clung to Naomi, saying, "Do not make me leave you. Wherever you go, I will go, and wherever you stay, I will stay. Your people shall be my people, and your God shall be my God."

Naomi saw that Ruth was determined to go with her, and so they walked on until they came to Bethlehem around harvest time. The whole town recognised Naomi and welcomed her with Ruth. Because they had few possessions and nothing to eat, Ruth said to Naomi, "Let me go to the fields to gather any grain left behind by the people harvesting the barley." Naomi agreed.

Around noon, Boaz, the owner of the field, came to see the harvesters. Boaz greeted them and asked, "Who is that young woman?"

They replied, "She is Ruth, a Moabite who came back with Naomi. She asked to gather leftover grain. She has been working here all morning with only a short rest."

Boaz went to Ruth and said, "My daughter, do not go to any other fields. Stay with the women who work for me, and if you are thirsty, get a drink from the water jars the men have filled."

Ruth bowed low and asked, "Why have I found favour in your eyes, when I am a foreigner in this land?"

Boaz replied, "I have heard how loyal you have been to Naomi, your mother-in-law, and how you left your home to come and live with a people you do not know. May the Lord repay you for what you have done."

"May I continue to find favour in your eyes," Ruth replied.

At mealtime, Boaz invited her to join his people and share their bread. He gave orders to his men to let her gather leftover grain, and even to leave some stalks of grain from the sheaves for her.

Ruth gathered until evening, and then she threshed the barley – separating the grain from the husks – and carried the grain back to her mother-in-law. Naomi was amazed at how much grain she had brought back and asked where she had gathered it. Ruth explained where she had worked and how she had met Boaz, the owner of the land. "He even said to me, 'Stay with my workers until we have finished the harvest,'" said Ruth.

"The Lord bless him," said Naomi. "He is a relative of mine who has never stopped showing kindness."

Ruth and Boaz

Towards the end of harvest time, Naomi said to Ruth, "My daughter, I must find a husband and a home for you. It is the custom among our people that when a woman's husband dies, she can only marry a relative of her husband, who is known as a kinsman-redeemer because he helps his relative. Boaz is related to us, and I know he will take good care of you. Will you marry Boaz?"

"Yes, I will do as you say," said Ruth.

"Now listen carefully. Tonight, Boaz will be threshing barley at the threshing floor. Wash, put on perfume and dress in your best clothes. Then go there, but don't let him see you. After he has finished eating and drinking, he will go to sleep. Find him and lie down at his feet."

Ruth did everything Naomi told her. When Boaz finished his meal, he went to lie down at the far end of the grain pile. Ruth crept after him quietly and lay down at his feet.

In the middle of the night, Boaz awoke. "Who are you?" he asked in the dark.

"I am your servant Ruth," she replied. "You are the kinsman-redeemer of our family."

"The Lord bless you," he replied. "Your kindness is great. Although it is true that I am the kinsman-redeemer of your family, there is another man more closely related to your family than I am. But leave it with me, I shall speak with him."

Before daybreak, Boaz said to Ruth, "Before you leave, hold out your shawl." When she did so, he filled it with grain. Then she returned to Naomi with the grain and told her everything that had happened.

At dawn, Boaz went to the town gate and waited. When the other relative he had mentioned came along, Boaz said, "Come here and sit down." Boaz also called ten elders of the town and asked to sit down with them.

He then said to the relative, "Naomi, who has come back from Moab, is selling a piece of land that belonged to her husband, your relative. I thought I should tell you so you can buy it, because no one can buy it except a relative. But if you don't want it, then tell me, for I am next in line."

"I will buy it," said the relative.

Then Boaz said, "When you buy the land from Naomi, you will also have to marry Ruth the Moabite, the widow of her son, in order to keep the property."

The relative became worried. He did not want to marry a foreign woman, so he made up an excuse: "I cannot do it because it would endanger my own property. You can buy the land."

So Boaz announced to the elders and all the people at the town gate, "Today you are witnesses that I have bought all the property from Naomi, and I will marry Ruth the Moabite. You are my witnesses!"

The elders replied, "We are witnesses. May the Lord bless the woman who is coming into your home, and may your family be remembered for generations to come."

Ruth married Boaz. In time they had a son called Obed, and Obed became the father of Jesse, who became the father of King David.

Samuel's childhood

There was once a man named Elkanah whose wife Hannah had no children. Every year they went to Shiloh, the mountain where the Ark of the Covenant stood, and Hannah prayed to God to give her a child, promising, "Lord Almighty, if you look upon your servant and give her a son, I will give him to the Lord for all the days of his life."

She was praying silently, deeply in her heart, but her lips were moving. Eli, the priest at Shiloh saw this. Thinking she was drunk, he said to her, "Put away your wine."

Hannah answered, "I am not drinking wine, I am praying to the Lord out of my deep anguish."

When Eli heard this, he replied, "Go in peace, and may the God of Israel grant what you have asked for."

In the course of time, Hannah gave birth to a son and named him Samuel, which means "God heard". When Samuel no longer needed his mother's milk, his parents took him to Shiloh and presented him to Eli.

Samuel grew up serving God under Eli, the priest. Each year his mother made Samuel a white linen robe and brought it to him when she and her husband came to make their annual sacrifice. Eli would bless them.

Eli's two sons were also priests, but they were wicked. People would bring meat offerings to sacrifice to the Lord, but the sons would take the meat for themselves. They also sought favours from people.

Eli was very old when an angel of God came to him and said, "I chose you and your family to be priests, but your sons are not honouring me. I will destroy your sight, and all your descendants will die before they are old. Your two sons will both die on the same day. I will choose another to be priest, and his family will be my true priests always."

Later, Eli asked his sons, "Why do you do such things? Anyone who sins against the Lord will be put to death." But they did not listen to their old father.

One night, Samuel, who was sleeping in the house of Eli and his family, heard a voice call his name.

He ran to Eli and said, "Here I am, you called me."

But Eli said, "I did not call you. Go back to sleep."

Samuel returned to his bed, but again he heard a voice call his name, and again he ran to Eli. Eli told him to go back to sleep. The same thing happened a third time. This time Eli realised that God was calling Samuel, and he told him, "Lie down again, but if you hear the voice, say, 'Speak, Lord, for your servant is listening.' And tell me in the morning what he said."

Soon after, Samuel was once again lying in his bed when he heard the voice call, "Samuel! Samuel!"

Then Samuel said, "Speak Lord, for your servant is listening."

God said to Samuel, "I am about to do something that will make all who hear it shudder. I will do everything to Eli's family that I told him I would. I warned him that I would judge his family forever because of the wicked deeds of his sons, but they have not stopped."

Samuel lay down until morning and then opened the doors of the house. He was afraid to tell Eli what he had heard, but Eli called him, asking, "What did the Lord say to you? Do not hide it from me."

Samuel told him everything he had heard. Eli replied, "He is the Lord. Let him do what is good in his eyes." Eli spent many years waiting for God's punishment, knowing that one day it would come.

The Lord was with Samuel as he grew up, and Samuel became his true priest. All the Israelites from the very north to the far south of the land recognised Samuel as a prophet of the Lord, because the Lord continued to appear at Shiloh and speak to him.

The capture and return of the ark

When Eli was ninety-eight years old, the Israelites went out to fight against the Philistines. The Philistines called all their men together to fight and they defeated the Israelites, killing many of them. Then the elders of Israel said, "Let us bring the Ark of the Covenant from Shiloh to our camp, so that the Lord is with us in battle and can save us from our enemies."

Men, including Eli's two sons, were sent to Shiloh to fetch the Ark of the Covenant. When the ark arrived in the camp of the Israelites, the people raised such a great shout of joy that the ground shook.

The Philistines heard the great shout, and soon learned that the ark had reached the Israelite camp. They were afraid, saying, "A god has come into their camp. We are doomed! It is the god who brought the plagues to Egypt and led the Israelites through the desert. We must be strong! Otherwise, we will become slaves to the Israelites."

The Philistines fought like never before and defeated the Israelites again, killing many, including Eli's two sons. The Ark of the Covenant was captured.

One of the Israelites who escaped ran to Shiloh in his torn clothes. When he arrived, Eli was sitting on his chair, waiting, because in his heart he feared for the ark. When the man came into the town, Eli heard the commotion and asked him what had happened.

"Israel fled from the Philistines, and many were killed. Your two sons are dead, and the Ark of the Covenant has been captured," he replied.

When Eli heard about the ark, he fell off his chair, broke his neck and died.

The Philistines brought the captured Ark of the Covenant to the temple of their god Dagon in one of their cities, and set it beside the great statue of Dagon. When the people rose early the next morning, they saw the statue of Dagon had fallen on its face before the ark. They carefully raised it back into place. The next morning, the statue of Dagon had fallen again, but his head and hands had broken off.

The people said, "The ark of Israel must not stay here."

So they moved it to another Philistine city. But after the ark's arrival, people were afflicted with terrible diseases. They discussed moving it again, but the rulers of the Philistines said, "We must send the ark back to the Israelites, otherwise it will kill all our people."

They called their priests and wise men, who said, "If you send the ark back, you must send it with gifts. Then you will be healed. Get a new cart ready with two young cows that have never pulled a cart before."

The Philistines put the ark onto the cart along with a chest of gold, and let the two cows pull the cart wherever they wanted. The cows went straight towards the hill country, reaching a town of the Israelites, and came to rest by a large rock. As soon as the Israelites saw the ark, they rejoiced. They sacrificed the two cows on the rock as an offering to God.

The ark was then taken to Kiriath-Jearim, a hilltop in Judea close to where Samuel lived. In the time of Samuel, the Israelites recaptured the towns the Philistines had taken from them, and the land was at peace for the rest of Samuel's life. The Ark of the Covenant was safe.

The Kingdom of Israel

Saul

The Israelites want a king

When Samuel was old, he appointed his sons as leaders. But Samuel's sons did not follow his ways: they were dishonest and took bribes. The elders of the Israelites went to Samuel and told him so, pleading, "Appoint a king to lead us, so that we are like other nations."

Samuel was troubled by their words, for he knew that the king of the Israelites could only be the Lord, the God of Israel. He prayed to God, who answered, "The people have rejected me as a king. But listen to them. Tell them what a king ruling over them will do."

Samuel told the elders what God had said, adding, "A king who rules over you will make your sons serve him with his chariots and horses. He will take the best of your fields, vineyards and olive groves, and the best of your flocks. You will become his slaves. But when you cry out to the Lord to free you from the king that you asked for, he will not listen to your cries."

But the elders refused to listen, saying, "No. We want a king. Then we shall be like other nations, with a king to lead us and fight our battles."

Samuel prayed again to God, who answered, "Listen to them and give them a king."

Saul is anointed king

Once, a man of the tribe of Benjamin lost his donkeys, which had wandered off, so he said to his son Saul, a tall and handsome boy, "Take one of the servants with you and go and look for the donkeys."

Saul and the servant took some provisions and searched for several days, but did not find the donkeys. "Let us return home now," Saul said to the servant, "or my father will stop thinking about the donkeys and start worrying about us."

But the servant replied, "Look, we are near the town of Samuel, the man of God. Let us go and ask him."

Saul said, "But what shall we offer him? Our food sacks are almost empty."

The servant replied, "I have a silver coin. I will give it to the man of God."

The day before, the Lord had said to Samuel, "Tomorrow at this time I will send you a man from the tribe of Benjamin. Anoint him as king. He will rule over my people and deliver them from the Philistines."

Saul and his servant set out for the town. As they drew close, they asked some women, "Where is the man of God?"

"There he is ahead of you," replied the women. "Hurry, for the people are preparing a sacrifice at the holy place on the hilltop."

They hurried up to the town. When Samuel saw Saul approaching, God said to him, "This is the man."

Samuel spoke to them as if he knew them. "Come with me to the holy place, for today you shall eat with me. In the morning I shall send you on your way."

Samuel led the way to the hilltop, where he blessed the sacrifice that the people had made to the Lord. He invited Saul and the servant to be seated at the head of the table in the place of honour before all other guests. After they had eaten, Samuel took Saul and the servant to his house, where they slept on the flat roof, as was the custom for guests in that land.

In the morning Samuel called to Saul, "Get ready, and I will send you on your way. Tell the servant to go on ahead of us: you must stay behind so that I may give you a message from God."

When the servant had left, Samuel took a flask of olive oil and poured it on Saul's head. He kissed him, saying, "The Lord has anointed you ruler over all his people."

Saul could not believe what he had heard. "How can I know this is true?" he asked.

Samuel replied, "When you leave me, you will meet two women near Rachel's tomb, outside the village of Bethlehem. They will say to you, 'The donkeys you were looking for have been found, and your father is now worrying about you.'

"Then you will meet three men going to worship at Bethel. One will be carrying three goats, another three loaves of bread, and the third a skin of wine. They will greet you and offer you two loaves of bread, which you will accept.

"After that, as you approach a Philistine town, you will hear lyres and pipes playing, then meet a procession of prophets coming towards you. You will talk with them, and you will be changed into a different person. Once all these signs have been fulfilled, do whatever your heart tells you, for God is with you."

As Saul left the town to catch up with his servant, God lifted Saul's heart. And everything happened as Samuel had foretold. But Saul did not speak to anyone about what Samuel had said to him.

Saul is crowned king before the people

Some time later, Samuel summoned all the people of Israel and said to them, "The Lord, the God of Israel, brought you out of Egypt and delivered you from all your enemies, but you have rejected him and said you want a king to rule over you. So now present yourselves before the Lord."

Samuel asked one man from each tribe to come and draw lots, and the tribe of Benjamin was chosen. Then one man from each clan of the tribe of Benjamin came, and then each family from the chosen clan drew lots, and finally Saul was chosen. But when the people looked for him, he could not be found.

They prayed to the Lord, and God said, "Saul has hidden himself among the supplies of food and bedding."

They ran to there and saw him standing among the servants, for he was a head taller than any of the others. They brought him before Samuel, who said to everyone, "You see the man the Lord has chosen."

The people shouted, "Long live the king!"

Samuel explained to the people the rights and duties of a king, and he wrote them down in a scroll. Then he sent all the people home.

Saul, too, returned home to Gibeah, a town in the north of Judea. Almost all the people rejoiced, but some had doubts, asking, "How can this young fellow save us?" They despised Saul and brought him no gifts.

But Saul took no notice. He ruled over Israel and won many battles against the neighbouring peoples.

Saul loses his kingship

Saul and the Israelites had attacked some of the outlying Philistine villages, so the Philistines assembled a great army to fight back. Samuel said to Saul, "Summon all the Israelites at Gilgal, in the Jordan valley, and wait there for seven days until I come to offer a sacrifice."

The Israelites gathered at Gilgal, but when they saw the vast army of the Philistines in the distance, they became afraid. Some hid in caves and others fled. But Saul remained at Gilgal with many of his men. Every day he sent lookouts to see if Samuel was coming, and every day Saul saw that in the night more of his men had fled. After seven days Samuel had still not come, so Saul made a burnt offering to the Lord at the altar in Gilgal.

Just as he had finished making the offering, Samuel arrived. Saul went out to greet him, but Samuel asked, "What have you done?"

Saul answered, "When I saw the men were scattering and you still had not come, I was afraid the Philistines would come down against us at Gilgal, so I made a burnt offering to seek the Lord's favour."

"You have done a foolish thing," said Samuel. "Only the priests are allowed to make burnt offerings. You have not kept the commandments of the Lord your God, and now your kingdom will not endure. The Lord will choose another man as a worthy leader of the people."

Saul pleaded with Samuel, promising never again to disobey the commandments of the Lord, but Samuel left.

Saul now only had six hundred men with him, but when he went to fight against the Philistines, his men were victorious. The Philistines fled to their coastal lands.

Some time later, Samuel told Saul, "The Lord Almighty commands you to fight against the Amalekites. Do not spare them. Kill all their cattle and herds, leaving nothing alive."

The Amalekites were a bitter enemy of the Israelites and had fought them when they were travelling through the desert from Egypt.

Saul summoned a great army and led them south into the desert, where they attacked the Amalekites and took some of their best cattle.

Then God spoke to Samuel: "Saul has again turned away from me, and not obeyed my commandments."

Although Samuel was strict and fierce with Saul, he looked upon him as his son. Troubled, he argued with the Lord all that night, but the Lord did not hear him.

Early the next morning, Samuel went out to meet Saul as he returned to Gibeah. When they met, Saul said, "The Lord bless you! I have carried out the Lord's commands."

God had not told Samuel what Saul had done wrong, but when Samuel saw the cattle he asked, "What is the bleating of sheep and the lowing of cattle that I hear?"

Saul answered, "Our soldiers brought the best of the Amalekites' sheep and cattle to make a sacrifice to the Lord."

But Samuel asked, "Which pleases the Lord more: burnt offerings or people who obey his word?"

Then Saul was ashamed and answered, "I have done wrong. I went against the Lord's command and against your instructions. But I was afraid how the men would react if I ordered them to leave the battle empty-handed. Now I beg you, forgive my wrongdoing and come with me, so that I may worship the Lord."

Samuel said, "I will not go back with you. You have rejected the word of the Lord, and so the Lord has rejected you as king over Israel. The Lord is giving the kingdom to a man who is better than you."

Then Samuel turned and left, and never went to see Saul again. And from that day, the spirit of God left Saul.

David

Samuel anoints David king

God asked Samuel, "How long will you continue to mourn for Saul? I have rejected him and have chosen another. Fill your horn with oil and go to Bethlehem, to the house of Jesse, because one of his sons is to be king."

But Samuel replied, "How can I go? If Saul hears I have anointed another, he will kill me."

God replied, "Say that you have come to make a sacrifice to the Lord. Invite Jesse and all his sons to the sacrifice and I will show you what to do."

When Samuel came to Bethlehem the people were afraid, because prophets often criticised their wrongdoings. But Samuel said, "I have come in peace to make a sacrifice to the Lord. Go and purify yourselves – bathe, put on fresh clothes – and come to the sacrifice with me."

Samuel went to Jesse's house and invited him and all his sons to the sacrifice. Jesse called his sons, and when Samuel saw the eldest he thought, "This must be the one, for he is tall and handsome."

But God said to Samuel, "Do not consider his height or appearance. The Lord does not look at people like that – he looks at their heart."

Then the second son stood before Samuel, but God said, "I have not chosen this one."

And the same happened when the third and the fourth son came, and the fifth, sixth and seventh. Samuel asked Jesse, "Are these all of your sons?"

"There is still the youngest," Jesse replied. "He is tending the sheep, and he is too young to take part in sacrifices."

Samuel said, "Send for him. Let us sit down until he arrives."

Jesse sent a messenger to call David, who left his father's flock with the messenger and ran back to the house. Samuel saw that he was glowing with health. Then God told him, "Rise and anoint him. He is the one."

David knelt down before the wise man, but did not know what Samuel was going to do. Samuel took the horn of oil and poured some on David's head, anointing him in front of his father and his brothers. The family did not really know what this meant, because Samuel said no more to them before returning home. They knew that oil was used to bless kings and priests, but Saul was king and David was not from a priestly family. But from that day on, the spirit of the Lord was with David.

David comes to Saul's court

The spirit of the Lord had left Saul and now an evil spirit tormented him. Saul's servants said, "Let us search for someone who can play the harp, so that the soothing music will calm you when the evil spirit comes and make it leave."

One of the servants had heard that in Bethlehem, Jesse's youngest son could play the harp, so Saul sent a messenger to him, commanding, "Send me your son David to play his harp for me."

Jesse took a donkey, loaded it with bread, a skin of wine and a young goat as gifts, and sent them with David to Saul at Gibeah.

Saul liked David very much, and asked Jesse if he would let David remain in his service. Whenever the evil spirit visited Saul, David would play the harp, then the evil spirit would leave Saul and he would feel better. Yet David was often allowed to return home to his family and watch the sheep until he was called again to Saul's court.

David and Goliath

One day the Philistines, the seafaring people from the coast, gathered their army on the ridge of a hill in Judah. Saul called the Israelites together, and they stood on the opposite ridge, facing the Philistines, with a valley below between them.

A champion of the Philistines named Goliath came out towards the Israelites. He was a giant of a man – more than six cubits high. (A cubit was the length of an arm from fingertip to elbow; most people are about four cubits high.) He had a bronze helmet and bronze armour covering his body and his legs, and he held a spear and a sword of iron. Goliath shouted out to the Israelites, "Why line up for battle? Choose a man and send him down to me. If he is able to kill me, we will become your subjects, but if I kill your man, you will serve us."

On hearing this, Saul and the Israelites were terrified. For forty days, this giant of the Philistines came out every day and taunted the Israelites with his challenge.

David's father Jesse told him to take some grain, bread and cheese for Saul and David's three oldest brothers, who were among the Israelite army. David left early the next morning and reached the camp where the two armies were facing each other. As he was talking with his brothers, Goliath stepped forward and shouted his usual taunts.

The men surrounding David explained, "This man keeps coming out to defy Israel. Our king will give great wealth to the man who kills him. He will also give his daughter in marriage to him, and his family will not have to pay taxes."

David's oldest brother was annoyed that he was wandering around talking with all the men in the army, and said, "What are you doing here? You should be watching the sheep instead of trying to watch the battle."

"Can't I even ask questions?" asked David, who was used to his brother's bad temper.

Word of the curious young man reached Saul, and he sent for him. Saul was so wrapped up in his worries that he did not recognise the youth who often played the harp for him. David said, "No one should lose heart on account of this godless Philistine. I will go out and fight him."

Saul replied, "You cannot go out and fight him: you are only a boy, and you have never been a soldier."

But David told Saul, "I have been keeping my father's sheep. Each time a lion or a bear carried one off, I went after the beast, struck it and rescued the sheep from its mouth. When the beast turned on me, I seized it by the hair, struck it and killed it. I have killed both lion and bear, and I will do the same to Goliath. The Lord God who saved me from the lion and the bear will save me from this Philistine."

So Saul said, "Go then, and the Lord be with you."

Saul gave David his armour, helmet and sword. But when David put them all on and tried to walk around, he could barely move. He told Saul, "I cannot take these, I am not used to them."

David took off the armour, then chose five smooth stones from the bed of a stream and put them in his bag. As he approached the giant Philistine, he held his sling in one hand and his staff in the other.

Goliath came closer, looked at the boy and laughed out loud, saying, "Am I a dog? Is that why you come to me with a stick? Come here and I'll feed your flesh to the birds!"

David said, "You come against me with a sword and spear, but I come against you in the name of the Lord Almighty, the God of Israel. The Lord will deliver you into my hands, and I will cut off your head."

As Goliath moved closer to attack, David ran to meet him. Reaching into his bag and taking out a stone, he slung it and struck Goliath. The stone sank into his forehead and he fell to the ground. David ran and stood over him. He took Goliath's sword and cut off his head. The Philistines turned and ran, and the Israelites gave chase, pursuing them to the gates of their cities.

Saul asked Abner, the commander of his army, "Who is this young man?" Abner found David and brought him to Saul.

When the king asked who he was, David replied, "I am your servant. I am the son of Jesse, in Bethlehem."

Saul then recognised him as the soothing harp-player. He kept his promise about the reward for killing Goliath and allowed David to marry his daughter Michal.

Saul tries to kill David

David and Saul's eldest son, Jonathan, became best friends. Jonathan made a promise that they would always remain friends, and as a sign he gave David his robe, sword and bow.

David was successful whenever Saul sent him to fight, and the soldiers

were pleased with David's leadership. Once when they returned from a great battle with the Philistines, the women from the towns came out to greet Saul and David. They danced and sang, "Saul has slain thousands, but David has slain tens of thousands."

Though it was true, Saul was angry and jealous, and the evil spirit came upon him. As he always did when this happened, David played the harp to soothe the king. But this time the evil spirit had taken such a strong grip of Saul that he picked up his spear and hurled it at David. David simply dodged the spear and continued playing. Again, Saul tried to spear David, but again David dodged his throw.

Jonathan promised David that he would speak to his father. He went to Saul the next day and said, "Let the king do no wrong to David, for he has served you well. Everything he has done has benefited your kingdom. Why would you kill David for no reason?"

Saul listened, and promised, "As the Lord lives, David will not be put to death."

Jonathan told David what his father had promised. But soon the evil spirit took hold of Saul again, and for a third time he tried to kill David. This time David escaped to his home. The evil spirit was seething in Saul, and he sent men to David's house to watch over it and kill him when he came out in the morning. But Michal, David's wife, spotted them. Because she knew about her father's anger, she helped David escape through a window in the back of the house, and he fled.

Michal took a wooden statue, laid it on David's bed, covered it with garments and put some goats' hair on its head.

Saul grew impatient and sent soldiers to bring David from his house. But Michal said, "He is ill."

Then Saul, in his rage, sent the soldiers back, saying, "Bring him to me in his bed so that I may kill him."

The soldiers rushed into the house, picked up the bed and brought it to Saul. When Saul saw that it was only a statue he raged at Michal, "Why did you trick me and let my enemy escape?"

She did not tell the truth to her father, but replied, "He said that I had to let him escape, otherwise he would kill me."

In the meantime, David had fled to Samuel the prophet and told him everything. Saul, still raging, heard where David was and sent out men to capture him. When the men arrived, they saw Samuel standing as a leader among a group of prophets, singing. The spirit of the Lord came upon Saul's men and they joined the singing.

Saul was told about it and sent more men. But the same thing happened again. Finally, Saul himself went to visit Samuel, and when he arrived the spirit of God came over him too, and he also joined the group of prophets singing.

David spares Saul's life

Not long after Saul returned to his court at Gibeah, the evil spirit came over him once more and David had to flee again. He hid in a cave in the wilderness of Judea. Soon, several men who were unhappy with Saul joined David, and he became the commander of a group of four hundred men.

While hiding there, he heard that the Philistines were fighting and looting the threshing floors of Keilah, a town in Israel. David asked the Lord, "Shall I go and attack the Philistines?"

And the Lord answered, "Go, attack the Philistines and save Keilah."

But David's men argued, "We are in enough danger here, hiding from Saul. Don't make us face even greater peril, fighting against the mighty Philistines."

Once again David asked the Lord, and the Lord answered, "Go and fight. I will grant you victory over the Philistines."

So David and his men fought the Philistines and won, making their enemies flee back to their cities on the coast. The town of Keilah was freed.

When Saul was told about David's victory, the evil spirit made him jealous. He gathered his men and set out to find David. However, David and his company had again hidden in the caves of Judea, moving from place to place. Day after day Saul searched, but God did not let him find David.

While Saul was searching in the desert of Judea, he stopped to rest at the mouth of a cave. At the back of the cave, in the dark, David and some of his men were hidden. The men whispered to David, "This is the day the Lord spoke of when he said, 'I will give your enemy into your hands.'"

David crept up silently behind Saul, but he did not really want to harm the king, so he cut off a corner of his robe instead. Then David felt guilty and said to his men, "I pray the Lord will never let me do such a thing to my king. None of us must ever attack Saul or lay our hands on him, for he is the Lord's anointed."

When Saul started to walk away, David moved forward and called out, "My lord, my king!"

When Saul looked behind him, David bowed low with his face to the ground. He asked Saul, "Why do you listen when men say, 'David wants to harm you'? Today you were in my hands, but I spared you. See, I cut off the corner of your robe, but I did not kill you. Why do you hunt me down?"

"Is that your voice, David, my son?" Saul asked, and he wept for shame. "You are more honourable than I am. You have treated me well, but I have treated you badly. I know that one day you will be king. But swear to God that you will not kill any of my children or grandchildren."

David gave Saul his solemn promise, then Saul returned home.

Nabal and Abigail

The evil spirit came over Saul often, so David fled into the desert of Judea where he remained with his men. While he was away, Saul in his jealousy made his daughter Michal, David's wife, marry another man.

Very close to where David and his men were hiding there lived a very wealthy man named Nabal, who owned thousands of goats and sheep. Nabal's flocks often grazed by the caves, but David and his men never stole any sheep, though they were often hungry. When the time came for shearing the sheep, the people of this region used to hold a great festival.

David sent messengers to Nabal. They said, "Greetings from our master, David. He wishes you and your household long life and good health. It is near the time of the festival of shearing. When your shepherds were near us, we did not mistreat them, and in the whole time we were close to your land, nothing of yours went missing. Ask your servants: they will tell you this is true. So, since we are here at this festive time, please will you spare us some food as a favour to our master?"

In those lands it was very rude not to offer food and shelter to a stranger who was looking for help. Although David was known by many as a great leader who had many times been victorious over the Philistines, Nabal was a mean, grumpy fellow.

"Who is this David?" he replied. "Are his men just servants who have run away from their masters? Why should I share my bread and meat with these men who come from who knows where?"

When the messengers returned, David was angry at Nabal's insulting reply. He ordered a group of his men to take their swords and go with him to fight Nabal and his servants.

Meanwhile one of Nabal's servants, who had heard his master insulting David's messengers, ran to Nabal's home. He told Abigail, Nabal's wife, what had happened. "But David's men were good to us," he said. "The whole time we were grazing the flocks near where they were hiding, nothing went missing, and they protected us night and day. Now, I think a disaster is hanging over the master. He is a wicked man who will not listen to anyone."

Abigail acted quickly. She took supplies of bread, wine, meat, grain and cakes, loaded them onto donkeys, and rode out to meet David and his men. When she saw them coming towards her, she quickly got off her donkey and bowed down at David's feet.

"Pardon your servant, my lord," she said. "Please pay no attention to that foolish man Nabal. He is just like his name." (Nabal means "fool".) "I did not see the messengers you sent, but I have heard that your men have always been good to ours. Let this gift which I have brought to you be given to the men who follow you. And may the Lord your God always bless you."

David said, "Praise be to God for sending you. You have kept me from shedding blood this day. We were on our way to fight Nabal and all his men, and we would not have left one of them alive." He accepted Abigail's gifts and said, "Go home in peace."

On Abigail's return home, Nabal was holding a banquet like a king. She told him nothing, because he was in high spirits and very drunk. In the morning, when Nabal was sober, she explained what she had done. He was seized by fury and became rigid like stone. Ten days later, God struck Nabal and he died.

When David heard that Nabal was dead, he said, "Praise the Lord, because he has dealt with Nabal and kept me from doing wrong against him."

He sent word to Abigail, asking her to become his wife. She immediately climbed onto her donkey, went along with the messengers, and married David.

David spares Saul again

The evil spirit did not leave Saul, and when he heard that David was hiding in the desert of Judea, he set out after him with three thousand men. David carefully spied out Saul's camp, and at night, he and a companion crept in.

They found Saul asleep in his tent. Abner, the commander of the army, who was supposed to be guarding Saul, was also asleep. David's companion whispered, "Let me kill him with a thrust of his spear."

But David replied, "Do not lay a hand on the Lord's anointed. The Lord will set his time to die. I will take his spear and the water jug by his head. Then let us go."

They left silently. No one saw them, and no one woke up. David crossed to the other side of a dry riverbed, stood on a hill and called, "Abner! Guards! Why did you not guard your king when someone came to harm him? Where are the king's spear and water jug?"

Saul recognised David's voice and shouted, "Is that your voice, David, my son?"

David replied, "Yes, it is, my lord and king. Why are you pursuing me? What have I done wrong?"

Saul said, "I have done wrong. Come back to me! You spared my life today. I will not harm you again."

David answered, "Here is the king's spear. Let one of your men come and get it."

Saul returned home to Gibeah. But David and his men stayed away and lived among the Philistines.

The death of Saul

One day the Philistines raised an army to fight against Israel. However, they told David to stay behind in their city. Though they liked him, they did not completely trust him.

Saul gathered his men and set up camp opposite the Philistines, but when he saw their vast army he was terrified. By this time Samuel had died, so Saul could no longer go to him for advice. He prayed to the Lord, but the Lord did not answer him. He asked his people for advice and found an old woman who could communicate with the world of spirits. He asked her to contact Samuel.

The woman sat in silence as she tried to reach Samuel's spirit, and finally she said, "I see an old man wearing a robe."

Saul knew it was Samuel, so he bowed down to the ground and said, "I am in great distress. God did not answer me, so I called on you. The Philistines have assembled a vast army to fight against me."

The old woman told Saul how Samuel replied: "Why do you disturb me? The Lord has departed from you and become your enemy. You did not obey the Lord, so he has given your kingdom to David. Tomorrow the Lord will give victory to the Philistines, and you and your sons will be with me."

Saul was filled with fear, and all his strength left him.

The next day the Philistines fought against Israel, and the Israelites fled. Many died. The Philistines pursued the king. Saul, his eldest son, Jonathan, and two of his other sons were all killed.

When David heard of the death of King Saul and of Jonathan, his dearest friend, he tore his clothes, wept and fasted until evening.

David wrote a song of mourning for Saul and Jonathan, and everyone in the land of Israel sang it. Throughout his life, David wrote songs of praise when he was filled with joy, or laments when he was filled with sorrow, all of which showed his deep trust in God. (The Book of Psalms contains one hundred and fifty of David's songs, which are sung to this day.)

David is crowned king

David knew that the time had come for the fulfilment of God's promise that he would become king. But to be sure of God's will, he prayed to the Lord, asking, "Shall I go to one of the towns in the hill country of Judah?"

The Lord answered, "Go up to the town of Hebron."

So David went with his men and all their families to Hebron, where Abraham, Isaac and Jacob were buried. The people of the tribe of Judah came to Hebron and anointed David as their king.

However, Saul's commander, Abner, was faithful to Saul and his family. He pronounced as king Saul's only surviving son, Ishbosheth. The eleven other tribes of Israel recognised Ishbosheth as their king, but the tribe of Judah remained loyal to David.

For years there was a war between the followers of Saul and the followers of David, but in time David grew stronger and stronger.

One day Ishbosheth insulted Abner, accusing him of taking something from Saul. This made Abner very angry. "Am I a dog?" he demanded of Ishbosheth. "To this day I have been loyal to the house of Saul, and have not betrayed you to David. But now I must do what the Lord promised and hand over the kingdom to make David king over all of Israel."

Abner sent messengers to David in Hebron, saying, "Make an agreement with me, and I will help bring all the tribes of Israel over to you."

David replied, "I will make an agreement with you, but I demand one thing. You must bring me my wife Michal, daughter of Saul." Though David had had many other wives since his first marriage, he still longed to see Michal, his first love.

Abner spoke with the elders of the tribes of Israel, reminding them that God had promised David would be king. Then he took Michal and a few men to Hebron, where David prepared a feast for them. Abner said to David, "Let me go at once and assemble all the Israelites so that they will make you their king."

David agreed and Abner left. But when the commander of David's army heard that Abner had come to visit David, he was sure the king was being tricked, so he found Abner and killed him.

When David heard this news, he called out, "My kingdom and I are innocent of this man's death."

David and all his people mourned the death of Abner, and they buried him in Hebron. David sang a great lament for Abner, because he had been a worthy foe. All the people of Israel heard this song, and knew that David had no part in Abner's murder, for they could see how noble David was.

Soon, the leaders of the tribes of Israel came to Hebron and asked David to be their king. He was crowned before a huge gathering of his people and they celebrated with a great feast. David was thirty years old when he became king, and he reigned for forty years.

The conquest of Jerusalem

At that time, the kingdom of Israel extended from Dan in the north, below the snowy peak of Mount Hermon, to Beersheba, in the desert in the south. But there was one city that the Israelites had not conquered: Jerusalem, which lay in the hills of Judea between Gibeah, where Saul had lived, and Bethlehem, where David was born. It was the holy place where, hundreds of years earlier, Abraham met the priest-king Melchizedek.

David and the Israelites marched to Jerusalem to attack the Jebusites who lived there. The Jebusites guarded the sacred city and tried to ward off the Israelites in an unusual way: they paraded their blind and lame people on the city walls, perhaps to warn the Israelites what would happen to them if they came into the city, or perhaps to show that they felt so safe behind their walls that even the blind would stop the invaders.

David asked if any of his men would be willing to creep into the city through the shaft that carried water inside the walls. One of his men agreed. He crawled through the shaft and then opened the gates from inside, so the Israelites could conquer the city.

From that time on, David lived in Jerusalem and built up the city around his fortress. Because the Lord was with him, he became a powerful king, and his fame spread to all the neighbouring lands. King Hiram of Lebanon in the far north sent cedar logs, skilled carpenters and stonemasons to build a palace for David.

David also prepared a tent on a hill just outside the city for the Ark of the Covenant. When the ark was brought into Jerusalem, David and all the Israelites celebrated with dancing and singing.

Michal, David's first wife, watched from a window. When she saw David leaping and dancing for joy, she despised him, because she thought it was beneath the dignity of a king to dance. When he finally came home, she asked, "How can the king of all Israel be seen dancing and leaping about like any vulgar fellow?"

But David replied, "I rejoiced and danced before God. Before the splendour of the Lord I am only a humble, common fellow."

David and Bathsheba

One evening, when the heat of the day had died away, David went up onto the roof of his palace to enjoy the cool breeze. From there, he saw a woman bathing. He was struck by her beauty and sent a messenger to invite her to his palace. When she arrived, she told him that her name was Bathsheba. David could not stop thinking about Bathsheba and wanted her to be his wife, even though he had several wives already. But Bathsheba was married to Uriah, a loyal soldier in his army.

David sent for Uriah and gave him a letter for the commander of the army. Without knowing what was in the letter, Uriah gave it to the commander. At their next battle, the commander followed David's instructions and sent Uriah to lead some men into the most dangerous part of the battle. The enemy attacked the group of Israelites and Uriah was killed.

When Bathsheba heard that her husband had died, she mourned for him. After the time of mourning was over, David sent for her and asked her to become his wife, and she accepted. Their wedding was celebrated, and after a time she bore him a son. But David's actions had displeased God.

At that time, a holy man called Nathan lived in Jerusalem. He was known as a prophet, because he spoke the words of God. The Lord sent Nathan to visit David, and Nathan told David a story.

"There was once a rich man who had a great number of sheep and cattle. In the same town lived a poor man who had only one lamb," Nathan said.

"He loved this lamb, cared for it, fed it, and even let it sleep in his arms. One day a traveller asked the rich man for food and shelter, but the rich man did not want to use one of his own sheep to prepare a meal for the traveller. Instead, he took the lamb of the poor man and prepared it for the traveller."

David was angered, and said, "As the Lord God lives, that rich man must die for the wrong he did, and he must pay for the lamb four times over because he did not have any pity."

Then Nathan told David, "You are the rich man. The Lord, the God of Israel, says, 'I anointed you king over Israel, and delivered you from Saul. I gave you all of Judah and Israel, and I gave you your house and all your wives. Why did you despise my word and do this evil thing? You killed Uriah with the sword of your enemies and took his wife to be your own.'"

David admitted, "I have done wrong before the Lord God."

Nathan replied, "The Lord has taken pity on you, and you will not die. But the son who was born to you and Bathsheba will die."

After Nathan left, Bathsheba's child became ill. David pleaded with God for his son. He fasted day and night for a week, and lay on the ground wearing only a rough sackcloth tunic instead of his kingly robes. On the seventh day, the child died.

David's attendants were afraid to tell him the news, but David noticed them whispering among themselves and asked, "Is my son dead?"

"Yes," they replied. "He has died."

David got up, washed himself, put on fresh clothes and went to the tent of the Ark of the Covenant to pray. Then he returned to his palace and asked for food and drink.

His servants were surprised and asked, "While the child was alive you did not eat or drink, but now that he is dead, you get up and eat. Why do you act like this?"

He answered, "While my son was alive, I fasted in the hope that the Lord might be gracious and let him live. But now that he has died, I must accept the will of God."

David comforted his wife Bathsheba. Within a year she gave birth to another son, and they named him Solomon, which means "the peaceful one".

David's son Absalom

David had an older son, Absalom, a handsome young man with long flowing hair, who had hopes of becoming king one day. David was still full of health and strength, so Absalom resorted to a cunning plan.

Every morning he stood by the city gate. Whenever anyone came with a complaint or dispute to bring to the king, Absalom would greet them warmly, find out what their problem was and say, "Your claims are valid, but unfortunately the king does not have anyone to hear them. If only I could become a judge, everyone in the land would have justice." Absalom said this to everyone, both to the accused and the accusers, and so in time he won many friends and supporters.

After four years, Absolom said to his father, "Let me go to Hebron to fulfil a promise I made to God."

David loved Absalom and was unaware of his plans, so he agreed, saying, "Go in peace."

Absalom went to Hebron with his followers and had himself crowned king. He sent secret messengers throughout the land to all the people he had befriended, telling them, "As soon as you hear the sound of trumpets, say, 'Absalom is king in Hebron.'"

Soon afterwards, a man arrived at David's palace and told him, "Your son has been crowned king, and the hearts of the people of Israel are with Absalom."

David immediately called all his officials and said, "Come, we must flee, or none of us will escape from Absalom. He will move quickly and overtake us, bringing ruin on the city."

David and all his household and followers set out through the Judean desert and across the River Jordan. Absalom came after him with all the men of Israel. David divided his followers into three groups. He planned to lead one of them, but his men told him to stay behind, saying, "If we are forced to flee and half of us are killed, it does not matter. But you are worth ten thousand of us."

The battle took place in forested country, where David's experienced men soon put Absalom's followers to flight. Absalom was riding a mule when he met the commander of David's army with some soldiers. As the mule passed under the thick branches of an oak, Absalom's long hair got caught in the tree, and he was left hanging there while his mule trotted on.

As Absalom hung helplessly by his hair, the commander of David's army took a javelin and plunged it through Absalom's heart. Then David's men stopped pursuing the Israelites, who fled back to their homes.

When David heard of the victory, he immediately asked after his beloved son. On hearing that Absalom was dead, David wept and called, "O my son Absalom, my son Absalom!"

David's mourning lasted many days before he returned to Jerusalem.

David's census

An evil spirit came over David and gave him the idea of finding out exactly how many fighting men there were in his kingdom. So he told his nephew Joab, who commanded the army, to go through the land, from Dan in the north to Beersheba in the south, to count all the fighting men.

But Joab replied, "Why would my king want to do such a thing? If the Lord is with us, our troops' courage will be multiplied a hundredfold. Are they not all my king's subjects?"

However, the king insisted, so Joab went through the whole kingdom. After some months he returned to Jerusalem and reported to David. Then David began to have doubts about counting his people. Had Joab been right when he said that if God was with them, each man would have the strength of a hundred men? Did counting his people make him lose sight of God's will? He said to God, "I have done a great wrong and a very foolish thing. I beg you to take away the guilt of your servant."

The Lord sent Gad the prophet to visit David and tell him, "The Lord says, 'You must choose one of these three punishments: three years of famine, three months of fleeing from your enemies, or three days of the plague in your land.' Now, decide how I should answer the Lord who sent me."

David said to Gad, "Let me fall in the hands of the Lord, for his mercy is great, but let me not fall into human hands. So let it be three days of the plague."

So God sent a plague on Israel and very many people died. When the angel came to destroy Jerusalem, God called, "Enough!"

At that moment, David saw the angel of the Lord and fell face down. He said to God, "It is I who have done wrong. Let your hand fall on me and my family, but do not let this plague remain on your people."

Then Gad went to David and said, "Go to the threshing floor belonging to Araunah on Mount Moriah, the hill above the city, and build an altar to the Lord."

All the Israelites knew that Mount Moriah, the holy mountain of Jerusalem, was where, centuries earlier, Abraham had taken his son Isaac to be sacrificed. So David went to the threshing floor, and when Araunah saw him he bowed low, asking, "Why has my lord come to his servant?"

"To buy your threshing floor," David answered. "I must build an altar to the Lord God so that he will stop the plague."

"Let my lord the king take whatever he wishes, and here are oxen to sacrifice as a burnt offering."

"No," replied David. "I insist on paying for the threshing floor and for the sacrifice to the Lord, because I cannot make a sacrifice that cost me nothing."

So David bought the threshing floor and the oxen from Araunah, then built an altar and made a sacrifice. God answered his prayer and stopped the plague on Israel.

Solomon and Later Kings

Solomon is made king

David had many sons. After Absalom died, Adonijah was the oldest, and expected to become king upon David's death. When David was very old, Adonijah grew impatient and thought it was time for him to become king. He called together his followers, went to a spring near Jerusalem and made a great sacrifice of sheep and cattle. Then he invited his brothers and the royal officials to come and celebrate him becoming king. But he did not invite his brother Solomon, Bathsheba's son. Nor did he invite Nathan the prophet, who was now an old man, but from time to time still came to warn King David, or to rebuke him when he did things wrong. Neither did Adonijah invite the high priest Zadok, who made sacrifices every day before the Ark of the Covenant.

Nathan heard of Adonijah's plot and went to Bathsheba, Solomon's mother. "Have you heard that Adonijah has pronounced himself king, and our lord David knows nothing about it?" he asked.

He went on to tell her what to do to save her life and Solomon's. So Bathsheba went to King David and bowed low before him. "My lord, you yourself made a solemn promise to me before the Lord God that Solomon our son would be king after you. But now Adonijah has made himself king, and you do not know about it. All of Israel waits to learn from you who will sit on the throne after you."

Just then, King David was told that Nathan the prophet had come to see him, so Bathsheba withdrew. Nathan bowed before the king and asked, "Have you declared that Adonijah shall be king after you? At this moment he is eating and drinking with his followers, who are saying, 'Long live King Adonijah!'"

The king immediately said, "Call in Bathsheba."

When she came before him, he said, "Today I will carry out what I solemnly promised to the Lord God. Solomon your son will be king after me."

Then he called for the high priest Zadok, and gave him and Nathan instructions: "Have Solomon mount my royal mule and take him down to the spring of Jerusalem. There, anoint him king over Israel. Then blow the trumpet and shout, 'Long live King Solomon!'"

When Zadok and Nathan did this, all the people followed, playing pipes and rejoicing so loudly that the ground shook. When Adonijah and his friends heard what had happened, all his guests rose in alarm and ran away. Adonijah was left alone, trembling in fear. In those days, if someone falsely claimed to be king, they would be put to death.

Yet Solomon said, "If Adonijah shows himself to be worthy, not a hair on his head will be harmed. But if evil is found in him, he will die."

So Adonijah came and bowed down before Solomon. Solomon showed mercy and just said, "Go to your home."

When the time came for David to die, he blessed his son Solomon, saying, "Be strong and observe what the Lord God commands. If you do this, you will prosper in all that you do."

After David's death, he was buried in his city. He had reigned for forty years over Israel: seven years in Hebron and thirty-three years in Jerusalem.

Solomon's wise judgement

When Solomon became king, he went to Gibeon to make a thousand burnt offerings on the altar there.

During the night, God appeared to Solomon in a dream and said, "Ask for whatever you want me to give you."

Solomon answered, "You have shown great kindness to David, my father, and you have made me, your servant, king in his place. But I am still young and do not know how to be king. Give your servant wisdom and a discerning heart, so that I may lead these people justly."

The Lord God was pleased, and said, "Since you have asked for this, and

not for a long life or wealth for yourself, I will give you a wise and discerning heart, so that there will never be another like you. I will also give you what you have not asked for – wealth, possessions and honour – and, if you keep my commandments, I will give you a long life."

Some time later, two women came before Solomon in Jerusalem. "My lord," the first woman said, "this woman, who lives in the same house as me, had a baby three days after I had a baby. We were alone in the house. When this woman's son died, she got up in the night, took the son from my side while I was asleep and put her dead son next to me. But when I looked closely in the morning, I saw that it was not my son."

The second woman protested, "No! The living one is my son, the dead one is yours."

But the first woman insisted the living baby was hers, and so they argued before the king.

The king asked for a sword and gave an order: "Cut the living child in two and give half to one woman and half to the other."

Then the second woman, who had the living baby, pleaded with the king, "Please, my lord, give her the baby, and do not kill him."

But the first said, "Neither you nor I shall have him. Cut him in two."

Then the king delivered his judgement: "Give the living baby to the second woman, because she who does not want her child to be killed is his true mother."

When the people heard the judgement, they held their king in awe, because they saw that he had wisdom from God.

Solomon builds the temple

When Solomon became king, there was no temple yet in Jerusalem where he could make an offering. The Ark of the Covenant was simply housed in a tent, and there was an altar outside where daily offerings were made. But there was now peace in the land, so Solomon could at last build a temple to the Lord God. He sent word to King Hiram of Lebanon, to the north, asking for skilled carpenters, stonemasons and great cedar logs, like those he had sent when David built a palace.

Hiram was king of a powerful empire whose ships traded all along the coast of the Mediterranean Sea. He replied to say that his men were felling cedar and juniper trees and would drag them to the sea and float them down the coast to Joppa. Solomon sent seventy thousand men to haul the trees from there to Jerusalem, and eighty thousand men into the hills as stone cutters.

Then Solomon began to build the temple at the threshing floor that David had bought from Araunah on Mount Moriah, the hill above the city. The temple itself was sixty cubits long, twenty cubits wide and thirty cubits high (about the height of seven or eight adults). The floor was made of juniper, and the hall of the temple was panelled with cedarwood and carved with palm trees and flowers. At the back of the hall, he built the Holy of Holies, a small windowless room decorated inside with gold. No one was allowed to enter except the High Priest once a year. The Ark of the Covenant, containing the two stone tablets that Moses had placed in it some three hundred years earlier, would rest here.

All the furnishings of the temple were made of gold: the altar, the table for the bread, the lampstands, as well as all the dishes and implements.

In front of the temple stood two great pillars made of bronze, which Solomon named Jakin and Boaz. The pillars were eighteen cubits high and the carvings on top were in the shape of lilies. At the south side of the temple stood a great circular bowl, cast in metal, and supported on twelve bronze bulls. It stood higher than a man and measured ten cubits from rim to rim. An altar was built outside, in front of the temple, for making burnt sacrifices.

Solomon spent seven years building the temple with the help of Hiram's skilled men and the thousands of carriers and stonemasons. When it was finished, Solomon called all the Israelites together and had the priests carry the Ark of the Covenant into the Holy of Holies.

Solomon stood outside before the altar in front of all the Israelites, spread out his hands towards heaven, and spoke a great prayer of thanksgiving, promising that his people would keep to the ways of the Lord.

Then God appeared to Solomon and said, "I have heard your prayers and have made this temple holy. My eyes and my heart will always be here with you. But if you or your descendants turn away from me and serve other gods, this temple will collapse in a heap of rubble."

The queen of Sheba visits Solomon

When the temple was complete, Solomon built a great palace for himself. As Solomon's fame spread to distant lands, more and more visitors came to see him, bringing gifts of silver and gold, fine horses and weapons, robes and spices. He had 1,400 chariots and 12,000 horses. All the household items in his palace were made of gold, and his throne was covered in ivory – carved elephant tusks brought from Africa. His kingdom stretched from the land of the River Euphrates to the border with Egypt.

When the queen of Sheba, in the far south of Arabia, heard of Solomon's great fame and riches, she felt suspicious. She decided to visit him to see whether he really was as wise and good as people claimed he was. She travelled with a large retinue of servants and a very great caravan of camels carrying precious stones, gold and rare spices as gifts for the king.

She arrived to see the great temple, the palace and King Solomon's countless courtiers and servants. Solomon and the queen spent hours in deep conversation. He was able to answer all the difficult questions she posed – nothing was too hard for him – and the queen recognised his great wisdom. She said, "The reports I have heard in my country about your achievements are true, but I did not believe them until I saw them with my own eyes. Indeed, in wisdom and wealth you have far exceeded the reports. Praise be to the Lord your God."

King Solomon gave the queen of Sheba many gifts before she returned with her retinue to her own country.

The death of Solomon

When Solomon became king, he made peace with Egypt and married the pharaoh's daughter. He also had many other wives and, as his fame spread, he married women from nations God had forbidden the Israelites to marry. By the time he was old, he had seven hundred wives, and they turned his heart away from the Lord. To please his foreign wives, he built altars to their gods and even went to worship there with them.

The Lord God became angry with Solomon because he had not kept God's commands. He said, "I will tear your kingdom away from you, but for the sake of David I will not do it in your lifetime. I will tear it from the hand of your son and leave him just a small part of the land."

But because Solomon no longer followed the ways of the Lord, he could not hear God's word. He demanded more and more work and money from his people to maintain his extravagant court.

At that time there was a young man in Jerusalem, Jeroboam, who followed the ways of the Lord. He was one of Solomon's officials and saw how the king was turning away from the ways of the Lord and losing himself in all his splendour.

Once, when Jeroboam was leaving Jerusalem, Ahijah the prophet met him while they were alone in the countryside. Ahijah was wearing a new cloak, which he took and tore into twelve pieces. He said to Jeroboam, "Take ten pieces for yourself, because the Lord, the God of Israel, told me, 'I am going to tear the kingdom out of Solomon's hand and give ten tribes to Jeroboam. Only the tribes of Judah and Benjamin will remain under the rule of Solomon's sons.'"

The king somehow managed to hear of this. Solomon's wisdom had turned to cunning, and he wanted to prevent God's will being carried out by killing Jeroboam. But Jeroboam fled to Egypt, and Solomon never saw him again.

Solomon grew old, and when he died he was buried in Jerusalem, the city of David. He had reigned over Israel for forty years.

The kingdom is divided

As soon as Jeroboam heard of Solomon's death, he hastened home. To show that he was not only king of Judea but of all Israel, Solomon's son, Rehoboam, gathered the people of Israel at Shechem for his coronation. All the twelve tribes, who were the descendants of Jacob's twelve sons, were present (Jacob was also known as Israel).

After the coronation, the elders of Israel went to Jeroboam to ask him to speak for them. Jeroboam told King Rehoboam before the whole assembly,

"Your father put a heavy burden on us, demanding harsh labour and taxes. Lighten our burden now and we will serve you."

Rehoboam replied, "Come back to me in three days."

Rehoboam had grown up at the court of his father, Solomon, and was used to the respect people had shown him and all the great extravagance of the palace. He asked the older counsellors who had served his father, "How would you advise me to answer these people?"

They replied, "If you are kind to them and give a favourable answer, they will always be your servants."

But Rehoboam didn't like their advice, so he went to the young men who had grown up with him and asked them for their advice. These men had been brought up around the royal court and had never had to do any real work themselves. They answered, "Tell them, 'My father laid a heavy burden on you, but I will make it heavier.'"

Three days later, Jeroboam and the people returned to see Rehoboam in Shechem. The king rejected the advice of the elders and followed the young men's instead, saying, "My father laid a heavy burden on you, but I will make it heavier."

The new king did not listen to the people because God made him hard-hearted, so that the word the Lord had spoken to Jeroboam and Ahijah would be fulfilled.

When the people of Israel saw that the king refused to listen, they said to Rehoboam, "Go and look after your own house."

The ten tribes of the north rebelled against the king, stoning one of his officials. King Rehoboam managed to escape to Jerusalem in his chariot, while the ten tribes of the north called on Jeroboam and made him king over Israel.

The tribes of Judah and Benjamin remained loyal to Rehoboam. But when he raised an army to go to war against the northern tribes, they refused to go, because God had spoken to one of the prophets and commanded, "Do not fight against your fellow Israelites. Go home, for this is my doing."

From that day onwards, the kingdom was divided in two. The southern part around Jerusalem, ruled by Rehoboam, was called the kingdom of Judah or Judea, and the northern part in Galilee and Samaria, ruled by Jeroboam, was called the kingdom of Israel. And Israel was always in rebellion against Judea.

Jeroboam strays from God

Jeroboam had always been a devout man, following the ways of the Lord, but once he became king he lost his trust in God. He was afraid that his people might turn to Rehoboam instead if they had to go to Jerusalem three times a year to offer sacrifices at the temple to God. So Jeroboam made two golden calves. He set one up in the south of his kingdom, in Bethel, and one in the far north, in Dan. He said to his people, "It is too much for you to travel to Jerusalem to worship. Here are the gods who brought you out of Egypt."

Jeroboam fortified the cities of the north and built shrines on hilltops. The priestly tribe of Levi did not take sides, but remained loyal to the temple in Jerusalem. Fearing that his people might follow Rehoboam if they went to the temple in Jerusalem, Jeroboam appointed priests from all the other tribes. The Lord God was displeased.

One day, when Jeroboam was standing at the altar of the calf in Bethel making an offering, a man of God came from Judah and called out in a loud voice, "This is what the Lord has declared: this altar will be split apart and the ashes of the sacrifice will be poured out."

When King Jeroboam heard this, he stretched out his hand and ordered, "Seize him!"

But his outstretched hand shrivelled, and he could not pull it back. The altar was split apart and the ashes of the sacrifice poured out.

Then the king said to the man of God, "Talk with the Lord and pray that my hand may be restored."

So the man of God prayed, and the king's hand returned to the way it was before. Jeroboam offered, "Come home with me for a meal, and I will give you a gift."

But the man of God answered, "Even if you gave me half your possessions, I would not go with you, nor eat with you, for I was commanded by the Lord: 'You must not eat bread or drink water with Jeroboam, but return in haste.'"

The man of God went on his way. But Jeroboam still did not change his evil ways, and the kingdoms of Israel and Judea remained divided.

The Prophets

Elijah and Elisha

Elijah, messenger of God

Many years passed, and the kingdoms of Israel and Judah were still divided. Different kings came to the throne of Israel, and by and by the people of Israel lost their connection to the Lord God who had saved them again and again in the past. But there were a few who remained true to God. One such man was Elijah the prophet. He was a mysterious figure from east of the River Jordan, who would suddenly appear, remind the people of the ways of the Lord, and then wander away again, without anyone really noticing where he went.

Ahab, the seventh king of Israel after Jeroboam, had ignored the ways of the Lord. Like many others, he no longer sought a wife among his own people, but married the daughter of the king of Sidon, a country in the north. They did not worship the true God there, but instead made sacrifices to a false god called Baal. Ahab loved his wife, Jezebel, so he set up an altar to Baal for her and they worshipped there together.

One day, when Ahab was in his garden, he looked up and saw a figure wearing a cloak made of camel's hair standing before him. He knew it was Elijah the prophet. Elijah said to Ahab, "I stand before the Lord, the living God of Israel: there will be no dew and no rain in the next few years, unless I say so."

Before Ahab had a chance to ask anything, Elijah disappeared. Ahab was troubled, but he did not say anything to anyone about this strange encounter.

God told Elijah to go east of the River Jordan and hide in the ravine of the Cherith brook, where some ravens brought him food. But some time later, the brook dried up, because, as God had warned, no rain was falling over the land. The Lord said to Elijah, "Go to Zarephath, near Sidon. I have told a widow there to give you food."

When Elijah reached the town gate, he saw a widow gathering sticks. He asked, "Would you bring me a little water to drink?"

As she turned to go for the water, he called, "And please bring me a piece of bread."

The widow replied, "I don't have bread: I only have a handful of flour and a little olive oil. It is the last food I have. I am gathering a few sticks to make a fire so that I can bake a last meal for myself and my son, before we starve to death."

Elijah said to her, "Do not be afraid. Go home and do as you have said, but first make a small loaf of bread for me, and then make something for yourself and your son. The Lord God of Israel says, 'The jar of flour will not be used up and the jug of oil will not run dry until the Lord sends rain on the land.'"

She went away and did what Elijah had asked. From then on, there was enough food every day for Elijah, the widow and her son, and Elijah stayed with them in the upper room of her house.

Some time later, the son became very ill and died. The widow was deeply sorrowful, but also fearful of Elijah. She said to him, "What have you against me, man of God? Did you come to remind me of my wicked past and punish me with the death of my son?"

Elijah took her son from her arms, carried him to the upper room and laid him on the bed. He called out to God, "Lord, my God, why have you brought tragedy to the widow I am staying with?"

Then he breathed on the boy three times and cried out, "Lord, my God, let this boy's life return to him."

God heard Elijah's cry and the boy's soul came back, and he lived. Elijah carried him down to his mother, and said, "Look, your son is alive."

The widow replied joyfully, "Now I know that you are a man of God, and the words you speak are the true words of the Lord."

God sends rain on the land

After three years of waiting, God finally said to Elijah, "Go to visit King Ahab, and I will send rain on the land."

Elijah went south to Samaria, where the drought was severe and there was a terrible famine. He went straight to see the king, and appeared before Obadiah, the head of Ahab's household. Obadiah was a devout follower of the ways of the Lord. When he saw Elijah, he recognised him immediately and bowed to the ground.

Elijah said, "Go tell your master, 'Elijah is here.'"

Obadiah was afraid and said, "Have I not always served the Lord God? My master sent someone to look for you in every kingdom, and when they claimed you were not there, he made them swear it was true, on pain of death. Now you want me to tell Ahab, 'Elijah is here.' If I tell the king and then the spirit of the Lord carries you away when I leave you, the king will kill me."

But Elijah said, "Go. As the Lord Almighty lives, I will stand before Ahab today."

So Obadiah told Ahab, and Ahab went out to meet Elijah. When the king saw the prophet, he said, "Is that you, you troublemaker of Israel?"

"I have not made trouble for Israel," replied Elijah. "You and your family have. You have abandoned the commands of the Lord and followed Baal. Now, summon the people to meet me on Mount Carmel and bring all the prophets of Baal."

Ahab sent word throughout the land and assembled the prophets on Mount Carmel. The mountain, rising from the shores of the Mediterranean Sea, was usually covered in the most beautiful plants and trees and surrounded by lush valleys. But after three years of drought it was stony, bare and dry.

Elijah stood before the people and said, "If the Lord is God, follow him;

but if Baal is God, follow him. I am the only prophet of the Lord that is left, but Baal has four hundred and fifty prophets. Now, go and find two bulls for us. Let Baal's prophets kill one and put it on the wood ready to sacrifice, but do not set fire to it. I will prepare the other bull, but I will not set fire to it."

Turning to the prophets of Baal, Elijah said, "You call on the name of your god, and I will call on the name of the Lord. The god who answers with fire is the true God."

Two bulls were brought, and Elijah let the prophets of Baal choose one of them and prepare it. They laid it on a splendid altar to Baal that stood on Mount Carmel. (There were altars to Baal on many of the hilltops of the kingdom.) They called on the name of Baal from morning to midday: "Baal, answer us!" But there was no response.

At noon, Elijah taunted them, saying, "Shout louder! Maybe your god is sleeping and needs to be woken."

So the prophets shouted louder and danced around the altar in a frenzy until evening. But there was no response.

Then Elijah said to the people, "Come here to me."

He took twelve stones, one for each of the tribes descended from Jacob (who was also known as Israel), and he used them to repair the altar of the Lord, which had long lain in ruins. Elijah prepared the bull for sacrifice and laid it on the wood. Then he said to the people, "Fill four large jars with water and pour it on the offering and the wood."

Elijah asked them to do this three times, and they did. The offering was drenched and water flowed off the altar. Then, as the sun was setting, Elijah stepped forward and prayed, "Lord, God of Abraham, Isaac and Israel, let the people know that you, Lord, are God."

Then the fire of the Lord fell and burned up the sacrifice and the wood, and dried all the ground surrounding it. When the people saw this, they fell down and called, "The Lord, he is God!"

As God told him, Elijah commanded them to seize the prophets of Baal and kill them all, so that they could never again turn people away from God. Then Elijah said to Ahab, "Go, eat and drink, for I hear the sound of heavy rain."

Ahab was afraid. He could hear no sound and the sky was quite cloudless. However, he went off to eat and drink.

Elijah climbed to the top of Mount Carmel and bent down to the ground with his face between his knees, in deep contemplation. During the night he said to his servant, "Go and look towards the sea."

His servant looked at the clear, starlit sky, towards the sea. "There is nothing there," he said.

Seven times Elijah sent him back, and the seventh time, at dawn, the servant reported, "A cloud as small as a hand is rising from the sea."

"Go and tell Ahab, 'Prepare your chariot, and go home before the rain stops you.'"

Ahab was still fearful of Elijah, and did what he was told. As he rode off, the sky grew black, the wind rose and a heavy rain started falling. The spirit of the Lord came over Elijah and, tucking up his cloak, he ran ahead of Ahab all the way to Samaria.

God commands Elijah to find Elisha

When King Ahab reached his palace in Samaria, he told Jezebel everything that had happened and how Elijah had killed all the prophets of Baal. Jezebel's fury knew no bounds, and she sent a messenger to Elijah to say, "By this time tomorrow you will suffer the same fate as my prophets."

Ahab was still deeply shaken by what Elijah had done, and was not sure that Jezebel's threat would work, but he knew that nothing could stop her in her rage.

When Elijah heard this he was afraid, and he ran for his life and came to Beersheba, in the southern kingdom of Judea. There, he left his servant and went on alone into the desert. By evening he was tired, so he sat down under a bush and prayed: "I have had enough, Lord. Take my life." Then he lay down and fell asleep.

Suddenly an angel touched him and said, "Get up and eat."

Elijah looked around, and by his head there was some freshly baked bread and a jar of water. He ate and drank, and then lay down again.

A second time the angel touched him and said, "Get up and eat, for a great journey lies before you."

Elijah got up, and ate and drank. Strengthened, he journeyed for forty days and forty nights until he reached Horeb, the mountain of God in the Sinai Desert. There he spent the night in a cave.

God spoke to him, asking, "What are you doing here, Elijah?"

"I have fought for the Lord God Almighty," Elijah replied. "The Israelites have rejected your laws, torn down your altars and killed your prophets. I am the only one left, and now they are trying to kill me too."

God said, "Go and stand on the mountain in the presence of the Lord, because he is about to pass by." Elijah did so.

A great wind arose and shattered the rocks, but the Lord was not in the wind. Elijah could not hear him. After the wind came an earthquake, but the Lord was not in the earthquake. Elijah could not hear him. Then came a fire, but the Lord was not in the fire. Often before, Elijah had heard God speaking through fire and through thunder and lightning, but now he could not hear him.

After the fire came a gentle whisper. When Elijah heard it, he knew it was the voice of God, and he pulled his cloak over his face so that he would not see the Lord. God said, "Go back the way you came. Go to Damascus and anoint Elisha to succeed you as prophet."

Elijah had never heard of Elisha, and wondered how he would find him. But, like Moses and the children of Israel many years before, he walked back through the desert, across the great valley of Arabah to the mountains of Moab. Instead of turning west to cross the River Jordan, he continued on the east side until he was near Damascus.

As he was walking, he saw a man ploughing his field with his servants. There were twelve ploughs each pulled by a pair of oxen, and the servants were ahead of the master, who was at the rear with the twelfth pair. Suddenly he heard a voice inside him saying, "There is Elisha."

Elijah went up to the young man and threw his cloak around him. Elisha immediately understood that this meant he was to follow Elijah. First, he asked to go and kiss his father and mother farewell. Elijah replied, "Go back and do that, for the way ahead is hard."

Naboth's vineyard

One day, King Ahab was staying at one of his palaces in Jezreel. Much time had passed since he had last heard of Elijah, and he was again forgetting the commands of the Lord. From his palace, he looked out onto the neighbouring vineyard and imagined how wonderful it would be to have palace gardens there instead. So Ahab went to see Naboth, the owner of the vineyard, and offered to give him a better vineyard in exchange for the land, or to pay him a large sum of money for it.

Naboth was a hard-working, honest man who kept to the ways of the Lord, and did not allow himself to be dazzled by the sudden appearance of the king. He replied, "I inherited this vineyard from my ancestors, and the Lord forbids that I should give you this inheritance."

Ahab knew of the law of inheritance, which was one of the many laws that Moses had made for the people of Israel, but was angry about it. Returning to Samaria, he lay on his bed, sulking and refusing to eat. His wife Jezebel asked him what was troubling him, and he told her the story of Naboth and the vineyard. Jezebel said to him, "Is this how you behave as king of Israel? Get up and eat! I will get you Naboth's vineyard."

She wrote letters in Ahab's name, put his royal seal on them, and sent them to the elders of Naboth's city. The elders did as commanded in the letters, which they thought had been written by the king. They proclaimed a day of fasting, when people came together to pray, and they seated Naboth in a prominent place, with two scoundrels opposite him. As instructed by the elders, the scoundrels called out loudly before all the people, "Naboth has just cursed both God and the king!"

There was uproar. The crowd seized Naboth, dragged him outside the city and stoned him to death.

The elders sent word to the palace. As soon as Jezebel heard the news, she said to Ahab, "Get up. You can take Naboth's vineyard now because he is dead."

Ahab went straight to Jezreel and took possession of Naboth's vineyard.

Then God spoke to Elijah, and Elijah appeared before Ahab, who said, "So you have found me, my enemy!"

"I have found you," Elijah answered, "because you have done evil in the eyes of God. The Lord says, 'I will bring disaster on you and your descendants, and dogs will lick your blood in the place where they licked Naboth's blood.'"

When Ahab heard these words, he knew that he had behaved wickedly, so he fasted and wore a rough sackcloth tunic instead of his kingly robes. But his sorrow and remorse for his evil ways did not last long. Three years later, when he was riding a chariot into a battle against the Syrians, he was killed by an arrow. When his chariot stopped at the city walls of Jezreel and his men took out the body of their king, the blood flowed out of the chariot at the place where Naboth had been killed.

Elijah ascends to heaven

One day near the end of Elijah's time, he was walking with Elisha, and said, "Stay here, the Lord is sending me to Bethel."

Elisha said, "As surely as the Lord lives and as you live, I will not leave you."

So they went on to Bethel together. In Bethel they came across a group of prophets who were singing and dancing, proclaiming the word of the Lord. They came up to Elisha and asked, "Do you know that the Lord is going to take your master from you today?"

"Yes, I know," Elisha replied. "Keep silent."

Then Elijah said, "Stay here, Elisha, the Lord is sending me to Jericho."

But Elisha replied, "As surely as the Lord lives and as you live, I will not leave you."

So they went down to Jericho, in the hot Jordan valley. There, another company of prophets came to Elisha and asked, "Do you know that the Lord is going to take your master from you today?"

"Yes, I know," Elisha replied. "Keep silent."

Then Elijah said, "Stay here, Elisha, the Lord is sending me to the Jordan."

And Elisha again replied, "As surely as the Lord lives and as you live, I will not leave you."

So the two of them walked on while fifty men from the company of prophets followed at a distance. Elijah and Elisha stopped at the banks of the

River Jordan, at the same place where four hundred years earlier the children of Israel had crossed into their promised land. Elijah took off his cloak, rolled it up and struck the water with it. The water divided and the two of them crossed over dry ground.

When they had reached the far side, Elijah said, "Tell me, what can I do for you before I am taken from you?"

Elisha thought deeply before replying. "Allow your spirit to remain with me after you are gone, so that your spirit may be heard a second time."

"This is a difficult request," Elijah said. "But if you see me after I am taken from you, your wish will be granted."

As they were walking and speaking together, suddenly a chariot of fire and horses of fire appeared, separating them, and Elijah was taken up to heaven in a whirlwind.

Elisha called out to Elijah, "My father! My father! The chariots and horsemen of Israel!"

Elijah had been like a father not only to Elisha, but to all the people of Israel, and had protected the kingdom like an army of chariots and horsemen. Elisha saw Elijah no more, and he tore his own cloak in two as a sign of mourning. Then he picked up the cloak that had fallen from Elijah as he was taken up to heaven and walked back to the River Jordan. He stood on the banks and struck the water with Elijah's cloak. The water divided and he crossed over on dry ground.

The prophets who had followed from a distance watched, and said, "The spirit of Elijah is with Elisha."

Elisha lived for many years after that, performing great deeds and miracles, bringing light to the people of Israel, and often saving the kings of Israel from ambush.

When Elisha was old and ill, Jehoash, the tenth king of Israel, went to see him before he died. As he was with Elisha, the king suddenly saw a heavenly light, and called out the same words Elisha had called many years before, "My father! My father! The chariots and horsemen of Israel!"

After Elisha died, many trials still lay ahead for the people of Israel, and times were changing.

The Decline of the Two Kingdoms

Jonah

Many years later, far in the east, the kingdom of Assyria was becoming more powerful. It had swallowed up the kingdom of Babylonia to its south and Syria to its west. Several cities in Galilee had been captured, and the kingdom of Israel feared that the Assyrians would invade the rest of their country.

At that time, God spoke to Jonah, a prophet from Galilee, telling him, "Go to the great city of Nineveh and preach against the wickedness of its people."

Nineveh was the capital of Assyria, and Jonah had heard how the people lived there: they thought nothing of thievery, or even killing people, and had fashioned their own gods who did not object to their evil ways. Jonah did not want to go there at all. So, instead of joining a caravan of camels to travel east through the desert, he walked west to the sea and came to Joppa. There, he found a ship bound for Spain, far in the west, where he hoped to flee from God.

When the boat set sail, Jonah headed below deck and fell asleep. But they had not travelled far when a great storm arose. All the sailors were afraid and cried out to their own gods. The captain woke Jonah, saying, "How can you sleep? Pray to your god! Perhaps he will listen and we will not perish."

The sailors frantically prayed to their gods, and Jonah prayed to the Lord to save them, but still the storm raged, tossing the boat on the waves.

The sailors said to each other, "Come, let us cast lots to show us who is responsible for this calamity." (In those days people were sure that this would show them the right answer.) So they each drew a stick, and Jonah drew the shortest one. They already knew he was running away from his lord, by which they thought he meant his master. They asked, "What have you done to bring all this trouble on us?"

"I am an Israelite," he replied, "and I worship the Lord God who made the sea and the dry land."

This terrified them, for they had not realised he was running away from his God. They asked, "What can we do to make the sea calm down?"

"Pick me up and throw me into the sea," Jonah said. "I know it is my fault that this storm has come upon us."

So the sailors called to the Lord, "Please do not let us die for taking this man's life," then they threw him overboard.

Immediately the sea grew calm.

But Jonah did not die. Instead, God sent a huge fish to swallow him, and he lived inside its belly for three days and three nights.

From inside the fish, Jonah prayed to God. "In my distress I called on you, O Lord. I was hurled into the depths, but then you, O Lord, lifted me out of the pit of death. I will make sacrifices to you, and I vow I will follow your commands from now on."

Then God commanded the fish to spew Jonah out onto dry land.

Again God said to Jonah, "Go to Nineveh and proclaim there what I told you."

This time Jonah obeyed, and in great fear he went to Nineveh. On the far bank of the great River Tigris, he saw the high city walls built of brown-red clay bricks. Once he entered through the vast gates, he found splendid buildings. The wide streets thronged with people dressed in all manner of colourful clothes. Because Jonah had heard how the people of Nineveh thought nothing of thieving or even killing, he trembled with fear. But he remembered what the Lord had commanded and took courage.

The city was so large, it took Jonah three days to walk through it. Everywhere he went, he proclaimed what God had told him to say: "In forty days Nineveh will be overthrown, because your ways are wicked."

Jonah was surprised to see the citizens taking notice of what he was saying. The king of Assyria decided to hold a fast to repent for their bad behaviour, and all of the people, from the richest to the poorest, humbled themselves and promised to follow the ways of God. Even the king proclaimed, "Let everyone give up their evil ways."

When God saw this, he relented and did not bring destruction on the city. To Jonah, it seemed very wrong that these people would not be punished, and he became angry. They had been so wicked and evil, and now just by holding a fast, God was forgiving them and not destroying the city.

Jonah left the city, made himself a shelter and waited to see if God would punish the people of Nineveh. He prayed to God, "This is just what I thought, Lord, when I was still at home. You are a compassionate God who would not send calamity to this evil people. That is why I tried to flee on the ship. Now, Lord, take away my life. It is better for me to die than to live."

God said to him, "Is it right for you to be angry?"

Jonah remained silent because he did not know what to say. Was the Lord God not always right, and all-powerful?

Then God made a leafy plant grow up over Jonah to give him shade in the heat of the day, and Jonah felt some relief.

At dawn the next day, God sent a worm to chew the plant, which made it wither. A scorching wind blew from the desert and the sun blazed down on Jonah. He felt very faint and even more angry. By nightfall, the leafy plant had died.

God said, "Is it right for you to be angry that this plant has died?"

"It is," said Jonah. "And I am so angry that I wish I were dead."

God answered, "You are angry that this plant, which I gave you for shade, has died, though you did not look after it or care for it. So should I not care for the great city of Nineveh, which has more than 120,000 people?"

Jonah became silent. His anger abated as he pondered the mysterious ways of the Lord God: perhaps the vengeful God from the times of Moses, Joshua and Saul had become compassionate and caring?

Job

Once there lived a wealthy man called Job, who had seven sons and three daughters. He was good and just; he prayed to God and shunned evil. Everyone knew he was a devout man, the most respected among all the people around him.

One day there was a great gathering before God of all the angels – the messengers and servants of God – and the evil one named Satan was among them. God said to Satan, "Where have you been?"

"I have been roaming the earth, seeing how people have fallen away from your commandments," replied Satan.

God replied, "Have you considered my servant Job? There is no one like him: he is blameless and upright, and he shuns evil."

"That's easy for him," Satan answered. "You have blessed him with riches, health, and sons and daughters. If you take away everything he has, he will surely curse your name."

God said to Satan, "Everything he has is in your power to change, but if you choose to test Job you must spare his life."

Satan departed and began making trouble.

As Job's sons and daughters were feasting at the eldest brother's house, Job sat outside his own house admiring his fields, feeling grateful to the Lord for all that he had. He saw a messenger come running, who said, "I have terrible news. While your oxen were ploughing and your donkeys grazing, a tribe of wild men from the south came and made off with them. They killed all your servants, and I am the only one to escape."

While he was still speaking, another messenger came running up and said, "Fiery lightning fell from heaven, and all your sheep and your servants were burnt in a great fire. I am the only one to escape."

Before he had finished speaking, a third messenger hurried towards them and said, "A tribe of wild men from the north came along in three raiding parties and made off with your camels. They killed all your servants, and I am the only one to escape."

He had not finished speaking when another messenger rushed towards him, calling, "Your sons and daughter were feasting at your eldest son's house when a mighty wind suddenly swept in from the desert and the house collapsed onto them. They are all dead. I am the only one to escape."

Then Job stood up, tore off his robe and shaved his head in mourning. He fell to the ground in worship, and said, "Naked I was born, and naked will I die. The Lord gives, and the Lord takes. May the name of the Lord be praised."

When Satan saw that he had not succeeded in making Job curse God's name, he caused Job to break out with painful sores from the soles of his feet to his head. Job's wife saw him scratching and suffering, and said, "What has God done to you? Curse him and then you will die," because she could see no other way for him to end his suffering.

Job replied, "You are talking foolishly. Should we only accept good from God, and not accept any trouble?"

Three of Job's friends heard about his troubles and went together to comfort him. When they saw him from a distance, they hardly recognised him: they wept aloud, tore their robes in two and sprinkled dust on their heads, to show their humility and sympathy. Then they sat on the ground with him for seven days and seven nights. No one said a word to Job because they saw how great his suffering was.

Finally, Job spoke: "May the day I was born be cursed. Why did I not die when I was born? I have no peace, only turmoil."

His oldest friend replied, "May I offer you advice, as a friend? Does the Lord punish the innocent? Perhaps you should look into the past, to times when you strayed from the laws of the Lord."

But Job answered, "You speak with clever arguments, but you do not know the truth. Look at me – is there wickedness on my lips?"

Then Job spoke to God of his anguish and pain, asking for his life to end: "Why do you make so much of human beings and give us so much attention? Look away from me and leave me alone."

One after the other, Job's friends tried again and again to make him look to his past, because surely God would not punish someone who had committed no evil. And each time, Job would again claim he was blameless, and asked God to end his wretched life. However much Job bemoaned his fate, he never once spoke against God. Despite all his pain and the sores on

his skin, he said, "I know that my Lord lives, and that he stands on the earth. He will redeem me and heal my flesh. I will see him with my own eyes. How my heart yearns for him."

His friends were at a loss as to what more they could say to Job, because he remained convinced that his woes were God's will, even though he could not understand why God was doing this to him.

Finally, the Lord appeared out of a whirlwind and asked Job, "Who created the world; who guided the fate of all peoples and nations; who makes rain fall and the sun shine?"

Job replied, "I know that you can do all these things, Lord. Until now I had only heard of you from what was written in the holy books, and I spoke without understanding, but now I see you with my own eyes. Therefore, I regret what I have said, and I despise myself."

Then the Lord turned to Job's friends and said, "I am angry with you, because you have not spoken from your hearts, as Job has; instead you came with clever thoughts, saying that God would not punish someone who had committed no evil. Go and sacrifice a burnt offering of seven bulls and seven rams. My servant Job will pray for you."

After they had made their sacrifice and Job had prayed for them, God restored Job's fortunes. He had twice as many sheep, donkeys, oxen and camels as before. And over the years his wife had seven sons and three daughters.

The fall of Israel

The northern kingdom of Israel strayed far from the commandments of the Lord. The people worshipped foreign gods and idols, they quarrelled with each other, and there was hardly a king who came to the throne who had not killed the ruler before him.

To stop the powerful Assyrians from conquering the land, Israel had to pay a great tribute of silver to them. But God was angry with the kings of Israel and the people of the kingdom for their evil ways. Again and again, he had sent prophets to warn them, but they did not listen, or soon forgot. So God withdrew his help and blessing.

The king of Assyria invaded the entire land of the northern kingdom, captured and imprisoned the king of Israel, and laid siege to the capital city of Samaria, allowing no food or anything else to come into the city. After three years the city surrendered, and Israel and its people were taken to Assyria as slaves.

Isaiah

The smaller kingdom of Judah, in the barren hills of Judea around Jerusalem, was largely cut off from the surrounding world. Its people were mainly from the tribe of Judah, and so they were called Jews. Although they had the temple in Jerusalem, they often worshipped the old gods at ancient holy places and sanctuaries on hilltops, so God had to remind the people of his commandments.

Once in a dream a young man called Isaiah saw the Lord seated on a throne high in heaven, with his robe trailing down and filling the temple of Jerusalem. Above the Lord flew Seraphim, the mightiest of angels, each with six wings. They were calling, "Holy, holy, holy is the Lord Almighty! His glory fills the whole earth!" At the sound of their voices, the whole temple shook and was filled with smoke.

When Isaiah awoke he was deeply moved, and understood his dream in an instant: the trembling of the temple was a sign of how unworthy the people were of God's protection. He was also afraid, for he had seen the Lord God.

"Woe is me!" he cried. "I am an unworthy man who has done much wrong, and live among a people full of wrongdoings, and my eyes have seen the Lord Almighty."

Then one of the Seraphim flew to Isaiah with a burning piece of charcoal and touched his mouth, saying, "Your lips are pure now and your wrongdoings have been taken from you."

Isaiah then heard the voice of the Lord asking, "Who shall I send? Who will speak to the people for us?"

And Isaiah immediately answered, "Here I am. Send me."

God said, "Go and tell the people: 'Be ever hearing, but never understanding. Be ever seeing, but never taking in.' Make their ears dull and close their eyes."

The young man was troubled when he heard this strange message, and asked, "For how long, Lord?"

God's answer was even more troubling: "Until the city lies ruined and without any people; until the fields are uncared for; until the Lord has sent everyone far away and the land is utterly neglected."

From that day on, Isaiah was known as a prophet. He could see a terrible future coming for the people of Judah: Jerusalem would fall and they would be taken captive by Babylonia, but then a king would allow them to return to Judah. And beyond that he saw also a distant time when a son would be born named Immanuel, which means "God with us".

King Hezekiah and the siege of Jerusalem

One of the kings of Judah, Hezekiah, was a just and devout man. He heard what Isaiah proclaimed and followed the commandments of the Lord. He repaired the walls, doors and lamps of the temple in Jerusalem and cleaned it.

Some years after the capture of Samaria, a new king of Assyria, Sennacherib, attacked the cities of Judea. In Jerusalem, Hezekiah quickly set about repairing the city walls and closing off the water springs in the surrounding area to prevent the Assyrians from getting water. He reassured the people, "Be strong and courageous. Do not be afraid of the vast army of the Assyrians, for the Lord God is with us."

He sent messengers to Sennacherib, offering to pay if he left them in peace. The Assyrian king demanded a huge amount of silver and gold. To pay this, Hezekiah had to strip off the gold from the doors of the temple and take the silver from its treasury.

However, Sennacherib was not satisfied. He surrounded Jerusalem and sent one of his commanders who spoke Hebrew (the language of the Israelites) to shout below the city walls: "Hear the words of the great king of Assyria! Do not let Hezekiah convince you to trust in the Lord. He is deceiving you. Has the god of any other nation helped against the power of the king of Assyria?"

The people remained silent.

When Hezekiah heard what Sennacherib had told his people, he ripped up his fine clothes, put on a rough sackcloth tunic and went to the temple to pray with the priests. He sent messengers to ask advice from Isaiah the prophet.

Isaiah said, "Tell your master that the Lord says, 'Do not be afraid of what you have heard. The king of Assyria will not enter this city or shoot an arrow here. I will defend the city and save it.'"

That night, the angel of the Lord visited the Assyrian camp that surrounded Jerusalem and put to death 185,000 of their soldiers. Sennacherib withdrew and returned to Nineveh, where he was killed by his own sons. After his death, the great Assyrian Empire lost its power.

Jeremiah and the fall of Jerusalem

Many years later, a young man called Jeremiah lived in Jerusalem. One day the word of the Lord came to him, saying, "Before you were born, I set you apart from other people. I appointed you a prophet to all people."

Jeremiah was shaken and did not know what he should do. He was a quiet and shy man, and he could not imagine himself as a prophet. So he replied, "Alas, Lord, I do not know how to speak, and I am too young."

But God said, "Do not say, 'I am too young.' Go to everyone I send you to and say what I command you to say. Do not be afraid."

After Hezekiah died, most of the kings who followed him were not just or devout, and they ignored the laws of God. On many occasions Jeremiah warned the people of the disasters that lay ahead, asking, "Will you steal and murder and burn incense to false gods, and then come to stand before the Lord in the temple and plead, 'Keep us safe'?"

He foretold, "This whole country will become a desolate wasteland, and you will be taken to Babylonia as slaves to serve their king for seventy years. After that, the Lord will bring you back."

But they took no notice of Jeremiah, and even the priests of the temple and the king forbade him from speaking in the courtyard of the temple.

In the east, the king of Babylonia had conquered the Assyrians. The Babylonians' power spread westward. The Egyptians moved against them, but the kingdom of Judah lay between these two great powers. The Babylonian king Nebuchadnezzar marched to Jerusalem and took the king and all of the leading families and skilled workers back with him to Babylon, the capital city of Babylonia, leaving Zedekiah, the king's uncle, to rule in his place over the poor and unskilled people who were left.

But Zedekiah did not follow the ways of the Lord, and Jeremiah spoke loudly against the king and his evil ways. Zedekiah had him imprisoned in a dungeon.

Tired of having to pay a huge tribute of gold to the Babylonian king every year, Zedekiah made an alliance with the pharaoh of Egypt. When Nebuchadnezzar heard this, he returned to Jerusalem and his army encircled the city, stopping anything from going in. After two years, there was no food left for the people to eat.

The Babylonian army entered the city. Nebuchadnezzar released Jeremiah, but the king and many of his followers were killed. Those who were left were taken captive to Babylonia. Nebuchadnezzar sent his commander to burn the temple and destroy the city. Anything of value (like the great bronze pillars in front of the temple, the golden vessels and the lamps) was taken back to his kingdom.

The city of Jerusalem fell into ruins, and only a few very poor people were left to tend the land. Jeremiah wrote a great song of lamentation about the fate of his people and the city:

> *How the gold has lost its lustre and the sacred gems are scattered at every street corner. Joy has gone from our hearts. The crown has fallen from our head. Our hearts are faint because the holy mount of the holy city lies desolate. Restore us Lord, that we may return!*

While the people of Israel and Judah were banished to the Babylonian kingdom, they prayed to the Lord to allow them to return to their land. But it was many years before God granted their wish.

Babylonian Exile

Ezekiel and Daniel

Ezekiel

When King Nebuchadnezzar first attacked Jerusalem, he took the king of Judah and all the leading families and skilled workers with him to Babylonia. Among them there was a young priest from the temple called Ezekiel. After the Jews had been settled in their new surroundings for some years, the word of the Lord came to Ezekiel.

In a whirlwind, Ezekiel saw a great cloud, glowing like a brilliant fire, with flashing lightning. In the centre he saw four creatures in human form, but each had four wings and four faces: the face in the centre was human, the right was the face of a lion, the left the face of an ox and above was the face of an eagle.

Each creature had two wings that spread up, touching the wings of its neighbour, and another two wings covering its body. The creatures moved back and forth like flashes of lightning, but all the time facing straight ahead. Beside each creature was a wheel with eyes all around its rim. When the creatures moved, the wheels moved too.

High above the archways formed by their great wings was a throne of a precious blue stone, and on the throne was a figure like a man, full of fire, with brilliant light spreading all around him.

When Ezekiel saw what appeared as the glory of the Lord, he bowed down to the ground, and then heard a voice saying, “Son of man, stand up, and I will speak to you.”

Ezekiel rose to his feet, and the voice continued, “Son of man, I am sending you out to talk to my people, for they have rebelled against me. Do not be afraid, but speak my words to them.”

For seven days, Ezekiel was overwhelmed by the vision. Then he went to speak to the Jews, reminding them that they were banished to this foreign land, far from Jerusalem, because they had not followed the commandments of the Lord.

When the Jews in Babylon heard that Jerusalem and its temple had been destroyed, and the remaining people of Judea had also been brought to Babylonia, there was great mourning. Ezekiel spoke words of comfort to them, for he saw in a vision that they would return home one day.

In another vision, Ezekiel was taken to Jerusalem and saw in great detail the temple being rebuilt. At the eastern gate of the city, he saw the glory of God coming.

The people who heard Ezekiel describe this wonderful vision yearned strongly for God’s spirit to return, in all its glory, and for the new and perfect temple. Would it happen soon or in the distant future? Would it happen on earth or in heaven?

King Nebuchadnezzar’s dream

When King Nebuchadnezzar took the Judean families to Babylonia, he ordered his court officials to bring some of the young Jewish boys to his palace. They were to learn the language and wisdom of the Babylonians, and train for three years before serving the king.

Among them was Daniel and three of his friends. They were given Babylonian names: Daniel was named Belteshazzar, and his friends were named Shadrach, Meshach and Abednego. Daniel and his friends were concerned that the food they were given had not been prepared according to the Lord's commandments, so Daniel said they would prefer not to eat it. The official who served the boys was quite willing to help, but he admitted, "I am afraid of the king. If he sees you looking thinner and less healthy than the others, he will blame me and have me executed."

Then Daniel said, "Test us for ten days. Just give us vegetables and water. Then compare our appearance with those who eat the royal food."

The official agreed. After ten days, Daniel and his friends looked healthier and better nourished than the others, so they were left to their simple meals.

After three years, the boys were brought before Nebuchadnezzar. The king found that Daniel and his three friends surpassed all the others in every matter of wisdom and understanding. They were ten times cleverer than all the magicians – the wise and learned men – in the whole kingdom.

Some time later, Nebuchadnezzar had some unusual dreams. He summoned his magicians and said, "I have decided that you must tell me what I dreamed and what it means. If you cannot, you will be put to death and your houses will be destroyed."

"Tell us your dream and we will interpret it," said the magicians.

"No. You are just playing for time. You must tell me my dream and what it means."

The magicians answered, "There is no one on earth who can do what the king asks! Only the gods can reveal what the king has dreamt, and they do not live among us."

This made the king so angry that he ordered the execution of all the magicians of Babylon, and sent his guards to look for Daniel and his friends.

Daniel asked the commander of the king's guards, "Why has the king given such a harsh order?"

When the commander explained, Daniel asked that he might have some time to think about the king's dream. Then he went to his friends Shadrach, Meshach and Abednego, and urged them to pray to the Lord for mercy that they might not be killed along with the wise men of Babylon.

During the night, God revealed the mystery to Daniel. Daniel praised God, saying, "You have given me wisdom and power."

Then Daniel went to the commander of the guards and said, "Do not execute the magicians of Babylon. Take me to the king and I will describe and interpret his dream."

The commander took Daniel to the king, who asked, "Are you able to tell me what I saw in my dream, and what it means?"

Daniel replied, "No wise man or magician can explain the mystery the king has asked about, but there is a God in heaven who reveals all mysteries. God has revealed the mystery to me, not because I have greater wisdom than anyone else, but so that Your Majesty may know what is going to happen.

"In your dream, an enormous, dazzling statue stood before you. The head was made of pure gold, its chest and arms of silver, its belly and thighs of bronze, its legs of iron, and its feet partly of iron and partly of clay. While you were watching, a rock came down and struck the statue, smashing its feet. Then the clay, iron, bronze, silver and gold were all broken into pieces, and were swept away by the wind like chaff from the threshing floor. But the rock became a huge mountain that covered the earth."

The king was astonished, because Daniel had described his dream exactly. Then Daniel continued, "Now I will interpret the dream. Your Majesty, you are the greatest of kings. You are that head of gold. After you, there will be another king who will not be as great, the silver one; then a third king, the bronze one, who will be weaker still; the fourth king will be weaker still, and the kingdom will become divided. Finally, the God in heaven will send a king who will endure for ever. The great God in heaven has shown the king what will happen in the future."

Then King Nebuchadnezzar called out, "Surely your God is the God of gods and the Lord of kings!"

And he placed Daniel in a high position at court, and Daniel's friends Shadrach, Meshach and Abednego were appointed as rulers over the provinces of Babylonia.

The men in the fiery furnace

King Nebuchadnezzar, remembering his dream, had a huge golden statue made, sixty cubits high – as tall as a ten-storey building. He summoned all the governors and officials to its unveiling ceremony. A herald proclaimed, "People of every language, as soon as you hear the sound of a horn, flute, lyre or any kind of music, you must bow down and worship King Nebuchadnezzar's golden statue. Whoever does not obey will be thrown into a blazing furnace."

At that time there were some Babylonian magicians who were jealous of the Jews. They went to Nebuchadnezzar, saying, "May the king live forever! Some men are ignoring your decree to bow down to the golden statue. They are Shadrach, Meshach and Abednego."

These three Jewish men were Daniel's friends, whom Nebuchadnezzar had appointed rulers of the provinces. Furious, the king summoned them and asked, "Is it true that you do not worship my golden statue?"

They answered, "We will not serve your gods or worship an image of gold."

Nebuchadnezzar was enraged. He ordered that the furnace should be heated seven times hotter than usual, and that Shadrach, Meshach and Abednego should be tied up and thrown inside. The fire was so hot that the soldiers who threw the three men into the furnace burst into flame and were killed.

The king watched and then leapt up in amazement. "Look, I see four men walking freely and unharmed inside. The fourth man looks like a son of the gods!" King Nebuchadnezzar shouted into the furnace, "Shadrach, Meshach and Abednego, come out!"

They walked out, and everyone was astonished to see that their hair was not singed and their robes were not scorched. Nebuchadnezzar said, "Praise be the god of Shadrach, Meshach and Abednego, who has sent an angel to rescue them. Therefore, I decree that, on pain of death, no one must say anything against the God of the Jews."

Then he restored Daniel's three friends to be rulers of the provinces again.

Belshazzar's feast

King Nebuchadnezzar ruled for many years, but he became arrogant and was forced to give up his throne. For seven years he lived in madness in the wild, but then he looked up to God again and was restored to his kingdom.

Many years after he had died, his grandson King Belshazzar gave a great banquet. He ordered that the gold and silver goblets that had been taken from the temple in Jerusalem be brought out for the occasion. While his guests were drinking from the goblets, they praised the Babylonian gods of gold and silver.

Suddenly the fingers of a human hand appeared and wrote on the wall. As King Belshazzar watched, he turned pale, his legs became weak and his knees knocked together. He summoned his magicians and wise men, and said, "Whoever can read this writing and tell me what it means will be richly rewarded."

Not one of the king's wise men could read the writing and the king became even more frightened. But the queen said, "Do not be alarmed. There is an old man in your kingdom who was appointed chief counsellor by your grandfather, King Nebuchadnezzar. Call Daniel, and he will tell you what the writing means."

So Daniel was brought before the king, who said, "If you can read this writing and tell me what it means, you will be richly rewarded."

Daniel answered, "You may keep your gifts or give them to someone else. Nevertheless, I will read the writing and tell you what it means. Your grandfather Nebuchadnezzar held the God of the Jews in great respect. But when he became arrogant, the throne was taken from him and he was stripped of his glory.

"You, Belshazzar, knew all this, but you have not taken any heed. Instead, you had the goblets from the temple of God in Jerusalem brought for your companions to use, and you praised the gods of gold and silver. Therefore, God sent the hand. This is what it wrote on the wall: *Mene, mene, tekel, upharsin,* which means: 'numbered, weighed and divided'.

"God has numbered the days of your reign and brought it to an end. You have been weighed and found wanting. Your kingdom will be divided and given to the kingdoms of Media and Persia."

Though the message was grim, Belshazzar was thankful. He had a gold chain placed around Daniel's neck and made him the third highest ruler in the kingdom. But that very night Belshazzar was killed, and Darius of Media took over his kingdom.

Daniel in the lions' den

When Darius the Mede became king, he made Daniel one of three overseers of all the governors of his provinces. Daniel did his job so well that the king wanted to make him chief overseer, but the other two overseers and the governors were jealous and plotted Daniel's downfall. They knew they would not find any fault with his work – Daniel was honest, he did not accept bribes, and he did everything he was asked to do. Instead, they cunningly persuaded the king to decree that for thirty days no one should worship any god, except the king, on pain of being thrown into a den of lions.

Three times a day, Daniel would go upstairs and kneel down to pray at the open window facing Jerusalem. He carried on this routine even when he learned about the new law. The overseers and governors knew about Daniel's habit, so they went to watch him praying, then reported to the king, "Daniel pays no attention to you, Your Majesty. He still prays three times a day to his god."

The king was greatly distressed that his favourite overseer had broken the law, and he did everything he could to save Daniel. But the governors reminded him, "Remember, Your Majesty, that no law made by the king can be changed."

So Daniel was thrown into the den of lions. The king said, "May your God, whom you serve, save you!"

A large stone was placed over the mouth of the den, and the king sealed it with his own seal and the seals of the governors. Then the king returned to his palace and spent the night praying, because he could not sleep. In the den, Daniel prayed to God.

At dawn, the king hurried to the lions' den and called, "Daniel, has your god rescued you from the lions?"

Daniel answered, "Your Majesty! God sent his angel, and the lions have not hurt me. I have never done you any wrong."

Then the men who had accused Daniel were thrown into the den and the lions devoured them.

King Darius let it be known throughout his kingdom that his people must respect the God of the Israelites and of Daniel. Daniel was made overseer once again and continued to prosper.

Daniel's vision

Once when Daniel was standing at the banks of the River Tigris, he looked up and saw a shining figure: a man dressed in white linen, with a belt of fine gold, his body gleaming yellow like topaz, his face like lightning and his eyes like flaming torches. The others who were with Daniel did not see the vision, but they felt something terrible in the air, so they fled and hid.

As Daniel gazed at the vision, all his strength left him and he fell into a deep sleep. The shining figure said, "Daniel, you are favoured. Do not be afraid. Your prayers have been heard, and I have been sent to you. Stand up and listen carefully to the words I speak. This vision concerns things that are yet to come." Then he touched Daniel's lips and said, "Peace! Be strong now."

Daniel felt his strength return. "Speak, my Lord," he replied.

The shining figure told him, "I will return soon to fight against the archangel of Persia, and when I go, the archangel of Greece will come to these lands. But the archangel Michael, the angel of your people, will be my helper."

He went on to describe the many battles that were to come and the distress and suffering that the Jews would face. Then he said, "Michael, the great archangel who protects your people, will arise. You, Daniel, must keep the words you have heard secret until that time comes."

Then Daniel awoke and remembered everything he had seen in his deep sleep.

Tobit and Tobias

Tobit becomes blind

Tobit was an Israelite who had been taken with his wife to Nineveh when the Assyrians conquered the northern kingdom of Israel. However, he was a devout man who still followed the ways of the Lord.

In Nineveh he kept to his ways, not eating the foreign foods of the Assyrians, and giving money and clothes to his own people who were poor. He also buried the bodies of Israelites who had been killed and thrown over the city walls by the Assyrians, though he knew he would be put to death if anyone found him doing this.

One night in the heat of summer, Tobit, his wife and their only son, Tobias, were sleeping outside. As Tobit awoke, sparrow droppings fell in his eyes, stinging and itching, and his vision blurred. He went to many doctors, but their ointments made things worse, and soon he became blind. His neighbours and friends turned away from him – surely he could not be a good and righteous man if God punished him like that?

Tobit prayed to the Lord in his misery, asking that his life be ended so that he would not have to hear any more insults.

On the same day, Sarah, a young woman who was a distant cousin of Tobit, also prayed to God to let her die. Sarah and her parents had been taken by the Assyrians too but were settled far in the east, in the city of Ecbatana in Media. Sarah had been married to seven husbands, but a wicked demon had killed each one of them on their wedding night. Her father's maid accused Sarah, "You are the one who kills your husbands! Go with them and die!"

God heard the prayers of both Tobit and Sarah, and arranged to heal both of them through his angel Raphael.

Tobit remembered that he had left a large sum of money with a kinsman named Gabael in Media for safe-keeping, and decided, as he had now asked to die, that he should send his son Tobias to collect it. He called his son and said, "Tobias, please always follow the ways of the Lord, and give to those who are poor. Marry an Israelite woman. When I die, bury me in a proper grave. Care for your mother. We may seem poor, but fear not: we have great wealth that I left with Gabael. Go to Media now and bring back our money."

Tobias answered, "I will do as you ask. But will he give me the money if he does not know me? Also, I do not know the road to Media."

Tobit replied, "He gave me his bond – we wrote our agreement and cut it in two. He has one half with the money, and I have the other half, which I will send with you. Now, find a trustworthy man to go with you, and we will pay his wages until you return."

So Tobias went out to look for a man to guide him to Media. He found the angel Raphael standing in front of him, but he did not see that he was an angel. Tobias asked the man, "Where do you come from?"

"From your kindred, the Israelites," he replied, "and I have come here to work."

Tobias asked, "Do you know the way to Media?"

"Yes," he replied. "I have been many times, to stay with my kinsman Gabael who lives there."

"If you travel with me to Media, I will pay your wages," said Tobias. "Wait for me here while I tell my father."

So Tobias went to tell his father. Tobit asked to meet the young man, and Tobias fetched him. When Tobit asked the young man's name, he replied, "I am Azariah, the son of Hananiah, one of your kinsmen."

Tobit remembered that Hananiah was a good and devout man, so he said, "Your kinsmen are good people! Go with my son. I will pay your wages and your expenses for each day."

Tobit gave his half of the bond to his son, and he set off to Media.

When Tobias and the angel left, his mother began to weep and asked Tobit, "Why have you sent our child away? Do we not have enough money to live on?"

Tobit replied, "Do not worry. Our child will return in good health. A good angel will accompany him."

Tobit did not know how true his words were.

Tobias and Sarah

After a day's journey, they stopped by the River Tigris. As Tobias sat on the riverbank washing his feet, a large fish suddenly leapt up and tried to bite his foot. The angel said to Tobias, "Catch hold of the fish and hang on to it."

Tobias grasped the fish and threw it on land. Then the angel said, "Cut open the fish and take out its gall, heart and liver. Keep them with you, because they are effective medicine."

Tobias cut open the fish and found the heart, but was not so sure where the liver and gall were, so the angel showed him. After he had safely gathered the liver and the bitter gall, they roasted and ate some of the fish.

Over the next few days, they continued on their way to Media. Tobias had been wondering all the while why his friend had advised him to gather those parts of the fish, so he asked, "Brother Azariah, what use is the fish's heart, liver and gall?"

"If you burn the fish's heart and liver in front of someone afflicted by a demon or evil spirit, the demon will flee and never bother that person again. If you anoint a blind person's eyes with bitter gall then blow on their eyes, they will be healed," he explained.

When they arrived in Media, the angel Raphael said, "Brother Tobias, we must stay the night at the home of Raguel. He is your relative and has no children except his one daughter, Sarah. She is sensible and brave. As you are a relative, you have a right to ask for her hand in marriage."

Tobias answered, "I have heard that she has already been married seven times and, because of a demon, each husband died on their wedding night. Since I am the only son of my parents, I am afraid to die and leave my parents with no one to care for them or bury them when they die."

But Raphael said, "I know that this very night you will marry Sarah. When you go to bed, take some of the fish's liver and heart and put them on the embers of the fire. When the demon smells the smoke, he will flee. Do not fear, because Sarah was chosen to marry you before the world was made."

When Tobias heard these words, his heart was drawn to Sarah. They came to Raguel's house and were made welcome, and when Tobias met Sarah he felt even more certain that he wanted to marry her. He immediately asked Azariah to speak to Raguel about the marriage.

Raguel replied, "My daughter Sarah has married seven of our kinsmen, and each died on the night of their wedding. Now eat and drink, and we will talk of the matter later."

But Tobias insisted, "I will not eat or drink until we have discussed this."

And so Raguel and Sarah agreed that she would marry Tobias, and they were married that evening. The welcoming meal turned into a marriage feast. When Tobias and Sarah went to bed, he took the fish's liver and heart out of his bag and put it on the embers of the fire. The smoke rose, and the demon was so repelled that he fled to the remotest part of Egypt. The angel Raphael followed him and chained his hands and feet there.

In the night, Raguel called his servants to go and dig a grave secretly because, he said, "When Tobias dies, our neighbours and friends will look down on us and make fun of us." Then he sent a maid to the bedroom to see if Tobias was alive, whispering to his wife, "If he is dead, don't worry, we can bury him without anyone knowing."

The maid returned with the news that Tobias was alive and that he and Sarah were both sound asleep. Raguel blessed the God of heaven with a prayer of thanks. Then he ordered his servant to quickly fill the grave before daybreak.

In the morning, Raguel joyfully made Tobias promise to stay for two weeks to celebrate the wedding. As Tobias was concerned about the delay in returning to his parents in Nineveh, he said to his companion, "Brother Azariah, will you go to Gabael, give him the bond, get the money, and invite him to the wedding celebrations? You know that my father must be counting the days until my return."

The angel did as he was asked and returned with Gabael, who joyfully joined the celebrations.

Tobit is healed

Meanwhile, in Nineveh, Tobit counted the number of days Tobias would need for his journey. When Tobias did not return after those days had passed, Tobit began to worry. Perhaps Gabael had died and there was no money; or, worse, perhaps some disaster had befallen Tobias and he had perished on the journey. Tobit's wife rushed out every day to watch the road, and when she did not see her son coming, she began to weep and mourn.

When the fourteen days of wedding celebration ended, Tobias asked Raguel to allow him to return. "Otherwise, my father and mother will not believe they will ever see me again," he said.

Reluctantly, Raguel allowed him to leave. He gave Tobias half his property: servants, cattle and sheep, donkeys and camels, clothing and money. He embraced Tobias and kissed his daughter, Sarah, farewell, saying, "May the Lord of heaven let you prosper."

As they were approaching Nineveh, the angel Raphael said to Tobias, "Let us go ahead to prepare your parent's house while the rest of the company follows. And have the fish's gall ready."

Tobias' mother was sitting looking intently down the road. When she caught sight of him, she cried to Tobit, "Your son and the young man who went with him are coming!"

When they reached the house, his mother ran to him and threw her arms around his neck, weeping with joy. Tobit came stumbling out of the courtyard door. Tobias went up to him, smeared the gall of the fish on his eyes and blew on them. Then he peeled the white film from his eyes, and Tobit could see again. He rejoiced and praised God with a great prayer of thanks.

Tobias reported that he had not only brought the money from Gabael, but he had also married Sarah, Raguel's daughter, who was approaching the gate of Nineveh. Tobit ran out to welcome her, and his friends and neighbours were surprised to see him going without a guide.

For a week there was great rejoicing among the Israelites in Nineveh: Tobit's sight had returned and his son was married.

After the feast, Tobit told his son that he should pay the wages of the young man who went with him, and give him something extra. Tobias said, "I would like to pay him half my possessions, for he led me back safely, cured my wife, brought back your money and healed you."

Tobit agreed, and called the young man, who answered, "Now I will tell you the whole truth. God heard your prayer and Sarah's prayer, and he sent me to heal you both. I am Raphael, one of the seven angels who stand before God to carry out his will in the world."

Tobit and Tobias were shaken, and fell face down, afraid. But the angel said, "Do not be afraid. Write down everything that has happened to you. I am ascending back to God, who sent me."

When they looked up, they could no longer see him. For all their lives, they continued to worship God and sing his praises among their people.

The Return from Babylonia

The Jewish people return

Fewer than fifty years after King Nebuchadnezzar had destroyed Jerusalem and taken the Jewish people to Babylon, the Babylonian Empire was conquered by Cyrus, king of Persia. Cyrus was generous and did not destroy the places he conquered, but instead kept everything he liked and which could be useful. He found Daniel at the court of the Babylonian king and kept him on as a wise old counsellor.

Soon after he arrived in Babylon, Cyrus announced throughout the land: "The Lord God of heaven has commanded me to build a temple for him at Jerusalem, in Judea. Any of his people may go to Jerusalem to build this temple."

Many families prepared to leave, and those that remained were encouraged to give money to help rebuild the temple of Jerusalem. King Cyrus found the golden vessels and other treasures that Nebuchadnezzar had taken from the old temple, and he gave them to Zerubbabel, the descendant of the last king of Judea, who now led the return.

Some of the elderly people could remember clearly where they had lived, and their families settled in their old towns. After they had all settled, Zerubbabel called the people together in Jerusalem. They built an altar where the old temple had stood and made a burnt offering.

They sent for masons and carpenters from Lebanon, in the north, from where they also collected great cedar logs that had been sent by sea, just as when the first temple was built by King Solomon. When the foundations were laid there was much rejoicing, but many of the old priests and people also wept, because it reminded them of the splendour of the first temple.

When the enemies of the Jews who lived nearby heard that a temple was being built, they wanted to stop it. They went to Zerubbabel and said, "Let us help you build this new temple, because we have been worshipping God here since you left."

But Zerubbabel, sensing their deceit, replied, "We do not need your help to build our temple. We alone shall build it, as King Cyrus commanded."

Instead, the enemies tried to discourage people from helping with the building and bribed officials to frustrate their plans.

Seven years later, King Cyrus died. The enemies then wrote to the new king of Persia, who was an evil man, saying, "The people who came to Jerusalem are rebuilding the city. The king should know that they are rebellious and wicked people, and will not pay taxes to Your Majesty. You will see in the records that this city has always been rebellious, and that is why it was destroyed."

In the old records the king found that this was true, and ordered the work to be stopped.

The temple is rebuilt

After eighteen years, the evil king of Persia died, and Zerubbabel resumed the work of rebuilding the temple. The Persian governor of the local province heard about this and asked, "Who allowed you to rebuild this temple?"

Zerubbabel and the people answered, "We are rebuilding the temple which stood here for many years until Nebuchadnezzar, king of Babylon, destroyed it. King Cyrus issued a decree that this house of God should be rebuilt."

The governor immediately wrote to the new king of Persia, Darius, asking what he should do. King Darius ordered the archives of King Cyrus to be searched, where a scroll was found. Not only did it describe exactly how big the temple was to be, but it also said that the costs were to be paid by the royal treasury.

Darius replied to the governor, "Do not interfere with the work on this temple. I decree that the builders' expenses will be paid by the royal treasury from the money you raise in your province."

Six years later, the temple was finally finished. The people of Israel made a great sacrifice of bulls and rams on the altar in front of it, to dedicate the temple as the house of God. Many more Jews from Babylonia returned to Judea when they heard the temple had been completed.

That temple lasted for nearly six hundred years and still stood during the life of Jesus.

Esther

Esther becomes queen

After King Cyrus had conquered Babylonia, many Jews decided to stay there. King Darius' son King Xerxes, also known as Ahasuerus, ruled over the vast Persian Empire, which stretched from the River Indus in India to the River Nile in Egypt, and included Babylonia, Israel and Judea.

King Xerxes wanted to find a wife. His counsellor suggested that they search for young maidens throughout the kingdom, treat them to royal luxuries and healthy food for a year, and then the king could choose one of them to be his queen. The king's order was proclaimed in every province of his vast empire.

Right beside Xerxes' palace lived Mordecai, a Jew who, like many others, had not returned to Judea. When Mordecai's cousin died, he adopted his orphaned daughter, Esther, and loved her as if she were his own daughter. She was ordered to go to the palace. Before leaving, Mordecai told her, "Do not tell anyone who your family is or where they come from. If you become queen, it will be the Lord's doing, so that you can help God save his people."

"I will do as you ask, and hope to become queen," Esther answered.

Every day Mordecai would walk back and forth near the courtyard of the palace where the maidens were staying, to find out what was happening to Esther. After a year of royal treatment, she was taken to meet King Xerxes. As soon as the king saw her, he liked her so much that he set a royal crown on her head and made her queen. He proclaimed a holiday to celebrate their marriage, and held a great banquet for all his nobles and officials.

One evening soon after this, Mordecai was sitting at the palace gates, as he often did. After the sun sets in those parts, it gets dark very quickly, and as the air cools, people come out of their houses. As Mordecai was quietly sitting in the shadows, he overheard two of the king's guards plotting to kill King Xerxes.

Mordecai sent a message to Esther (for no man was allowed to visit the queen's palace) and told her about the plot. She reported it to the king, telling him that she had heard this from a man called Mordecai. The king immediately called for more soldiers to protect him and ordered the two scheming guards to be found and killed. King Xerxes made sure the details of the plot were written down in a great book that recorded all the important events of the kingdom.

Haman plans to kill the Jews

Some time later, King Xerxes made a vain man called Haman his highest counsellor. Haman was evil at heart, and he always sought more wealth, power and fame. Every time Haman passed through the palace gates, it was the law that everyone nearby had to kneel down in his honour. Only Mordecai, sitting in his usual place by the gates, did not do this. The royal officials spoke with him day after day, but he refused to bow. So they told Haman about this man who, by following the laws of the Jews, refused to bow down before another human being.

Haman was enraged and became determined to find a way to destroy all the Jews in the whole kingdom. He went to the king and said, "There are people in your kingdom who do not obey your laws, but follow other customs. I will give ten thousand sacks of silver to the royal treasury if you make a law to destroy these people."

The king, who was barely listening, handed Haman his signet ring and merely replied, "Keep the money, Haman, and do whatever you think best with the people."

So, without telling the king, Haman ordered the king's scribes to write a new law proclaiming that, at the end of the year, all the Jews in the land were to be killed. Haman sealed the scroll with wax and stamped it with the king's signet ring. The decrees – the scrolls announcing the new law – were sent to every part of the kingdom.

When Mordecai heard this terrible news, he walked over to the palace gates and asked to speak to Queen Esther's attendant. When the attendant came, Mordecai told him everything and gave him a copy of the decree, then asked that Esther go to the king and beg for mercy.

Esther sent a message back to Mordecai, saying, "All the people in the palace know that, on pain of death, no one – not even his wife – can approach the king unless he holds out his gold sceptre. It has been thirty days since I was called to the king. Gather all the Jews in the city, pray and hold a fast for three days, and my servants and I will also pray and fast for three days. Perhaps God will help us. After this, I will go to the king, even if I am put to death."

On the third day, Esther put on her most beautiful royal robes and stood in the inner courtyard in front of the king's window. When he saw Esther, he was pleased and held out his gold sceptre to her. She approached him and he asked, "What is your request, Esther? I will give you anything, up to half my kingdom."

"If it pleases the king," she replied, "let the king, together with Haman, come to a banquet today that I have prepared."

So that evening the king and Haman went to the banquet. Again, the king asked her, "What is your request, Esther? I will give you anything, up to half my kingdom."

Esther merely answered, "If it pleases the king, let the king, together with Haman, come to a banquet tomorrow. Then I will tell the king my request."

Haman went home that evening in high spirits. But when he passed the palace gate and saw that Mordecai did not bow down, he was again filled with rage. At home, he boasted to his wife and friends that he was the king's favourite, saying, "I am the only person Queen Esther invited to accompany the king to her banquet, and she has invited me again tomorrow."

But one thing was spoiling his sense of triumph: Mordecai. Haman told his wife and friends about this Jewish man who refused to bow down to him, and they suggested, "Order your men to set up a high pole, and in the morning ask the king to have Mordecai impaled on it."

This idea cheered Haman up, so he gave orders for the pole to be set up.

That night the king could not sleep, so he asked his attendants to bring the great book that recorded all the important events of the kingdom. There he found a record of how Mordecai some years earlier had reported the plot to kill him, something he had quite forgotten. The next morning, he asked his attendant, "What honour or recognition did Mordecai receive for this?"

"Nothing was done for him," the attendant answered.

The king asked, "Who is in the court?"

Haman had just entered the court to ask the king about impaling Mordecai. The king's attendant looked and answered, "Haman is there."

"Bring him in," the king ordered. When Haman entered, the king asked, "What should be done for a man the king wants to honour?"

Haman assumed that the king was thinking about him, so he answered, "Let him be clothed in a royal robe the king has worn and seated on a royal horse the king has ridden, then lead him through the streets, proclaiming, 'This is how the king honours those who serve him well!'"

The king was delighted with the answer, and commanded Haman, "Go at once, get the robe and the horse, and do exactly as you have suggested for Mordecai the Jew."

Haman managed to hide his dismay and obeyed. He had to lead Mordecai through the city streets, proclaiming, "This is how the king honours those who serve him well!" He rushed home afterwards, overcome with grief and embarrassment.

Later Haman was summoned to Queen Esther's banquet. After they had eaten, the king asked Esther, "What is your request? I will give you anything, up to half my kingdom."

This time Esther answered, "If it pleases the king, grant me my life and spare my people. For it has been ordered that my people and I should be killed."

King Xerxes asked, "Who has dared to order such a thing?"

Esther pointed at Haman and said, "That man sitting there!"

The king was in such a rage that he had to go outside into the garden to calm down. The terrified Haman fell at Esther's feet and held them, begging for his life. Just then the king returned and became even more enraged, because Haman had touched the queen. He called his guards to capture Haman.

One of the guards reported, "Haman has set up a high pole on which he intended to impale Mordecai – the very man who saved the life of the king."

The king gave orders that Haman be impaled on the pole he had set up. That same day, the king gave Queen Esther all of Haman's possessions. When Esther told him that Mordecai was her relative, the king made Mordecai his counsellor and gave him his signet ring. And so it was that, through Esther, God saved his people.

Awaiting the Messiah

The Maccabees

Mattathias defies the Greek rulers

Over a hundred years after the reign of Queen Esther and King Xerxes, the Persian Empire was conquered. As the prophet Daniel had seen in a vision, it was a young king from Greece, Alexander the Great, who swept through Egypt and right across Babylonia and Persia as far as the River Indus, in India. But Alexander died suddenly, while he was still young, and his generals divided his vast empire among themselves.

Across all these lands, there was excitement in the air. People were expecting a great event, a turning point, and for a saviour to appear who would bring justice to the world and end the evil ways of its rulers. Some prophets had foretold the coming of this saviour, or Messiah (from the Hebrew word for the "anointed one"), and it was written down in the Jewish scriptures.

About one hundred and fifty years after Alexander died, King Antiochus, who was descended from one of Alexander's generals, ruled Babylonia, Syria, Israel and Judea. Antiochus was an evil man, swollen with pride, and he liked to think that he was this long-awaited Messiah, so he added the word Epiphanes – Greek for "God appears" – to his name. (But behind his back some people nicknamed him Epimanes, meaning "mad one".)

Antiochus passed laws against the Jews, forbidding them from preparing food according to their customs; from resting on their holy day, the Sabbath; and from celebrating their traditional festivals. He also ordered them to worship idols of Greek gods. Many Jewish people, fearful of the king's punishments, followed these laws.

Next, Antiochus came to the temple at Jerusalem and entered the Holy of Holies – the inner chamber where only the High Priest was allowed to enter once a year – and stole the golden altar and all the golden vessels and implements.

Not far from Jerusalem, on the road down to the coast, lived a devout man called Mattathias, who had five sons. Like some of the Jewish people, Mattathias still followed the commandments of the Lord, and he told his sons many stories from the old books. Far from the hustle and bustle of the great cities, Mattathias and his family only ate food that was allowed by the laws of Moses, and they faithfully rested on the Sabbath. The people in the town looked up to Mattathias as one of their wise elders.

However, one day Antiochus' officials arrived and disturbed the peace. They called together all the townspeople and ordered them to offer sacrifices to false idols. One officer said to Mattathias, "You are a leader in this town. Be the first to come and make a sacrifice as the king has commanded. The king will reward you with gifts."

But Mattathias answered loudly, "My family will never abandon the law of our ancestors. We will not obey the king's command."

Instead, another man, who was afraid of the official, hastily stepped forward to make the sacrifice. When Mattathias saw this, his spirit was stirred up. How could a Jew, waiting for the arrival of the true Messiah, make an offering for a madman who called himself "God appears"? Mattathias killed the man at the altar, then killed the king's officer and tore down the false altar. Then he shouted out to all the people in the town, "Everyone who supports the law of the Lord, come with me."

Many people followed Mattathias as he fled to the hills of the Judean desert with his sons, leaving all his possessions behind.

When the king's officers and troops heard of this, they pursued Mattathias and his followers. The troops set up camp at the caves where some of the followers were hiding, and decided to fight them on the Sabbath, because they knew that devout Jews would not do any work or take up arms on their holy day. When the troops attacked, the devout people in the caves said, "Let us die innocently and not break the laws of the Sabbath."

Many were killed that day. Mattathias mourned them deeply, then said to his remaining followers, "If we all do as our people have done, there will soon be no one left to follow the commandments. The Sabbath was made for human beings. Therefore, it is better to break it than to break God's trust in people. If anyone attacks us on the Sabbath, we shall fight."

From that day on the Jewish people fought, and many more people came to join them. They rescued their people from the power of the rulers, making sure they followed the commandments of the Lord.

When Mattathias was old and the time of his death drew near, he called his sons and told them, "Remember the deeds of your ancestors: Abraham, Joseph, Joshua, King David, Elijah and Daniel. Do not fear the words of the unbelievers, show courage, be strong and keep the law. Simon, the oldest, is wise. Always listen to him like you would to a father. Judas has been a powerful fighter since he was a boy, so he will command the army and lead the battles."

Then he blessed them all and died.

Judas Maccabee restores the temple

Mattathias' son Judas won many victories against King Antiochus' troops. The king sent out a large force to fight him, but Judas and his followers defeated them. Then the commander of the Syrians gathered a great army, and Judas went to meet him with a small group of men. Judas spoke to his followers, reminding them that they were fighting for the true God. They rushed out suddenly, surprising their enemy, and crushed the Syrian army.

Because Judas hammered his enemies, people called him Maccabee, which means "hammer" in Hebrew. When King Antiochus heard of his reputation, he became very angry and sent another huge army to defeat Judas. They tried to surprise Judas' followers by night, but they were again defeated. Finally, after many more battles and defeats, the king withdrew his troops from Judea.

Judas travelled to Jerusalem and found the temple deserted and empty. His followers set about clearing the sanctuary, rebuilding the altar in front of it and setting everything in order again. When they finished, they celebrated the rededication of the temple with a feast that lasted for eight days.

Even though Judas had not lost a battle, he was worried about the power of the king. Judas heard about the Romans, who were strong and had conquered great parts of the lands around the Mediterranean Sea, and sent two of his men to Rome to form an alliance with them. They made an agreement that if either the Jewish people or the Romans were attacked, they would help each other.

Strangely, from that time on, Judas no longer won every fight. In one frantic battle, during which many on both sides were wounded and killed, Judas himself died. The whole of Israel mourned for him for many days. His brother Jonathan became their leader and renewed the alliance with Rome, which encouraged the Romans to come to the Holy Land many years later.

After Judas died, all his followers became known as the Maccabees, for they fought bravely against Antiochus and the arrogant kings who followed him. (One of those kings even called himself Soter, which means "Saviour".)

But the Maccabees were still awaiting the true saviour, the Messiah, and they remembered the words of the Lord, spoken by the prophet Malachi and written in the Jewish scriptures, which said:

The day is near when the Lord is coming. I will send my messenger who will prepare the way before me. Remember the law of my servant Moses that I gave for all of Israel. I will send the prophet Elijah to you again before the day of the Lord.

The New Testament

Jesus Christ

The Birth and Childhood of Jesus

An angel appears to Zechariah

There was a priest named Zechariah who had a wife called Elizabeth. They were both old and they did not have any children. In those days, having children was always seen as God's blessing.

Once when it was Zechariah's turn to serve in the temple in Jerusalem, he went inside to burn incense while the people prayed outside in the large space in front.

An angel of the Lord appeared to Zechariah, who was startled and afraid. But the angel announced, "Do not be afraid, Zechariah. Your wife Elizabeth shall give birth to a son and you are to call him John. He will be great in the sight of the Lord and have the spirit and power of the prophet Elijah."

God had told his people that Elijah would appear again before the coming of the Messiah (or saviour). But Zechariah was in awe, and asked, "How can this be? I am an old man, and my wife is old too."

The angel replied, "I am the angel Gabriel, and I have been sent to tell you this good news. But because you did not believe me, you will be silent and unable to speak until the day this happens."

Meanwhile, the people outside were waiting and wondering why the priest had stayed so long in the temple. When Zechariah came out, he could not speak. He made signs to them, and they realised that he had seen a vision.

After the time of serving in the temple had passed, Zechariah returned home. His wife Elizabeth became pregnant, but she could not imagine how this was possible at her age, so she felt ashamed and hid herself.

An angel appears to Mary

Six months after the angel appeared to Zechariah, God sent Gabriel to Nazareth, in Galilee, to visit Mary, a young maiden who would soon be married to Joseph, a descendant of King David who had ruled a thousand years earlier. The angel appeared to her and said, "Greetings, to you who are highly favoured."

Mary was confused and troubled by these words, but the angel Gabriel announced to her, "Do not be afraid, Mary, for you have found favour with God. You are going to give birth to a son, and you must name him Jesus. He will become a great man and the Son of God Most High. The Lord God will give him the throne of King David, and he will reign for ever and his kingdom will never end."

"How will I have a baby," asked Mary, "since I am not yet married to a man?"

"The Holy Spirit will come to you, with the power of the Most High, so your child will be the Son of God," the angel answered. "Even Elizabeth, your relative, is going to have a child in her old age, for with God, nothing is impossible."

With complete trust, Mary simply replied, "I am the Lord's servant. May your words be fulfilled."

Then the angel left her.

The next day, Mary hurried to Judea to visit Elizabeth. When she entered

Zechariah's home and greeted her relative, Elizabeth felt the baby kicking in her womb. Filled with the Holy Spirit, Elizabeth exclaimed, "Blessed are you, and blessed is the child you will bear!"

Mary replied with a great song of praise that began with the words, "My soul glorifies the Lord God, and my spirit rejoices in God, for the Mighty One has done great things for me."

Mary stayed with Elizabeth for nearly three months, as they happily awaited the births of their babies, and then returned home.

The birth of John

When the time came, Elizabeth gave birth to a son, and her neighbours and relatives shared her joy. After a week it was time to name the child, and everyone expected him to be named after his father, Zechariah, but Elizabeth spoke up: "No! He shall be called John."

In those days it was the custom to name children after someone in the family, and so the neighbours replied, "But you have no relatives with that name." They went to Zechariah and made signs to him, as if he could not hear (though he could), asking what he would like to name his son.

He got out a writing tablet and, to everyone's astonishment, wrote, "His name is John."

Immediately Zechariah's tongue was set free, and he began to say a great prayer of praise to God, ending with words about his son: "You, my child, will be called a prophet of the Most High, for you will go before the Lord to prepare his way."

All the neighbours were filled with awe, and word of these happenings spread throughout the hill country of Judea. People wondered about this child and who he was going to be, for they knew God's hand was on him.

The birth of Jesus

The Roman Empire now ruled all the land around the Mediterranean Sea, including Judea and Galilee, and in each province the emperor had installed a ruler – sometimes a king, sometimes a governor. Caesar

Augustus, the emperor, commanded that all the inhabitants of the Roman Empire should be counted. Each family had to go to their home town for their name and details to be recorded, so Mary and Joseph travelled from Nazareth, in Galilee, to Bethlehem, in Judea, the home town of Joseph's ancestor King David.

While they were in Bethlehem, the time came for Mary's child to be born. Because so many people had come back to be counted, the town was crowded and there was no room at the inns. They were sheltering in a stable when the baby was born. Mary wrapped him in some cloth and placed him in a manger, a trough for feeding cattle.

Nearby, shepherds were keeping watch over their flocks at night. An angel of the Lord appeared to them, and they were terrified. But the angel said, "Do not be afraid. I bring you good news of great joy: today in the town of David a saviour has been born, who is the Messiah, the Lord. You will find the baby wrapped in cloth and lying in a manger."

Suddenly a great company of angels appeared alongside the first, saying, "Glory to God in the highest, and on earth peace to all people of good will."

When the angels left, the shepherds were amazed to hear that the long-awaited Messiah had finally come. They said to one another, "Let us hurry to Bethlehem and look for this baby."

When they arrived, they found Mary and Joseph resting in a stable, and the baby lying in a manger. As soon as they saw him, they told Mary and Joseph about the angels who had visited them and told them that the child would be the Messiah. Mary and Joseph were amazed, and Mary kept these things in her heart.

The shepherds returned to their fields, joyfully praising God for all that they had heard and seen.

Wise men visit from the East

After Jesus was born in Bethlehem, in lands to the east beyond the Roman Empire, three wise men, Caspar, Melchior and Balthazar, saw signs in the stars telling them that a very special event had taken place. They travelled to Jerusalem and asked at the court of King Herod, who ruled Judea but took orders from the Roman emperor, "Where is the child

who will become king of the Jews? We have come to worship him."

Herod was greatly troubled by their question. He was king of Judea and of the Jews. He had made sure that anyone with even the slightest claim to the throne had been killed – he had even put two of his own sons to death for plotting against him.

Herod called together the chief priests and teachers of the land, and asked them where the king of the Jews, the Messiah, was expected to be born. They immediately replied, "In Bethlehem, for the prophets foretold that."

Then Herod called the wise men secretly to find out exactly when they saw the sign in the stars. He sent them to Bethlehem, saying, "Go and search for the child, and when you have found him, come and report to me immediately so that I too may go and worship him."

The wise men went on their way. As soon as they left Jerusalem, they could clearly see the signs in the stars again and were overjoyed. The signs led them to the child they had been searching for. When they saw Jesus with his mother, Mary, they bowed down and worshipped him. They presented him with gifts: gold, a noble metal signifying wisdom; frankincense, a costly incense evoking reverence; and myrrh, a precious healing medicine.

The wise men were warned in a dream not to return to Herod, so they took a different route back to their country.

The escape to Egypt

When the wise men had left, an angel of the Lord appeared to Joseph in a dream, saying, "Get up, take the boy and his mother, and escape to Egypt. Stay there until I tell you, for Herod is going to search for the child and kill him."

So Joseph got up and, taking Jesus and Mary, immediately set out on a journey, walking through the desert to Egypt.

After some days, Herod realised that he had been tricked by the wise men. In a rage, he ordered his soldiers to kill all baby boys in and around Bethlehem. There was much weeping and mourning in the land after the soldiers carried out Herod's brutal command.

A year or two later, Herod died, and an angel of the Lord appeared to Joseph in Egypt, saying, "Take the child and his mother and return to your land, because those who were trying to take his life are dead."

Joseph was ready to go home with Jesus and Mary, until he heard that Herod's son Archelaus had become king of Judea. He was still too afraid to return, so the family headed further north to live in Nazareth, in Galilee.

The twelve-year-old in the temple

Every year in springtime, the Jewish people celebrated the great festival of Passover, when all the families in Judea and nearby would make a pilgrimage to the temple in Jerusalem. When Jesus was twelve years old, like every year, he went with his parents, relatives and friends from Nazareth to Jerusalem.

After the festival was over, Jesus and Mary set out for home, assuming that Jesus was following behind them in the company of friends and relatives. Instead, the boy had stayed in Jerusalem. After a day of travelling, his parents began to look for him, but could not find him in the crowds. They anxiously returned to Jerusalem to search for him.

After three days, Mary and Joseph found Jesus in the courtyard of the temple, sitting among the priests, scribes (who wrote and taught the law) and learned teachers, listening and asking questions. Everyone who heard him speak was amazed at his understanding and his answers. His parents were astonished too.

His mother asked, "Why have you treated us like this? Your father and I have been worrying and searching for you."

Jesus surprised them with his answer: "Why were you searching for me? Did you not know that I would be in my Father's house?"

But they did not understand what he meant. Jesus obediently went back to Nazareth with his parents, and his mother remembered his words, keeping them in her heart. Jesus grew in wisdom, maturity and grace.

Jesus grew in wisdom, maturity and grace.

Jesus Meets John the Baptist

John preaches in the wilderness

In those days, many people were expecting the Messiah – the saviour who would put all things right again with the world. So there was great anticipation when word got round of a young man preaching in the Judean desert by the River Jordan. Was this the man of whom the prophets had said, "I will send my messenger ahead of you to prepare my way"?

In the desert, John, the son of Zechariah, wearing simple garments made of camel's hair, spoke to anyone who would listen to him. He called, "Repent! Change your ways! The kingdom of heaven is near."

John was preaching in the hottest part of the country, in the Judean Desert close to the Dead Sea. Despite the dryness and the heat, more and more people from far and near flocked to hear him preach. They asked him, "What shall we do?"

John answered, "Anyone who has two shirts should share with someone who has none, and anyone who has food should do the same."

If they vowed to change their ways and become better human beings, John led them to the river and baptised them there, to purify them. They waded into the river until, for a moment, they were completely underwater.

Some people wondered in their hearts whether John was the Messiah. But when they asked him, he answered, "After me will come one who is greater than I am, and I am not worthy to stoop down and untie the straps of his sandals. I baptise with water, but he will baptise you with the Holy Spirit."

Jesus is baptised

When Jesus was about thirty years old, he came from Nazareth to be baptised by John. When John saw him, he recognised him and knew that this was the man God had sent to be the Messiah.

John asked Jesus, "Why do you come to me? I should be baptised by you!"

But Jesus replied, "Let it be done, as I have asked."

John agreed and led him into the River Jordan. As Jesus rose out of the water, John saw the heavens open and the spirit of God descend onto Jesus like a dove. And he heard a voice from heaven saying, "This is my son, whom I love. Through him I shall show myself."

John spoke to all the people around, telling them what he had seen, and added, "I have seen, and I can say that this is God's Chosen One."

From that moment onwards, Jesus truly became the chosen or anointed one, which in Hebrew is the Messiah, and in Greek is the Christ, but he did not yet tell all the people.

The temptation

Immediately after Jesus was baptised in the River Jordan, he was led away from the crowds by the Holy Spirit and into a secluded place in the desert. There, he fasted for forty days and forty nights, praying in solitude.

After this time, Satan, the devil, came to tempt him away from God, saying, "If you are the Son of God, turn these stones into bread so that you can eat."

Despite his great hunger, Jesus answered, "It is written by the Lord's prophets that: 'Man shall not live by bread alone, but from God's word.'"

The devil did not like losing, and did not like to hear words from the Old Testament being quoted to him. (The Old Testament was written down over the course of a thousand years, and existed before Jesus was born.) But the devil knew the Old Testament too, so he whisked Jesus up to the holy city of Jerusalem, which stood high in the mountains above the deep valley of the River Jordan.

He took Jesus to the highest point of the temple and said, "If you are the

Son of God, throw yourself down, for it is written that: 'He will command angels to guard you carefully, so that you will not strike your foot against a stone.'"

Jesus answered, "It is also written: 'Do not put the Lord your God to the test.'"

The devil was maddened that he had lost again. He took Jesus to a very high mountain and showed him all the kingdoms of the world in their splendour, in the hope of persuading this Son of God to become ruler over all the world. The devil said, "I will give you all this if you will bow down and worship me."

This time Jesus answered, "Get away from me, Satan! For it is written: 'Worship the Lord your God, and serve him only.'"

The devil was furious, but finally he gave up and left Jesus, waiting for another time to tempt him away from God. Angels came and watched over Jesus in the desert.

The Early Work of Jesus

Jesus calls his disciples

After Jesus' baptism and the forty days he spent praying in the wilderness of Judea, he returned to Galilee. He left Nazareth and went to Capernaum, by the Sea of Galilee. One morning, Jesus was standing by the shore talking, and people crowded around him to listen. Jesus saw two boats at the water's edge. He climbed into one of the boats, which belonged to two fishermen, Simon (also known as Peter; there were no surnames in those days, so people often had two names, like Simon Peter) and his brother Andrew. Jesus asked Peter to row out from the shore a little, then he taught the crowd of people from the boat, telling them to change their ways because the kingdom of heaven was near.

When he had finished speaking, he said to Peter, "Row out into deep water and let down your nets."

Peter answered, "Master, we have worked all night and haven't caught anything." But then he added, "Because you say so, I will let down the nets."

Peter and Andrew caught so many fish that their nets began to break, so they called to James and John, the fishermen in the other boat (who were also brothers), to come and help them. Together they filled both boats so full that they began to sink. The fishermen were astonished at the enormous catch, and were afraid.

Jesus said to Peter, "Do not be afraid, because from now on you will no longer catch fish but be a fisherman of people. You will gather people and tell them about the word of God."

They pulled the boats ashore, and Peter, Andrew, James and John brought all the fish to the market, where the crowds were amazed at the enormous catch. Then they left their work as fishermen and followed Jesus.

Before long, eight others decided to join them, and they became known as the twelve disciples. They were Peter, Andrew, James, John, Philip, Bartholomew, Thomas, Matthew, James (the son of Alphaeus), Thaddaeus, Simon and Judas.

Jesus turns water into wine

One day a wedding took place at Cana, in Galilee. In those days weddings were great events often lasting several days. Jesus' mother, Mary, was there, and Jesus and his disciples had also been invited.

After a time, all the wine was finished, and Mary said to Jesus, "There is no more wine."

Jesus replied, "Why does this concern you and me? My hour has not yet come."

Nevertheless, Mary said to the servants, "Do whatever Jesus tells you."

Nearby stood six large stone water jars, each the size of three large buckets. Jesus said to the servants, "Fill the jars with water." And they filled them to the brim.

Jesus gazed at the water and said to the servants, "Draw some out and take it to the master of the wedding feast."

They did so, and the master of the wedding feast took the cup that they offered him and tasted wine. He did not know where it had come from, though the servants who had drawn the water knew. He called the bridegroom aside and said, "Wherever I go as master of a wedding feast, everyone brings out the best wine first, and then the cheaper wine after the guests have had too much to drink. But you have saved the best till now."

After Jesus transformed the water into wine, a belief began to awaken in his disciples that Jesus was more than just a teacher.

The Samaritan woman at the well

Once, when Jesus and his disciples were returning from Jerusalem to Galilee, they passed through Samaria. The Samaritans, the people of Samaria, were descendants of Jacob (who was also known as Israel), but they had drifted apart from the Jews, Jacob's other descendants who lived in Judea and Galilee. At the time of Jesus, the Jews despised the Samaritans and barely spoke to them.

Around noon, in the heat of the day, Jesus and his disciples came to Shechem, which lay in the valley beneath the mountain on which the Samaritans worshipped. They stopped at the well that Jacob had dug there around two thousand years before. The disciples went to the town to buy bread, leaving Jesus at the well. (The deep well is still there today, and clear, cool water can be drawn up with a bucket on a long rope.) When a Samaritan woman came to the well to draw water, Jesus asked her, "Will you give me a drink?"

The woman was quite surprised, for she immediately knew that Jesus was a Jew, from the way he spoke and was dressed. She said, "You are a Jew and I am a Samaritan. How can you ask me for a drink?"

But Jesus saw in her soul a deep longing for the Messiah, and he replied, "If you knew who was asking you for a drink, you would have asked him and he would have given you living water."

Being a very practical woman, she pointed out, "Sir, you have nothing to draw water with, and the well is very deep. Where can you get this living water? Are you greater than our father Jacob, who gave us this well and drank from it himself?"

"Everyone who drinks from this water will be thirsty again," Jesus replied, "but whoever drinks the water I give them will never thirst again. Instead, they will have a spring of water that wells up to become eternal life."

The woman could immediately see what a wonderful gift this would be, for it was hard work walking from her house to the well, then pulling up water and carrying it home in a great earthenware jug.

"Sir," she said, "give me this water so that I won't get thirsty and keep having to come here to draw water."

Jesus replied, "Go and call your husband, then come back."

Now the woman was embarrassed and quickly said, "I have no husband."

"I know that you have had five husbands," Jesus told her, "and that the man you now live with is not your husband."

When Jesus said this, she realised that he could see right through her, and wondered if he could answer some of her most puzzling questions. She exclaimed, "I can see you are a prophet. Tell me, if our ancestors worshipped on this mountain, why do Jews say that we must worship in Jerusalem?"

"Believe me," replied Jesus, "the time will come when people will worship God neither on this mountain nor in Jerusalem. You Samaritans worship what you do not know, and we Jews worship what we know. A time is soon coming when all true worshippers will worship the Father in spirit: the place of worship will no longer be important. For God is spirit and his worshippers must worship in spirit and in truth."

The woman said, "I know the Messiah, the Christ, is coming. When he comes, he will explain everything to us."

Then Jesus told her something that he had not even told his disciples: "I myself am he."

Just then the disciples returned. They were surprised to find him talking with a Samaritan woman, but none of them asked why. The woman left her water jar, ran back to the town and called to the people, "Come, see this man who told me everything about my life. Could this be the Messiah?"

People came from the town and made their way to the well. After they had spoken with Jesus they urged him to stay, and he remained with them for two days. Many of the Samaritans said to the woman, "We believe not only because of what you told us about this man, but also because we have now heard him for ourselves, and we know that he really is the Messiah, the saviour of the world."

The Sermon on the Mount

Jesus teaches the disciples

When Jesus arrived back in Galilee, great crowds from all the surrounding areas followed him. Seeing the crowds, Jesus climbed up the hillside above the Sea of Galilee to spend some quiet time with his disciples. He sat down and taught them how to become better human beings.

First, Jesus showed them how to see beyond the immediate situation, saying, "Blessed are the poor, for theirs is the kingdom of heaven." He also said, "Woe to those who are rich, for they have already received their reward."

He spoke of many other situations in which people may feel lost and dissatisfied, but each time he showed a fresh way of looking at it.

Jesus went on to say that it was not enough to simply follow all the Jewish rules, which had grown ever more complicated, but that people must look into their own souls too. "You have heard it said, 'You shall not murder,' and that anyone who does murder will be judged by God," said Jesus. "But I tell you that anyone who is angry with another person will also be judged by God. So, before going to make a gift at the altar or praying to God, go first to make peace and be reconciled with the person with whom you were angry."

Finally, Jesus gave the disciples the most difficult challenge. "You have heard it said: 'Love your neighbour and hate your enemy,' but I tell you to love your enemy and pray for those who are against you. What good does it do to only love those who love you? What reward will that bring? Be perfect, as your heavenly Father, God, is perfect."

The Lord's Prayer

Jesus told the disciples: "When you pray, do not babble empty phrases like those who believe in false gods, and think their gods will listen because they use lots of words. Do not be like them, for your Father knows what you need before you ask him. This is how you should pray:

Our Father in the heavens,
Hallowed be your name,
Your kingdom come,
Your will be done,
On earth as it is in the heavens.
Give us this day our daily bread,
And forgive us our trespasses,
As we forgive those who trespass against us,
And lead us not into temptation,
But deliver us from the evil.
For yours is the kingdom, the power and the glory
For ever and ever,
Amen.

Jesus did not explain much about this prayer, but he added, "For if you forgive other people when they sin against you, your heavenly Father will also forgive you. But if you do not forgive others their sins, your Father will not forgive your sins."

Treasures in heaven

Jesus continued teaching the disciples as they were gathered around him on the hillside above the Sea of Galilee.

He said, "Do not store up treasures on earth – moths and mice can destroy clothes and food, and thieves might break in and steal precious stones or gold. Instead, by being a good human being, store up treasures in heaven – where moths and mice cannot cause damage, nor thieves break

in and steal. For where your treasure is, there your heart will also be."

Jesus added, "No one can serve two masters. You will hate one and love the other. You cannot serve both God and money.

"Therefore I tell you, do not worry about your life – what you will eat or drink, about your body, or what you will wear. Is life not more important than food, and the body more important than clothes?

"Look at the birds of the air, they do not sow or reap or store away food in barns, and yet your heavenly Father feeds them. Are human beings not much more valuable to God than the birds? Can anyone add a single hour to their life by worrying?

"And why worry about clothes? See the lilies growing in the field: they do not work or make clothes. Yet even King Solomon in all his glory was not dressed as finely as one of these lilies. If that is how God clothes the flowers in the field that are here today and perish tomorrow, how much more will he clothe you?"

The disciples had of course all heard of King Solomon, who had built the temple in Jerusalem and ruled over the land when it was at its greatest. Kings and noblemen from neighbouring countries brought him gifts, and so King Solomon had great wealth and fine clothes.

Jesus continued, "Do not worry, saying, 'What shall we eat?' or 'What shall we drink?' or 'What shall we wear?' Your heavenly Father knows that you need these things. Seek his kingdom first, and all these things will be given to you as well. Therefore, do not worry about tomorrow, for tomorrow will worry about itself. Each day has enough trouble of its own."

Do not judge others

Jesus spoke to the disciples about how it is always easier to see the fault in other people and not notice it in oneself: "Do not judge others, or you too will be judged. Forgive, and you will be forgiven. Give, and you will be given to.

"Why do you look at the speck of sawdust in your brother's eye and pay no attention to the plank of wood in your own eye? You are a hypocrite! First take the plank out of your own eye, and then you will see clearly to remove the speck from your brother's eye."

The disciples could think of many hypocrites – people who talked about doing the right thing, but in reality did the opposite.

Jesus continued: "Ask and it will be given; seek and you will find; knock and the door will be opened. Because everyone who asks receives; everyone who seeks finds; and to everyone who knocks, the door will be opened.

"Which of you, if your children asked for bread, would give them a stone? Or if they asked for a fish, would give them a snake? If people know how to give good gifts to their children, how much more will your Father in heaven give to those who ask him?"

Jesus finished his teaching by saying, "In everything, treat others as you would like to be treated. This sums up the law and the teachings of the prophets."

During all this time when Jesus was up the hillside with his disciples, the crowds below had fallen silent. One or two had crept up the hillside to try to hear what Jesus was saying. By the end of his teaching, many more people had heard his words, and they marvelled at what he had to say.

Jesus' teachings on the hillside overlooking the Sea of Galilee became known as the Sermon on the Mount.

Miracles and Healing

Raising the young man at Nain

Soon after his Sermon on the Mount, Jesus visited a town called Nain, in Galilee. His disciples and a large crowd followed him. As he approached the town gate, the body of a dead man was being carried out – the only son of his mother, who was a widow. Many people gathered around the grieving woman.

When Jesus saw her his heart was filled with compassion, and he said to her, "Do not weep."

Then he went up and touched the wooden frame on which they were carrying her son's body, and the bearers stood still. Jesus said, "Young man, I say to you, get up!"

The dead man sat up and began to talk, and Jesus guided him back to his mother. The crowds were filled with awe and praised God. "A great prophet has appeared among us!" they said.

Word about this deed spread throughout the land.

Calming the storm

Jesus and his disciples had spent all day by the Sea of Galilee. Jesus had been teaching the crowds through parables (stories with a deeper meaning) and had then withdrawn with the disciples to explain what the parables meant. However, the crowds had come to find them, asking Jesus to heal sick people. Finally, when evening came, Jesus said to his disciples, "Let us go over to the other side of the lake."

Leaving the crowds behind, and hoping for some peace, Jesus and the

disciples climbed into a boat. Jesus went to the stern of the boat, lay down and slept.

Even today, conditions on the Sea of Galilee can change quickly. At times, if a strong wind blows, the peaceful lake can be transformed, with great waves breaking on the shore. On that day, a furious squall rose up and waves surged over the boat, nearly swamping it.

The disciples feared for their lives and woke Jesus up. "Teacher," they urged, "don't you care if we drown?"

Jesus stood up and said sternly to the wind and the waves, "Quiet! Be still!"

The wind died down and the sea was completely calm.

Then he asked his disciples, "Why are you so afraid? Do you still have no faith?"

They were filled with awe, and asked each other, "What kind of a man is our teacher? He can even command the wind and the waves to obey him!" They saw that Jesus was lord of the elements.

From then on, in times of danger or when they were afraid, they only needed to call Jesus to feel his power, and they would feel their fear vanish.

Healing Jairus' daughter and the sick woman

After Jesus had returned by boat to Capernaum, a large crowd gathered around him. Jairus, one of the leaders of the synagogue – the place where Jewish people gathered to pray – came and knelt before Jesus, pleading, "My daughter is dying. Please come and put your hand on her, so that she may be healed and live."

Jesus went with him, and the crowd followed. There was a woman among them who was suffering a great deal with a wound that had been bleeding for twelve years. She had spent all the money she had on seeing doctors, but no one could heal her. She said to herself, "If only I could touch Jesus' cloak, I will be healed."

She reached out to touch it, and immediately the wound stopped bleeding and she felt her suffering come to an end. At once Jesus realised that some healing power had left him. He turned and asked, "Who touched me?"

"Just look how the people are crowding around and jostling against you," his disciples answered. "How can you ask, 'Who touched me'?"

But Jesus kept looking around to see who had done it. Then the woman, knowing what had happened to her, fell at his feet, trembling with fear, and told him the whole truth.

Jesus said to her, "Daughter, your trust and faith has healed you. Go in peace and be free from your suffering."

While Jesus was still speaking, some people arrived from Jairus' house and told him, "We are sorry, but your daughter has died. There is no need to bother the teacher."

But Jesus heard what they said, and told Jairus, "Do not fear. She will be healed."

He did not let anyone follow him except Peter, and the brothers James and John. When they came to Jairus' house they witnessed a terrible commotion, with people crying and wailing loudly. Jesus walked in and asked, "Why are you all grieving? The child is not dead, only asleep." But in the family's grief, they just laughed at him.

Jesus sent them all out of the house. Then, taking the child's father and mother and the three disciples who were with him, he stepped towards the twelve-year-old's bedside. He took her by the hand and said to her, "*Talitha koum*!" (This means "Little girl, get up!" in Aramaic, the language of those parts.)

Immediately the girl stood up and began to walk. Everyone was completely astonished. Jesus told her parents to give her something to eat, and not to tell anyone what had happened there that day.

Healing the paralysed man at Bethesda

Some time later, Jesus went up to Jerusalem for one of the Jewish festivals. In Jerusalem near the Sheep Gate there is a pool called Bethesda, surrounded by five covered archways.

Once in a while, the water in the pool began to bubble and stir. When this happened, the first person to get into the water would be healed of any illness or injury. So a great number of people – those who had become blind, lame, paralysed or ill – used to lie there, waiting for the waters to stir.

One man there hadn't been able to walk for thirty-eight years. When Jesus saw him lying under the covered archways and heard what troubled him, he asked the man, "Do you want to walk again?"

"Sir," replied the man, "I have no one to help me into the pool when the water stirs, and every time I try to get in, someone else climbs in before me."

Jesus said to him, "Get up! Pick up your mat and walk."

At once the man was healed: he picked up his mat and walked.

This miracle took place on the Sabbath: the holy day of rest, in memory of the seventh day of Creation, when God rested. Jewish leaders had made rules about what was allowed and not allowed to happen on the Sabbath, and carrying anything outdoors was considered to be "work", which was forbidden.

In the holy city of Jerusalem the rules were particularly strict because there were so many learned Jewish leaders there. When they saw the man who had been healed, they said to him, "It is the Sabbath: the law forbids you to carry your mat."

But he replied, "The man who healed me said, 'Pick up your mat and walk.'"

The leaders asked, "Who is this man?"

But he could not answer because he had no idea who had healed him. Jesus had slipped away into the crowd.

Later Jesus found the man in the courtyard of the temple and said, "See, you can walk again. Stop doing wrong, be good to others, or something worse may happen to you."

The man now knew it was Jesus who had made him well, and he told the Jewish leaders.

Instead of rejoicing about a man being healed, the Jewish leaders were only concerned with keeping to the rules of the Sabbath. After this, they watched Jesus carefully. But Jesus said to them, "My Father is always at work to this very day, and I too am working."

This enraged the Jewish leaders even more. Not only was Jesus breaking the Sabbath, but he was calling God his own father, making himself equal with God. They tried even harder to stop his work, and even to kill him.

Feeding the five thousand

Jesus returned to the north to preach in the towns of Galilee, and great crowds followed him. Jesus went with his disciples in a boat across the Sea of Galilee to speak with them in peace, away from the crowds, but many people saw him and ran on foot to get to the other side.

When their boat reached the shore, Jesus and his disciples climbed up a nearby hill. They saw that a large crowd had followed, and Jesus took pity on them, for they seemed like lost sheep without a shepherd. So he began to teach them and healed their sick ones.

By the time he had finished it was getting late, so his disciple Philip said, "This is a remote place and it is already very late. Send the people away to the surrounding villages so they can buy themselves something to eat."

But Jesus answered, "You can give them something to eat."

Philip replied, "That would cost a great amount of money! Should we spend so much money on bread for them?"

"How many loaves do you have?" Jesus asked.

Another disciple, Andrew, went to find out and returned, saying, "There is a boy with five small loaves and two fishes."

Then Jesus said, "Bring them to me, and ask the people to sit down in groups of about fifty."

The crowd sat down on the grass – there were around five thousand people! Taking the five loaves and the two fishes, Jesus looked up to heaven, gave thanks to God, and broke the loaves. Then he handed them to his disciples to share out among the people. They all ate and were all satisfied. The disciples picked up twelve baskets of broken pieces of bread and fish that were left over.

After people saw what Jesus had done, they became excited and whispered to one another, "Surely this is a new prophet." They wondered if he might even be the Messiah who was coming to bring peace to the world.

But Jesus knew that if they really thought this they would force him to be king, so he withdrew to a mountain alone.

Healing the deaf man

Jesus and his disciples travelled far and wide, spreading God's word to the people. Returning from the cities of Tyre and Sidon, on the coast of the Mediterranean Sea, they went to the other side of the Sea of Galilee to the Decapolis, the region of ten cities. Among the crowds was a deaf man who struggled to speak, and some people asked Jesus to help him.

Jesus took the man away from the crowd. The man, who had never heard a sound or a word in his life, now faced Christ. Jesus put his fingers into the man's ears and then he spat on his fingers and touched the man's tongue. He looked up to heaven, murmured in prayer, and said, "*Eph-phatha*!" which means "be open" in Aramaic.

Immediately the man's ears were opened to sound and his tongue was loosened to speech, and he began to hear and talk.

Jesus commanded the crowd to remain silent and not to speak of what he had done, because he feared that in their excitement they might want to make him their ruler. But the more he did so, the more they kept talking about it.

The crowd was utterly amazed, and people praised Jesus, saying, "This man is astonishing! He can even make the deaf hear and the mute speak."

Healing the ten men with leprosy

Later, when Jesus was on his way to Jerusalem for a holy festival, walking through a village between Galilee and Samaria, ten men who had leprosy came to meet him.

Leprosy is a disease that causes big red sores on the skin. Often those who have leprosy can no longer feel pain and do not notice if they burn or cut themselves, so many have badly burned arms or legs with wounds that do not heal. In those days, people with leprosy were cast out from towns and villages, because the inhabitants were afraid of catching the disease.

As Jesus was passing, the men called out, "Jesus, Master, have pity on us."

When he saw them, Jesus said, "Go, show yourselves to the priests," because it was the priests' job to declare whether people were diseased or not.

The men went to see the priests and found that they had been healed.

When one of the men saw that he had been cured, he came back and, praising God loudly, threw himself at Jesus' feet and thanked him.

Jesus saw that the only man who returned to praise God was a Samaritan. The other nine men were Jews. He said to those around, "Were not all ten men healed? Where are the other nine? Is it only this foreign man who has returned to give praise to God?"

Then he said to the Samaritan, "Rise and go. Your trust in God has made you well."

Healing the blind man at Jericho

Once, Jesus was walking near Jericho, down in the hot Jordan Valley near the Dead Sea. As he was leaving the city, surrounded by a large crowd, a blind man was sitting by the roadside begging. When the blind man heard the crowd going by, he asked them what was happening.

They told him, "Jesus of Nazareth is passing by."

The blind man had heard of him, and called out, "Jesus, son of David, have mercy on me!"

The crowd rebuked him, telling him to be quiet, but he shouted out all the more, "Jesus, son of David, have mercy on me!"

Jesus stopped and told the crowd to call the blind man over. So the blind man jumped to his feet and came to Jesus.

"What would you like me to do for you?" Jesus asked.

"Lord, I want to see," replied the blind man.

Then Jesus said, "Go, your trust in God has healed you."

Immediately the man received his sight, and he followed Jesus along the road joyfully, praising God. When all the people around saw what had happened, they praised God too.

Parables

Parable of the sower

Once when Jesus was by the Sea of Galilee, the crowd that gathered around him was so large that he stepped into a boat so he could speak to the people standing on the shore. He told them a parable (a story with a deeper meaning) about something they had all seen around them every day:

"A farmer went out to sow seeds. As he was scattering them, some fell along the path, and birds came and ate them up. Some fell on dry, rocky ground, and when they grew the plants withered in the hot sunshine. Others fell among thorny bushes, which grew up around them and choked the new plants. And some fell on good, fertile soil; they grew well and yielded a good crop – a hundred times more than was sown."

Then Jesus said, "Whoever has ears to hear, let them hear."

When he was alone with his disciples, they asked him what the story meant, and Jesus told them, "The secrets of the kingdom of God have been given to you, but to others I speak in parables, so that until they are ready to understand what is hidden, they look but may not see, and they hear but may not understand."

And then he went on to explain the meaning of the parable: "The seed is the word of God. Those that fell on the path are the people who hear the word of God before the devil takes it away from their hearts and they are lost. Those on rocky ground are the people who hear the word of God with great joy and believe for a while, but in time they forget and fall away. Those among thorny bushes are the people who hear the word of God but are choked by worries about everyday life and finding riches and pleasure.

"But the seeds that fall on good, fertile soil are the people with kind hearts: they hear the word of God and remember it, and by keeping it in their hearts they thrive from it."

Parable of the prodigal son

One day as Jesus was travelling through Galilee on his way to Jerusalem, he stopped to eat with some criminals and tax collectors (who were despised by the Jewish people because they worked for the Romans who occupied their country). Some strictly religious people, known as Pharisees, were gathered nearby and muttered among themselves, "This man encourages evildoers and eats with them."

While the Pharisees were still standing nearby, Jesus told the criminals and tax collectors a parable:

"There was once a man who had two sons. The younger one said to his father, 'Father, give me my share of what I will inherit when you die.'

"So the father divided his property between them. The younger son soon gathered all that he had and set off for a distant country, where he spent his money enjoying a good life. After he had spent all his money, there was a famine in that country and he had nothing to eat, so he found work feeding pigs in the fields, where he would have gladly eaten the pig's food if he had been given any. (No Jew would normally do this work, for to them pigs were unclean animals that should be avoided.)

"Then the young man came to his senses, thinking: all my father's servants have food to spare, and here I am starving to death. I will go back to my father and say to him, 'Father, I have done wrong against God and against you. I am no longer worthy to be called your son. Take me as one of your servants.'

"Dirty and in tattered clothes, he walked back to his homeland to visit his father. When he was still a long way off, his father saw him coming and was filled with compassion and love for him. He ran to his son, threw his arms around him and kissed him. His son said, 'Father, I have done wrong against God and against you. I am no longer worthy to be called your son.'

"But the father said to his servants, 'Quick, bring the best robes to clothe him, put a ring on his finger and sandals on his feet. Bring a fat calf and kill it, for we shall have a feast and celebrate. My son, who I thought was dead, is alive again; he was lost and now is found.'

"Meanwhile, the older son came back from working his fields and heard the music and dancing, so he called one of the servants to ask what was going on. 'Your brother has come home,' replied the servant, 'and your father has killed a calf to celebrate him being safely home again.'

"When he heard this, the older brother grew angry and refused to go inside the house, so his father went out to speak with him, begging him to come and join them. But the older brother answered, 'Look, all these years I've been working for you and never disobeyed you, yet you never gave me even a young goat so I could celebrate with my friends. But when this son of yours who has wasted your property on easy living comes home, you kill a calf for him!'

"'My son,' the father replied, 'you are always with me, and everything I have is yours. But we should celebrate and be glad, because your brother was dead and is alive again; he was lost and now is found.'"

Jesus did not explain the meaning of this parable, but perhaps the proud Pharisees who looked down on him for keeping company with evildoers felt the story was aimed at them.

Parable of the good shepherd

In the Holy Land, to this day there are flocks of sheep that are closely watched by a shepherd, who leads them to feeding grounds and to water. Sometimes several shepherds with their flocks will come together at a well, but when the sheep have finished drinking the shepherds go in different directions, and each sheep follows its own shepherd.

Once, when the Pharisees heard that Jesus had healed a man on the Sabbath, some said that he should not have worked on the holy day. Others disagreed: if Jesus had healed the man, surely he could not be accused of wrongdoing. To decide the matter, some of the Pharisees went to question Jesus, and he told them:

"Truly, I tell you, anyone who does not enter the sheep pen by the gate but climbs in some other way instead is a thief and a robber. The one who enters by the gate is the shepherd. The sheep listen to his voice as he calls them by name and leads them out. Then he walks ahead of them, and his sheep follow because they know his voice. But they will never follow strangers; in fact, they will run away from them, because they do not know their voices."

Jesus spoke in pictures, but the Pharisees did not understand what he was telling them, so he told them again:

"Truly, I myself am the gate for the sheep. All who came before me were thieves and robbers, but the sheep did not listen to them. I myself am the gate. Whoever enters through me will find a future life with purpose. They will enter and leave, and find a pasture to graze. The thief comes only to kill and steal, but I have come to guide the sheep to a full and happy life.

"I myself am the good shepherd. The good shepherd lays down his life for his sheep. Hired servants would not care for them as I do. If they saw a wolf coming, they would run away and let the wolf attack the flock.

"I myself am the good shepherd. I know my sheep and the sheep know me – just as the Father knows me and I know the Father. I lay down my life for the sheep. No one takes it from me; I sacrifice it of my own accord. I have authority from the Father to sacrifice my life and receive it back again."

Though Jesus was clearly speaking of his coming death, no one really understood him.

Parable of the vineyard workers

On another occasion, Jesus was speaking to the disciples about how different people would come into the kingdom of heaven, and he told them a story:

"The kingdom of heaven is like a landowner who went out at dawn to the marketplace to hire workers for his vineyard. For the day's work he agreed to pay them one denarius (a silver coin that was the usual payment for a day's labour) and sent them to his vineyard.

"Later, at nine in the morning, he went out again and saw others standing in the marketplace. He told them to go and work in his vineyard, and that he would pay them a fair wage. So they went.

"At noon, and again at three in the afternoon, he went out to the marketplace and did the same thing. At five in the afternoon, he found still others standing around, so he asked them, 'Why have you been standing here all day doing nothing?'

"They answered, 'Because no one has hired us.'

"So he said to them, 'You can also go and work in my vineyard.'

"When evening came, the owner of the vineyard said to his foreman, 'Call all the workers and pay them their wages, beginning with the last one hired.'

"The workers who were hired at five in the afternoon came and each received a denarius. So when those who were hired first came, they expected to receive more, but each of them also received a denarius.

"They grumbled to the owner, 'Those who were hired last only worked for one hour, and you paid them the same as us, even though we have carried the burden of the work and suffered the heat of the day.'

"But the owner answered, 'I am not being unfair to you, friend. Did you not agree to work for one denarius? Take your pay and go. I want to give the one who was hired last the same as I gave you. Can I not do what I want with my own money? Or are you jealous because I am generous?'"

Jesus added, "So the last will be first, and the first will be last."

Later Events in the Life of Jesus

Peter recognises Christ

Jesus and his disciples travelled all around the hot, dry country, preaching to the people. Far in the north, below the snow-capped peak of Mount Hermon, there is a special place: a region of plentiful growth, shaded by trees. From a cave in a tall rock, a river of fresh, cool water gushes out. It is the main source of the River Jordan, and has been considered a holy place since the most ancient times.

King Herod had built a temple of shining white marble there and dedicated it to the Roman emperor Caesar Augustus. After Herod died, his son Philip built a city there, which was called Caesarea Philippi.

When Jesus arrived there, he asked his disciples, "Who do people say I am?"

"Some think you are John the Baptist, others say that you are the prophet Elijah who has come again, and still others say that you are a new prophet," they replied.

"But who do you think I am?" asked Jesus.

Suddenly, Simon Peter said, "You are the Messiah, the Christ, the Son of the living God."

It was the first time someone had said out loud what many people quietly felt in their hearts.

Jesus replied, "Blessed are you, Simon; your true name is Peter." (Peter means "rock".) He continued, "On this rock I will build my church."

Then Jesus instructed his disciples not to tell anyone that he was the

Messiah. They all stood in awe and could not fully take in that Jesus was the Messiah.

He then began to tell the disciples about the path that lay before him: that he must go to Jerusalem and be rejected by the elders, the chief priests and the teachers; that he must be killed and, on the third day, be raised to life again.

The disciples could not understand this, and Peter took Jesus aside and sternly argued, "Never, Lord! We will not let this happen to you."

But Jesus saw clearly what his future must be, and he knew that turning away from it would be like accepting temptation from the devil. He turned and said to Peter, "Get behind me, Satan! You do not have in mind the will of God, but only human concerns."

The Transfiguration

About a week after Peter recognised Jesus as Christ at Caesarea Philippi, Jesus took Peter, James and John up Mount Tabor to pray. The mountain rises like a great dome from the plain between the mountains of Galilee and the hills of Samaria.

As Jesus was praying, the appearance of his face changed, and his clothes became dazzling white – whiter than anyone in the world could make them. Suddenly he looked more like a spiritual being than a man. (This event became known as the 'Transfiguration'.) And two figures, Moses and Elijah, appeared in glorious splendour, talking with Jesus about the end of his life and how it would take place in Jerusalem.

The three disciples had been drowsy, but they now fully awoke and saw Christ in all his glory standing with the two prophets. They were afraid and did not know what to think or say.

Peter, who could never remain silent, blurted out, "Lord, it is good that we are here. Let us put up three shelters – one for you, one for Moses, and one for Elijah."

While he was speaking, a cloud appeared and covered them. They heard a voice from the cloud saying, "This is my son, whom I love. Listen to him!"

The disciples fell to the ground, afraid and in awe. But Jesus came and touched them on the shoulder, saying, "Get up. Do not be afraid."

And when they looked up, the disciples saw no one but Jesus in his everyday appearance.

As they were walking back down the mountain, Jesus instructed them, "Do not tell anyone what you have seen, until the Son of Man has been raised from the dead."

They kept the matter to themselves. After Peter had recognised him as the Messiah, they had heard Jesus calling himself "the Son of Man"; they knew that, as well as being the Son of God, he was the son of a human being and came to the world to help all people. They quietly discussed what "raised from the dead" might mean. Like all good Jews, they knew that at the end of time, all the dead would rise again. They asked Jesus, "Why do the teachers say that Elijah must come before the Messiah and the end of time?"

Jesus replied, "Elijah must indeed come first, to prepare the way. But I tell you, Elijah has already come, and the people did not recognise him, but did to him as they pleased."

Then the disciples understood that he was talking about John the Baptist, who they heard had been killed by one of Herod's sons.

Jesus continued, "And it will be the same for the Son of Man."

The raising of Lazarus

While Jesus was in Jerusalem, crowds of followers accompanied him as he healed people. But some priests and their followers thought he was a madman and tried to attack him by throwing stones. Jesus escaped with his disciples and headed down into the deep valley of the River Jordan, crossing it where John had first baptised people.

Close to Jerusalem, in a village called Bethany, lived a young woman named Mary and her sister Martha. They were close followers of Jesus, who often stayed at their house when he visited Jerusalem. Their brother Lazarus was ill, and the sisters sent a messenger to Jesus, saying, "Lord, our brother, whom you love, is sick."

When Jesus heard this, he knew what Lazarus was going through, and said, "This sickness will not end in death." His disciples were reassured, for they knew that Jesus loved Lazarus and his sisters. But then Jesus added the puzzling words, "No, it is for God's glory so that God's Son may be glorified through it." Again, the disciples were left to quietly wonder what this might mean.

They stayed in the hot depths of the Jordan Valley for two days, and then Jesus said, "Let us go back to Jerusalem."

His disciples were alarmed, for only a few days earlier some people there had tried to stone him. But Jesus told them, "Our friend Lazarus has fallen asleep; I am going there to wake him up."

The disciples replied, "Lord, if he sleeps, he will get better."

So Jesus told them plainly, "Lazarus is dead, and for your sake I am glad I was not there, so that you may believe. Let us go to him."

As they climbed through the Judean desert towards Jerusalem, they came to Bethany and Jesus heard that Lazarus had already been buried in a tomb for four days. When Martha heard that Jesus was coming, she rushed out to meet him, while her sister stayed in the house.

Tearfully, and almost blaming him, Martha said to Jesus, "Lord, if you had been here, my brother would not have died." And then, remembering her trust in God, she added, "But I know that even now God will give you whatever you ask."

Jesus calmly said to her, "Your brother will rise again."

"I know he will rise again in the resurrection on the last day," Martha answered, for it was common knowledge among Jews that in the distant future, at the end of time, everyone would rise again.

Then Jesus spoke words that have become famous: "I am the resurrection and the life. Anyone who believes in me will live, even though they die; and whoever lives by believing in me will never die. Do you believe this?"

And suddenly Martha saw with complete certainty who the man in front of her was, and she replied, "Yes, Lord, I believe that you are the Messiah, the Son of God, who is to come into the world."

Martha then returned to the house and simply told Mary, "The teacher is here, and is asking for you."

Mary hurried out of the house and went to find Jesus, who was still outside the village of Bethany. She fell at his feet and, like Martha, spoke reproachfully out of her sorrow saying, "Lord, if you had been here, my brother would not have died."

When Jesus saw her weeping, he was deeply moved in spirit, and troubled. "Where have you laid him?" he asked.

"Come and see, Lord," she replied.

Then Jesus wept, and the people nearby said, "See how much he loved Lazarus."

But some of them also muttered, "If he could open the eyes of a blind man, why could he not have kept his friend from dying?"

Jesus, once more deeply moved, came to the tomb. It was a cave with a great round stone across the entrance.

"Take away the stone," he said.

"But, Lord," replied Martha, who had always been very practical, "by now it will smell terrible, for he has been there four days."

However, Jesus merely said, "Did I not tell you that if you believe, you will see the glory of God?"

So they rolled away the stone.

Jesus looked up and said quietly, "Father, I thank you, for you have heard me. I know that you always hear me, but I am saying this so that the people standing here may believe that you sent me to them." Then Jesus called in a loud voice, "Lazarus, arise!"

Lazarus walked out of the cave, his hands and feet wrapped with strips of linen, and a cloth around his face, which was how the body of a dead person was prepared in those times.

Jesus said to the people, "Take off his grave clothes and let him stand freely."

Many people saw what Jesus had done, and they were amazed.

The Last Days of Jesus

Jesus enters Jerusalem as king

Every year in springtime, the people of the Holy Land celebrated the festival of Passover to remember the time, long ago, when their ancestors had escaped from captivity in Egypt and God had sent ten plagues upon the Egyptians. During the last plague, God had killed all the first-born children in Egypt and told the Israelites to mark their doorposts with the blood of a slaughtered lamb so that the spirit of God would know to pass over those homes. Passover was an important festival, when all the families in the land made a pilgrimage to the temple in Jerusalem. The city would be full of people, with many staying in the surrounding villages too.

For some time, the chief priests and scribes had been scheming to arrest Jesus secretly and kill him. "But not during the festival," they said, "or the people may riot."

Jesus and his disciples also made their way to Jerusalem. They stayed with Mary and Martha in the village of Bethany, from where they could make their way every day over the Mount of Olives and into the city.

Some days before Passover, as they came to the village of Bethphage, Jesus sent two disciples ahead, telling them, "Go into the village, where you will find a young donkey tied. Untie it and bring it here. If anyone says anything to you, tell them, 'The Lord needs it and will send it back here shortly.'"

In the village the disciples found a foal outside in the street, tied to a doorway. As they were untying it, the owners asked them, "Why are you untying our donkey?" And they replied, "The Lord needs it."

They brought it to Jesus, spread their cloaks over it and helped him climb onto its back. As they travelled on to Jerusalem, more and more people

gathered, following Jesus. At first his disciples did not understand what was happening. Only later, after Jesus had risen again, did they realise that these things had been written down many centuries ago by the prophet Zechariah:

"Rejoice! Shout aloud! See, your king comes to you triumphant, but humble and riding on the foal of a donkey."

The large crowd recognised Jesus and threw their cloaks on the road before him. Others cut branches from the surrounding palm trees and spread them on the road. And the crowds ahead and those that followed shouted, "Hosanna!" and "Blessed is he who comes in the name of the Lord!" and "Blessed is the king of Israel!"

The greatest commandment

When Jesus was in Jerusalem, the Pharisees and Sadducees tried to trick him by asking him difficult questions.

One Pharisee scribe asked him, "Teacher, which is the greatest commandment God gave to Moses?"

Jesus replied, "'Love the Lord your God with all your heart and with all your soul and with all your mind.' This is the most important commandment. And the second is this: 'Love your neighbour as much as yourself.'"

Jesus is anointed at Bethany

On one of the following days, at Bethany, a meal was given in Jesus' honour. Martha's sister Mary took an alabaster jar of nard, a very expensive perfume. She poured it over Jesus' feet, anointing them, and wiped them with her hair. The house was filled with the fragrance of the perfume.

One of the disciples, Judas Iscariot, asked, "Why didn't you sell this perfume and give the money to the poor? It was worth a year's wages." Judas did not really care about the poor, but he was the keeper of the disciples' money bag. He was also a thief, and often helped himself to the contents of the money bag.

However, Jesus replied, "Leave her alone. You will always have poor people around you, and you can help them any time you want. But you will not always have me. She has poured perfume on my body to prepare for my burial."

Most of the disciples were troubled to hear Jesus speak of his burial. However, Judas went to visit the chief priests to betray Jesus instead. He said he would tell them where to find Jesus without crowds around him. The chief priests were delighted to hear this and promised to reward Judas with money.

The Last Supper

On the first day of Passover, it was customary to sacrifice a lamb for the Passover supper. The disciples asked Jesus, "Where shall we make preparations for you to eat?"

Jesus told two of his disciples to go into the city, where a man carrying a jar of water would meet them and take them to a house. There, they should say to the owner, "The teacher asks: 'Where is the guest room where I may eat the Passover supper with my disciples?'" Jesus continued, "He will show you a room upstairs which is furnished and ready. Make preparations for us there."

The two disciples left and went into the city. In those days it was very unusual for a man to carry water, because fetching water from the well was always women's work. But the disciples found that everything happened just as Jesus had told them it would, and they prepared for Passover.

When evening came, Jesus sat down at the table with the twelve disciples. He knew that the hour was coming for him to leave this world and go to God, the Father.

Jesus got up, laid aside his outer garment, poured water into a basin and knelt down to wash the feet of each disciple.

Then he sat down and said to them, "Truly, I will not eat again until

Passover is fulfilled in the kingdom of God." The disciples did not really understand what Jesus meant by this.

Jesus took some bread, and when he had given thanks, he broke it and gave it to his disciples, saying, "Take and eat, this is my body. Do this in remembrance of me."

Then he took a cup of wine, and when he had given thanks he gave it to them, saying, "Drink: this is the blood and the promise of God."

Then Jesus said, "Truly, I tell you, one of you is going to betray me."

His disciples were troubled and stared at one another, not knowing which of them he meant. One after another they began to say to him, "Surely you don't mean me, Lord?"

Jesus replied, "The one who has dipped his bread into the same bowl as me will betray me."

Then Judas said, "Surely you don't mean me, teacher?"

Jesus answered, "You yourself have spoken." And he added, "What you are about to do, do quickly."

The other disciples did not understand why Jesus said this to Judas. Some thought Jesus was telling him to buy supplies for the festival, seeing as Judas was in charge of their money.

As soon as Judas had taken the bread, he went out. And it was night.

Then Jesus told the remaining disciples, "This very night you will turn your back on me."

Peter replied, "Even if all turn away from you, I never will."

"Truly, I tell you," Jesus answered, "this very night, before the rooster crows at dawn, you will disown me three times."

But Peter said firmly, "Even if I have to die with you, I will never disown you." And the other disciples agreed.

Then Jesus said, "I will be going away, but in time I will come back and take you with me."

Thomas objected, "How will we know the way to go?"

Jesus replied, "I am the way and the truth and the life. To know God, you must follow my way. And if you know me, you know God."

The disciples were puzzled by these words.

Jesus is arrested at Gethsemane

After their Passover supper, Jesus walked with his disciples, as usual, towards the Mount of Olives on their way back to Bethany. Before climbing the Mount, just after they had crossed the Kidron Valley outside the city, they stopped at a garden called Gethsemane. Jesus took Peter, James and John – the same three disciples he had taken up the mountain when he was transfigured – a short distance away, and said to them, "Stay here and keep watch."

Jesus withdrew from them, then knelt down and prayed: "Father, not my will, but yours be done."

Jesus was in anguish; beads of sweat were falling from him to the ground as he prayed earnestly. An angel from heaven appeared to Jesus and gave him strength to continue with God's plan. Then he returned to his disciples and found them all sleeping. "Could you not keep watch for me for one hour?" he asked Peter.

He withdrew a second time to pray, and when he returned he again found them sleeping. Then he withdrew a third time to pray, and when he returned he said to them, "Are you still sleeping? Look, the hour has come when the Son of Man will be delivered into the hands of men who have turned away from God. Rise! Let us go! Here comes my betrayer."

While Jesus was still speaking, Judas approached them with a crowd of armed men sent by the chief priests. It was not always easy for strangers to distinguish Jesus from his disciples, so Judas had arranged a signal with the armed men: "The man I kiss is the one you are looking for; arrest him and lead him away."

Judas walked up to Jesus, saying, "Teacher!" and greeted him with a kiss on the cheek.

Then the armed men stepped forward, seized Jesus and arrested him.

Peter reached for his sword and struck the servant of the High Priest, who was among the armed men. But Jesus said to him, "Put away your sword. Do you think I could not call on my Father? How would the writings of our prophets be fulfilled any other way? They say that it must happen like this."

And then he said to the crowd of armed men, "Why have you come with swords and clubs to capture me? Am I leading a rebellion? Every day I have sat in the courtyard of the temple, teaching, and you did not arrest me. But now you have come when the hour is dark."

The armed men led Jesus away, and almost all the disciples deserted him and fled.

Jesus goes on trial and Peter's denial

In the middle of the night, the armed men took Jesus to the house of Caiaphas, the High Priest, where all the chief priests and scribes (known as the Sanhedrin) were gathered. Peter followed at a distance until he reached the courtyard of the High Priest's house. There, he sat with the guards, warming himself by the fire and waiting to see what would happen.

All of the Sanhedrin were looking for a reason to put Jesus to death, because they saw him as a rebel and feared that people would follow him. But they could not find a reason. False witnesses came forward to tell lies about Jesus, but their stories did not match and could not be proven. Jesus remained silent throughout the time the witnesses were questioned.

Finally, Caiaphas the High Priest ordered, "Tell us if you are the Messiah, the Son of God."

"If I tell you, you will not believe me," Jesus replied. "But you will see the Son of Man sitting at the right hand of Almighty God."

Then Caiaphas tore at his clothes in outrage and proclaimed to the Sanhedrin, "He has spoken blasphemy!" Blasphemy is speaking against God, which was a serious offence. "Do you agree?"

The whole assembly agreed with the High Priest's accusation and condemned Jesus, saying he should be put to death.

Meanwhile, one of the High Priest's servant girls was walking out in the courtyard and saw Peter waiting there. She looked closely at him and said, "You were with that man from Nazareth, Jesus," she said.

Peter denied it and went out to the gateway. Another servant girl saw him and said to the people gathered there, "This fellow was with Jesus of Nazareth."

Peter angrily denied it again: "I do not know the man."

A little while later, just before dawn, one of the gathered crowd went up to Peter and said, "Surely you are one of Jesus' followers. You have the accent of a man from Galilee."

Then Peter cursed and swore, "I do not know the man!"

Immediately a rooster crowed, and Peter remembered Jesus' words: "You will disown me three times." And he broke down and wept bitterly.

Jesus appears before Pilate

In the early morning, the chief priests took Jesus from Caiaphas' house to the palace of the Roman governor, Pontius Pilate. He came out and asked, "What charges are you bringing against this man?"

"If he were not a criminal," they replied, "would we be handing him over to you?"

Pilate said, "Well, take him away then and judge him according to your own laws."

The chief priests protested, "But we have no right to execute someone." Judea was a province of the Roman Empire, and only the Roman governor was allowed to pass a death sentence. So Pilate went back into his palace and summoned Jesus, while the chief priests and the crowd waited outside.

"Are you the king of the Jews?" asked Pilate. This was another way of asking Jesus if he was the Messiah, because Jews believed that the Messiah would restore their kingdom.

Jesus answered, "You have said it."

Then Pilate went out and announced to the chief priests and the crowd, "I cannot find any reason under Roman law to condemn this man."

But they insisted, saying, "He stirs up trouble with his teaching wherever he goes."

Pontius Pilate was in a difficult position. He could see no reason to imprison or execute Jesus, but he was also afraid of the large crowds of Jewish people who had gathered for the Passover festival. He knew they could also stir up trouble.

It was the custom of the governor at the important festivals to release a prisoner chosen by the crowd. There was a man called Barabbas in prison who had led an uprising against the Romans and committed murder. So Pilate asked the crowd, "Do you want me to release Barabbas or Jesus?"

Pilate expected the crowd to choose Jesus. However, the chief priests stirred up the crowd to demand that Barabbas be released. Pilate then asked, "What shall I do with the man you call the king of the Jews?"

A few days earlier, crowds had welcomed Jesus into Jerusalem, calling him king of the Jews and chanting "Hosanna!" Now, having been whipped into a frenzy by the chief priests, they chanted, "Crucify him!"

Once more, Pilate tried to find a reason for sentencing Jesus to death and asked, "Why? What crime has he committed?"

But the crowd just shouted all the louder, "Crucify him! Crucify him!"

Afraid of the crowd, Pilate saw he was getting nowhere. He took water and washed his hands in front of the crowd, saying, "I am innocent of this man's blood; it is on your head."

Then he released Barabbas and had Jesus flogged and handed over to his soldiers to be crucified.

The Crucifixion

The Roman soldiers made a large wooden cross, then led Jesus out of the palace. A man named Simon from Cyrene, in north Africa, was passing, and the soldiers made him follow and carry the cross. Outside the city walls was a small hill called Golgotha (which means "place of the skull" in Aramaic).

There, the soldiers crucified Jesus by nailing his hands and feet to the cross. Then they threw dice to share out his clothes among them, and sat down to keep watch.

Above Jesus' head they had fastened a notice prepared by the governor, Pontius Pilate. It read: Jesus of Nazareth, King of the Jews. Two criminals were crucified with him – one on the left and one on the right.

Those who passed by hurled insults at Jesus and mocked him. Even the chief priests jeered, "If you are the Son of God, come down from the cross and save yourself!"

INRI

Jesus murmured, "Father, forgive them, for they do not know what they are doing."

At noon a hot wind arose, blowing sand from the desert. A great darkness came over the whole land until three in the afternoon, and there was an oppressive, dry heat. One of the soldiers filled a sponge with wine vinegar, put it on a staff, and taunted Jesus by offering it to him to drink.

Jesus gave a loud cry, then breathed his last breath. At that moment, the earth shook, rocks split, and the curtain hiding the Holy of Holies inside the temple was torn in two from top to bottom.

One of the soldiers pierced Jesus' side with a spear; blood and water flowed from the wound onto the ground.

When the captain of the soldiers saw how Jesus died, he said, "Surely this man was the Son of God."

The burial of Jesus

The Jewish Sabbath – when no work could be done – begins at sunset on Friday and lasts until sunset on Saturday. Jesus' crucifixion was held on a Friday. As the beginning of the Sabbath was approaching, Joseph of Arimathea, a rich man who had secretly become a follower of Jesus, went to see Pontius Pilate and asked to have the body of Jesus, because he did not want to make the Sabbath unholy by leaving the body on the cross. Pilate ordered that it be given to him.

Joseph took the body from the cross, wrapped it in a clean linen cloth, and carried it to his own tomb, which had been carved out of the rock in a nearby garden at Golgotha, ready for when he died. He carefully laid the body of Jesus inside the tomb and rolled a large stone in front of the entrance.

Three women who were followers of Jesus – Mary Magdalene, Mary the mother of James (the disciple), and Salome – were watching and saw where Jesus had been laid. Then they all went home and rested on the Sabbath.

The chief priests told Pilate, "Lord, we remember that while he was alive this man claimed, 'After three days I will rise again.' Give orders that the tomb be made secure until the third day after his death, or his disciples may come and steal the body and tell the people that he has risen from the dead."

Pilate wanted to keep peace among the people, so he ordered his soldiers, “Secure the tomb and make sure it is guarded.”

The soldiers did as they were instructed: they sealed the tomb where the body of Jesus lay, and kept watch.

The Resurrection and Ascension

Mary Magdalene at the empty tomb

When the Sabbath was over on Saturday at sundown, the stillness of the city came to an end. People came out into the dark streets and shops opened by lamplight. Mary Magdalene, Mary the mother of James, and Salome bought spices to anoint Jesus' body.

Very early the next morning, just after sunrise, they went to the garden at Golgotha, where the body of Jesus lay. As they were walking, they asked each other, "Who will roll away the heavy stone at the entrance of the tomb?"

But when they arrived, they saw that the very large stone had already been rolled away. They entered the tomb. There they saw a young man dressed in a white robe, and they became afraid.

"Do not be afraid," he said. "You are looking for Jesus of Nazareth, who was crucified. He has risen. He is not here. Go and tell his disciples, 'He is going ahead of you; there you will meet him, just as he told you.'"

Trembling and bewildered, the three women fled, knowing that they had seen an angel.

Mary Magdalene stopped outside the tomb and wept. Then she turned around and saw a man standing there. He asked her, "Lady, why are you crying? Who are you looking for?"

Thinking the radiant and healthy man in front of her was a gardener, she said, "Sir, if you have carried him away, tell me where you have put him, so that I may return his body to the tomb."

Jesus said to her, "Mary."

Suddenly she recognised his voice and cried out in Aramaic, "*Rabboni*!" (which means "my teacher"). She reached out to him.

Jesus said, "Do not touch me, for I have not yet ascended to the Father. Go instead to my brothers and tell them I have risen."

Mary found the disciples and told them excitedly, "I have seen the Lord!"

When they heard that Jesus was alive and that she had seen him, they did not believe it. But Peter ran to the tomb anyway. When he saw it was empty, he went away, wondering to himself what had happened.

Jesus appears on the road to Emmaus

On that same day, two of the disciples were going to a village called Emmaus, to the west of Jerusalem, and talking about all the things that had happened over the last few days.

As they were walking, Jesus himself came and walked with them, but they did not recognise him.

He asked, "What are you discussing?"

They stood still, their faces downcast, and one of them asked, "Are you the only person in Jerusalem who does not know what has happened?"

"What should I know?" asked Jesus.

"About Jesus of Nazareth," the disciple replied. "He was a prophet. The chief priests handed him over to be sentenced to death, and he was crucified. We had hoped that he was the Messiah who was going to make all things right again in the world. It is now the third day since he was killed. Early this morning, some of our friends went to the tomb, but said his body was not there. They told us they had seen a vision of an angel who said he was alive, but we don't know whether to believe them."

Then Jesus said, "How foolish you are! Did the prophets not say that the Messiah had to suffer these things and then appear in his glory?" He explained what had been written in the scriptures – the sacred writings of Moses and the prophets Isaiah and Daniel – about the coming of a Messiah who would suffer, die and rise again.

As they were approaching the village of Emmaus, Jesus continued as if he were going further. But, filled with wonder at what they were hearing, the two disciples begged, "Stay with us, for it is nearly evening and the day is almost over."

So Jesus stayed with them at the house of some friends. When they were sitting at the table to eat, Jesus took bread, gave thanks and shared it with them.

In that moment their eyes were opened and they recognised him. But Jesus disappeared from their sight.

They asked each other, "Were not our hearts burning within us when he talked to us on the road and explained the scriptures to us?"

They were gripped with excitement as they began to take in what they had heard and seen. Though night was falling, they immediately got up and returned to Jerusalem.

There they found the other disciples and said, "It is true! The Lord has risen and he appeared to us." They told their friends everything that had happened on the way to Emmaus, and how they had only recognised Jesus when he broke the bread.

Doubting Thomas

While the disciples were still speaking about what had happened in Emmaus, with the doors of the house locked in case the chief priests tried to eavesdrop, Jesus came and stood among them. He said, "Peace be with you," and the disciples were overjoyed.

He showed them the wounds on his hands and his feet from the nails that had pinned him to the cross, and the wound in his side from the soldier's spear.

Again, Jesus said, "Peace be with you." And with that, he breathed the breath of God on them, saying, "Receive the Holy Spirit."

The disciples were deeply moved, bowing in awe. When they looked up again, Jesus had disappeared as mysteriously as he had appeared in the locked room.

Thomas, one of the disciples, had not been with the others when Jesus came. Later, the disciples told him, "We have seen the Lord!"

Thomas replied, "Unless I see the nail marks on his hands and put my finger in his wounds, I will not believe you."

A week later, the disciples were again in the house, and this time Thomas was with them. The doors were locked, but Jesus appeared and stood among them, saying, "Peace be with you." Then he pointed to the wound in his side and said to Thomas, "Put your finger here, and see my hands. Stop doubting and believe."

Immediately Thomas replied, "My Lord and my God!"

Then Jesus continued, "Because you have seen me, you have believed. Blessed are those who have not seen and yet have believed that I have risen again."

The Ascension

For forty days after he rose from the tomb, Jesus appeared to the disciples. On one occasion, when they were on the Mount of Olives, which overlooks Jerusalem and the temple, he told them, "Do not leave Jerusalem, but wait for the gift my Father has promised. John baptised with water, but you will be baptised with the Holy Spirit."

They gathered around him, but were still trying to grasp how Jesus could be the Messiah. People had been expecting the Messiah to be a king who would restore the kingdom of the Israelites from David and Solomon's time. So they asked, "Lord, are you going to restore the kingdom of Israel?"

He answered, "It is not for you to know the plans the Father has set. But you will receive power when the Holy Spirit comes to you, and you will be my witnesses in Jerusalem, in all Judea and Samaria, and to the ends of the earth."

After he had said this, he was taken up into the heavens before their eyes, and a cloud hid him from their sight. This became known as the Ascension of Christ.

The disciples were still looking intently up into the sky where Jesus had ascended when suddenly two figures dressed in white appeared and stood beside them.

"Men of Galilee," they said, "why do you stand here looking into the sky? This same Jesus, who has been taken from you into heaven, will come back to you one day, in the same way as you have seen him go into heaven."

The Apostles

The Acts of the Apostles

The Holy Spirit at Pentecost

Ten days after Christ ascended into the heavens, the Jewish people celebrated the Festival of Weeks, seven weeks or fifty days after Passover (Pentecost, another name for this festival, comes from the Greek word for "fifty"). Again, many people from many different countries came to Jerusalem to worship. On the day of the festival, the disciples were gathered together in the room where the Last Supper had taken place, the night Jesus was arrested.

Suddenly a sound like the blowing of a great wind filled the whole house. They saw what looked like tongues of fire settle over each of their heads, and they were filled with the Holy Spirit. The disciples began to speak loudly in different languages that they hadn't known before.

When the throngs of passers-by heard this sound, they stopped in wonder. There were visitors from Mesopotamia, Egypt, Crete, Rome and many other places, but each one heard their own language being spoken. They were amazed and asked each other, "Are these men not from Galilee?

How do they know our languages? What does this mean?"

But some made fun of the disciples and said, "They must have drunk too much wine!"

Then Peter, who had first recognised Jesus as the Messiah, stood at the open window and raised his voice to speak to the crowd: "Fellow Jews and all who are in Jerusalem, listen carefully to what I have to say. These people are not drunk, for it is only nine o'clock in the morning! No, this is what the prophets foretold: 'God says, the day will come when I will pour out my spirit on all people and you will prophesy and have visions. I will show wonders and signs: the sun will be turned to darkness and the moon to blood before the coming of the great and glorious days of the Lord.'"

Those people who had been in Jerusalem at Passover remembered the sun becoming dark and the full moon that night appearing red in the sky.

Peter continued, "Fellow sons and daughters of Israel, Jesus of Nazareth was shown to you by God to work miracles, wonders and signs, as you yourselves know. He was handed over to you by God's plan, and you, with the help of wicked men, put him to death by nailing him to the cross.

"But God raised him from the dead, freeing him from death because it was impossible for death to keep its hold on him.

"Let me remind you that King David, seeing what was to come, spoke of the resurrection of the Messiah, who would not be abandoned to the realm of the dead. God has raised Jesus of Nazareth, and we are witnesses of it. He is raised to the right hand of God. Therefore, let all Israel be told of this: God has made Jesus, whom you crucified, both Lord and Messiah."

When the people heard this they were deeply moved, and asked Peter and the other disciples, "What shall we do?"

Peter replied, "Change your ways, and be baptised in the name of Jesus Christ. Then you will be given understanding and peace in your hearts."

Many accepted what Peter had said and were baptised.

After that day, the disciples could only speak their own language, but from this time onwards, the disciples and followers who taught others were called apostles, which means "messengers" in Greek.

The apostles are persecuted

One day Peter and John were going to the temple in Jerusalem when they saw a man who had been lame from birth begging at the gates. Peter said to him, "Look at us!"

The man looked up, expecting to get something from them.

Instead, Peter said, "In the name of Jesus Christ of Nazareth, walk."

Peter took the man by the hand, and he jumped up and began to walk. He went with them into the courtyard of the temple, walking and jumping and praising God. Many people recognised the man and came running towards him. They were filled with wonder at what had happened.

Peter said, "Fellow Jews, it is through the power of Jesus of Nazareth, whom you handed over to be killed, that this man has been made strong and can walk." And Peter went on to explain how the prophets' predictions about the Messiah had come about through Jesus.

The priests, scribes and learned teachers who were gathered at the temple were greatly disturbed by the apostles, who were proclaiming to everyone they saw that Jesus had risen from the dead. They seized Peter and John and, because it was evening, locked them in prison until the next day.

The next morning, Annas, the new High Priest, had Peter and John brought before the Sanhedrin, the gathering of chief priests, scribes and teachers, for questioning. "Tell me by what power or in what name you do this work!" he demanded.

Then Peter was filled with the Holy Spirit and said, "Rulers and elders of the people, if we are being questioned here about an act of kindness to a man who was lame and is now healed, then know this: it is in the name of the Messiah, Jesus of Nazareth, whom you crucified and who rose from the dead, that this man has been healed."

The Sanhedrin conferred together and saw they could do nothing to stop the apostles, because so many people had seen the lame man being healed. Instead, they commanded the two apostles not to speak in the name of Jesus.

But Peter and John replied, "Which is right in God's eyes: to listen to you or to him? We cannot help speaking about what we have seen and heard."

As the chief priests and scribes could not find a reason to keep the apostles imprisoned or decide how to punish them, they let them go.

The apostles continued to perform many healings, and the chief priests and their followers were filled with jealousy, and worried about losing their power over the people. They arrested the apostles and put them in prison.

But during the night, an angel of the Lord came to the prison and let the apostles out. He said, "At daybreak, go and stand in the courtyard of the temple and tell the people about this new life of following Jesus Christ."

Meanwhile, the High Priest had called together the Sanhedrin. In the morning he ordered the captain of his guards to bring the apostles before them. But the captain soon returned to the Sanhedrin and reported, "We found the prison securely locked, with the prison guards at the doors, but when we opened them, there was no one inside."

Then a messenger came to tell them, "Look! The men you imprisoned are standing in the courtyard of the temple, teaching the people!"

The captain hurried with his men to the temple courtyard, where a crowd of people had gathered around the apostles. The soldiers didn't use force for fear that the people might stone them. Instead, they ordered the apostles to come and appear before the Sanhedrin. The apostles came willingly.

The High Priest said, "We gave you strict orders not to teach in this name, yet you have filled Jerusalem with your teachings."

Peter and the other apostles replied, "We have witnessed the events we are teaching about, and we must obey God, not people."

When the Sanhedrin heard this, they were furious and wanted to sentence all the apostles to death. But Gamaliel, a wise old teacher of the law who was greatly respected by the people, stood up and ordered that the apostles be sent outside while they discussed the matter further.

Gamaliel addressed the Sanhedrin: "Men of Israel, consider carefully what you intend to do to these men. Some time ago, others appeared and people followed them, but when they died, their preaching came to nothing and their followers were scattered. Therefore, I advise you to let these men go and leave them alone. If their purpose is human, it will fail. But if it is from God, you will not be able to stop them."

His speech persuaded the Sanhedrin not to kill them, but they called the apostles in and had them flogged, and they ordered them not to speak in the name of Jesus. Then they let them go.

The apostles rejoiced, glad that they had been worthy of suffering in Jesus' name. They continued to teach the people and proclaim that Jesus was the Messiah.

The death of Stephen

One of the new apostles who performed great wonders among the people was called Stephen. However, some Jews who were opposed to this new teaching proclaimed, "We have heard Stephen speak blasphemy – words against God and against Moses." They stirred up the people and the chief priests, who seized Stephen and brought him before the Sanhedrin. A false witness claimed, "This fellow never stops saying bad things about this holy city of Jerusalem and the laws of Moses. We have heard him say that Jesus of Nazareth will destroy this place and change the customs that Moses handed down to us."

When the chief priests and scribes of the Sanhedrin looked at Stephen, they saw that his face was as radiant as an angel's. The High Priest asked Stephen, "Are these charges true?"

Stephen spoke at length, telling them of the whole history of the Israelites from the time of Abraham and Moses to the time of King David and then the prophets, showing not only how God had guided and protected them, but also how there were always people who resisted.

Finally, Stephen concluded, "You stubborn people! You are just like your ancestors who always resisted the Holy Spirit. Was there ever a prophet your ancestors did not persecute or have killed? And now you have betrayed and murdered the Messiah."

When the members of the Sanhedrin heard this, they were furious. But Stephen, full of the Holy Spirit, looked up to heaven and saw the glory of God.

"Look," he said, "I see heaven open and the Son of Man standing at the right hand of God."

At this, the priests and scribes covered their ears. Yelling at the top of their voices, they rushed at Stephen, dragged him out of the city and began to stone him.

Stephen prayed on his knees, "Lord Jesus, receive my spirit. Do not hold this sin against them." Then he fell down beneath the blows and died.

Watching the stoning of Stephen with approval was a young man called Saul.

Paul of Tarsus

Saul's vision at Damascus

Saul was from Tarsus, in Asia Minor, a Greek-speaking city of the Roman Empire. At home and at the synagogue, Saul spoke Hebrew or Aramaic, but in the city he spoke Greek, and in Greek his name was Paul. He had studied in Jerusalem at the temple, under great teachers like Gamaliel, and much of that learning involved questioning ideas and looking for answers.

As a devout Jew, Saul was awaiting the Messiah, but like the chief priests he was convinced that the followers and disciples of Jesus were wrong. He was keen to see them persecuted so they would stop their silly preaching, which seemed to be catching on and spreading to other cities. Saul went from house to house in Judea, dragging off any followers of Jesus and imprisoning them. Any remaining apostles who had not been caught were scattered throughout the land and its neighbours.

Hearing that there were followers in Damascus, Saul went to see the High Priest in a state of high agitation, breathing murderous threats against the disciples of Jesus. He asked to go to Damascus to take prisoner any followers of this new way and bring them to Jerusalem. The High Priest agreed.

Damascus was three to four days' journey away by fast horse. As Saul and his companions were nearing Damascus around noon, suddenly a light from heaven flashed and he fell to the ground. He heard a voice say to him in Aramaic, "Saul, Saul, why do you persecute me?"

Despite the shock, Saul immediately asked, "Who are you, lord?"

"I am Jesus, whom you are persecuting," the voice replied.

In that moment Saul's whole world was turned upside down. He asked, "What shall I do, Lord?"

"Get up and go into the city, and you will be told what you must do."

The men travelling with Saul were speechless, for they saw the light and heard a sound, but could not understand the voice speaking to Saul.

Saul got up from the ground, but when he opened his eyes, he could not see. His companions led him by the hand to Damascus.

For three days Saul was blind, and he did not eat or drink anything.

In Damascus lived a follower of Jesus called Ananias. The Lord appeared to him in a vision, calling, "Ananias, go and find a man from Tarsus named Saul in the house on Straight Street. He has seen in a vision that a man named Ananias will come to him to restore his sight."

Ananias was deeply shocked and doubtful. "Lord," he replied, "I have heard many reports about this man and all the harm he has done to your disciples and followers in Jerusalem. He has come here with the authority of the High Priest to arrest everyone who honours your name."

But the Lord said to Ananias, "Go! I have chosen this man to proclaim my name to all the people in the world, as well as to the people of Israel, though he will bear much suffering for my sake."

So Ananias went to the house, put his hands on Saul, and said, "Brother Saul, the Lord Jesus Christ, who appeared to you on the road, has sent me here so that you may see again and be filled with the Holy Spirit."

Immediately, something similar to fishscales fell from Saul's eyes and he could see again.

Saul took some food and regained his strength. He spent some time in Damascus, preaching in the synagogues that Jesus was the Messiah, the Son of God.

All those who heard him were astonished and asked, "Is this not the man who raised havoc in Jerusalem among those who spoke the name of Jesus?"

After he had been preaching for many days, some of the strict Jews who were against the followers of Jesus plotted to kill Saul. Day and night they kept watch at the city gates of Damascus, waiting to capture him. But Saul learned of their plan. Under cover of darkness, his followers took him to a house built against the city walls and lowered him in a basket through a window. So Saul managed to escape from those who wanted to kill him.

Paul's travels

After withdrawing for a time in the desert of Arabia, Saul returned to Jerusalem, where he met Peter. (The other disciples were afraid to meet him.) Peter sent him to the city of Antioch, in Asia Minor. Antioch was the third largest city of the Roman Empire (after Rome, in Italy, and Alexandria, in Egypt) and many followers of Jesus lived there, both Jews and non-Jews. It was here that they were first given the name "Christians".

After spending some time teaching in Antioch, Saul set off for the island of Cyprus and then to the inland regions of Asia Minor. In these parts Saul spoke Greek and gave his name as Paul. Everywhere he went, he would find the synagogue or the marketplace and begin speaking about Jesus of Nazareth, the Messiah. Often someone would invite him to stay for a while and continue teaching, and often the Jews of the town would find his teaching strange and unsettling – was the Messiah not meant to bring peace and rule over the whole world? At times people were outraged and attacked Paul, and on one occasion he was even stoned and left for dead.

Paul spoke both to Jews and, increasingly, to other people who did not follow Jewish laws and customs, as Paul and the apostles did. The vision that Paul had at Damascus had made a deep impression on him, and Paul understood and was convinced that Christ, the Messiah, had come for *all* people on earth, not only for the Jews who awaited him.

One night he had a vision of a man from Europe calling him. He followed this by sailing to Greece and speaking in the towns and cities there. He visited Athens, which was famous for its learning. When he looked around the city, Paul was distressed to see so many statues of gods, because Jews were forbidden to make images of God. He debated with people in synagogues and marketplaces, and told them about Jesus and the resurrection.

When a group of philosophers heard him, they took him to the Areopagus: a rock near the famous temple known as the Acropolis, where people would gather to discuss and debate the latest ideas. The philosophers said to Paul, "Tell us about your new teachings."

Paul stood up and looked at the people gathered there. They were quite different from the crowds he usually addressed. There were no Jews familiar with the stories of the Patriarchs, Moses, the kings or the prophets.

"People of Athens!" Paul began. "I see that you are very religious in every way, for as I walked around your city I saw objects of worship everywhere. I even found an altar with the inscription: *To an Unknown God*. So you have built an altar to worship the very thing you know nothing about! Let me tell you about this God."

Paul spoke about God, who made everything and all the people on earth. Paul knew the Greeks' love of poetry and quoted their poets: "We are God's offspring," and "In him we live and move and have our being." They were spellbound by his speech.

He ended by speaking about the Messiah that God had sent into the world, who had died and was raised from the dead. This was something they had never heard of before, and many of them sneered at Paul, but a few became his followers.

While he was in Greece, Paul also travelled to Corinth where some people heard him and became Christians. Later, from his travels, he sent them two long letters about the promise the disciples had heard at the Ascension of Christ: Christ would appear again to people on earth (sometimes called the Second Coming). And, in the distant future, all human beings who follow Christ would overcome death and live close to God, like Adam and Eve in the Garden of Eden before the Fall.

The armour of God

Paul travelled widely through Greece and Asia Minor, attracting many followers and founding many communities (or congregations) of Christians. He often endured great hardship and was sometimes imprisoned. Even while in prison, he used his time to write long letters to his new communities. These would be taken by friends and, after several weeks of walking and sailing by boat, would be delivered to the Christian congregations.

Paul knew that the people of Rome were down to earth and, unlike the people of Athens, did not discuss ideas endlessly. So when he wrote to the community in Rome he told them that the church – the community of all Christians – was one body, the body of Christ. And like a body, in which each part had its own function, every member of this body of Christ also had their own task and purpose, but together they made a living being.

He also wrote to them about how Christ had taken on the life of a human being right through to the experience of death. This showed his love of humankind, gave people hope, and allowed them to know that, after they died, there was a life in spirit, close to God.

There was another community of followers at the city of Ephesus, in Asia Minor, which had a large temple dedicated to Artemis, the Greek goddess of hunting and nature. But at the time of Paul, few of the local people still believed in these ancient gods or respected the temple. Most of them were only interested in making money by selling trinkets to the great throngs of pilgrims from all over Greece and Asia Minor who came to visit the temple every year.

Paul ended his letter to the Ephesians by warning them of the power of evil that tempts people away from the world of God, to follow their own wishes and desires. He wrote about needing armour to protect against this evil, but not the heavy armour of soldiers, the armour of the soul:

> *Strengthen yourselves in the Lord and his mighty power. Put on the full armour of God, so that you can stand your ground when the day of evil comes and, having done everything, remain upright. Stand firm then, with the belt of truth around your waist, with the breastplate of righteousness in place, and with your feet fitted with the readiness that comes from the gospel of peace. Besides all this, take up the shield of faith, with which you can put out all the flaming arrows of the evil one. Take the helmet of salvation and the sword of the spirit, which is the word of God. And pray in the spirit at the right moments of time. This shall be your armour.*

Paul is arrested in Jerusalem

After Paul had travelled for many years through Asia Minor and Greece, he returned to Jerusalem, where he met the apostles. Many Jewish people had heard that Paul also preached to other people but did not tell them to follow all the Jewish laws. Some thought this was wrong.

When Paul went to the courtyard of the temple to purify himself and to pray, some Jewish people from Asia Minor recognised him and stirred up the crowd to seize him, shouting, "Fellow Israelites, help us! This is the man who teaches everyone everywhere against our laws."

The people came running from all directions and seized Paul.

Jerusalem was a city of narrow streets and alleyways, and the only open space where a crowd could gather was the open courtyard around the temple. And because there was always unrest in this part of their empire, the Romans had built a fort, the Fortress of Antonia, overlooking the temple courtyard, and a guard kept watch at all times for any signs of trouble.

When the guard saw the commotion, he immediately told his commander that the whole city of Jerusalem was in uproar. The commander took some officers and soldiers down to the courtyard. When the crowd spotted them, they stopped beating Paul.

The commander, thinking Paul had caused the unrest, put him under arrest and bound him in chains, asking who he was and what he had done. Some people in the crowd shouted one thing and some another. Because the commander could not make sense of anything amid the uproar, he ordered that Paul be taken into the fort. The violence of the mob was so great that Paul had to be carried by the soldiers.

As he was about to be taken inside, Paul spoke to the commander in Greek (for that was the language the Romans used in the eastern part of their empire), asking, "May I tell you something?"

"What, do you speak Greek?" replied the surprised commander, as he thought Paul was a rebel wanted by the Romans. "Aren't you the Egyptian who started a revolt here some time ago?"

Paul answered, "I am a Jew from Tarsus, a great city. Please let me speak to the people."

After receiving the commander's permission, Paul stood on the steps and made signs for the crowd to be silent. Then he said to them in Aramaic, "I am a Jew from Tarsus, but I was brought up in this city and studied under Gamaliel."

Gamaliel had long since died, but was still revered as a wise teacher, so the crowd fell silent.

Paul went on to tell them how he had persecuted the followers of Jesus, and about his experience of Jesus appearing to him on the road to Damascus, and how he was told to go and teach all people – both Jews and non-Jews.

At that point the crowd, who had listened in silence, began to shout, "Get rid of him! He is not fit to live!"

The commander, who did not understand Aramaic and still thought Paul had caused the unrest, ordered him to be taken inside the fort and flogged to find out why the people were shouting.

In those days most people in the outlying provinces of the Roman Empire were not Roman citizens. Only rich people could afford to buy citizenship for their families. Roman citizens had special rights: they were allowed a fair trial, and could appeal, even to the Emperor Caesar, if they thought they had been treated unfairly. No one was allowed to beat or torture Roman citizens either. Paul's family in Tarsus had been given Roman citizenship, and so Paul too was a Roman.

Paul waited until he was stretched out and tied down to be flogged, before quietly asking the soldiers, "Is it legal for you to flog a Roman citizen before he has had a fair trial and been found guilty?"

Immediately the soldier informed the commander, "This man says he's a Roman citizen. What are you going to do?"

The commander went to Paul and asked, "Tell me, are you a Roman citizen?"

"Yes, I am."

Looking at Paul in his old, tattered clothes, the commander could not believe that Paul was rich enough to buy Roman citizenship, and said, "I had to pay a lot of money for my citizenship."

"But I was born a Roman citizen," Paul replied.

Those who were about to beat and question Paul quickly left the room, and the commander himself was alarmed when he realised that he had put this Roman citizen in chains.

The commander released him and ordered the High Priest to gather all the members of the Sanhedrin, because he wanted to find out exactly why Paul was being accused.

Paul had spent years studying all different aspects of Jewish teaching, and he knew that some members of the Sanhedrin were Pharisees and some were Sadducees. Both were very religious Jews who strictly kept every law of Moses, but Sadducees did not believe in angels or spirits, or that there would be a resurrection of the dead, while Pharisees did believe these things.

Standing before the Sanhedrin, Paul said, "Brothers, I am a Pharisee, descended from Pharisees. I stand here on trial because I believe in the resurrection of the dead."

As soon as he said this, the Sadducees and the Pharisees began to argue with one another. The whole assembly was divided and there was a great uproar. Some of the Pharisees stood up and argued loudly, "We find nothing wrong with this man. What does it matter if a spirit or an angel spoke to him?"

The dispute became so violent that the commander was afraid Paul would be torn to pieces. He ordered his troops to take him to the Roman fort for safety.

Paul is taken to Caesarea

The next morning, a group of more than forty Jewish men swore an oath not to eat or drink until they had killed Paul. They went to see the High Priest, who was angry that Paul had changed from persecuting the Christians to proclaiming their beliefs loudly. The group of men told the High Priest, "We have taken an oath to kill Paul. Ask the commander to bring him back to the Sanhedrin for questioning, and we will ambush him on the way here."

But Paul's nephew heard of the plot and hurried to the Roman fort to warn him. The commander listened carefully as the young man explained, and warned him not to tell anyone of what he had reported.

The commander had a duty to ensure that no harm would befall a Roman citizen in his care, and he took it very seriously. He decided to send him to the Roman governor in Caesarea, the Roman city on the shores of the Mediterranean Sea. He ordered his officers, "Prepare a detachment of two hundred soldiers, seventy horsemen and two hundred spearmen to go tonight at nine o'clock to Caesarea. Provide horses for Paul so that he may be taken safely to Felix, the governor." He wrote a letter to Felix explaining the situation.

Carrying out their orders, the huge group of soldiers took Paul away in the dark of night, riding fast through the narrow valleys of Judea until they came to the flat coastal plain. The next day, the horsemen continued with Paul to Caesarea, the capital city of the province, which lay by the sea. From there, ships sailed across the Mediterranean to other parts of the Roman Empire.

When Felix, the governor, read the letter he did not really know what to do. He kept Paul under guard, because he secretly hoped to get a large sum of money from Paul's followers to set him free.

When the chief priests in Jerusalem asked the governor to send Paul back to Jerusalem, Paul, sensing a trap, replied, "I am standing in a Roman court. I have done nothing wrong. I appeal to Caesar!"

Next, Paul was sent to Rome with some of his companions. There he was allowed to live by himself and receive visitors, but a soldier guarded him at all times.

Legends of Paul

No more is told of Paul in the Bible, but there are legends of Paul's later life, saying that he was set free and travelled to Spain to visit and teach the small communities of Christians there.

Later he was in Rome again at the time of Emperor Nero when a great part of the city burnt. Nero blamed the Christians for the fire, and many Christians were imprisoned and put to death. Paul and the disciple Peter, who now lived in Rome, were both killed.

Paul was beheaded, and it is said that where his head hit the ground, three springs of water came forth. To this day there is a church to mark the spot, called San Paolo alle Tre Fontane (or St Paul at the Three Fountains).

The Revelation to St John

The coming of the Son of Man

Jesus' disciple John lived longer than any other disciple. When he was a very old man, the Romans, too, persecuted the Christians, because they feared these people would not simply and obediently follow their laws. John was banished from Jerusalem to the island of Patmos, where he lived like a hermit in a remote, simple hut, and rarely saw other people.

As John was praying one Sunday, the day of Christ's resurrection, he heard a loud voice like a trumpet behind him, saying, "John, you will see a vision. Write down everything you see on a scroll and send it to the seven Christian churches in Asia Minor: to Ephesus, Smyrna, Pergamum, Thyatira, Sardis, Philadelphia and Loadicea."

John turned around to see where the voice was coming from. He saw seven golden stands for flaming lamps, and among the lampstands was someone who looked like Christ, dressed in a robe reaching down to his feet and with a golden sash around his chest. His hair was like wool, and as white as snow, and his eyes were like blazing fire. His feet were like bronze glowing in a furnace, and his voice was like the sound of rushing waters. In his right hand he held seven stars, and coming out of his mouth was a sharp, double-edged sword. His face was like the sun, shining in all its brilliance.

When John saw him, he fell at his feet as though dead. But the figure put his right hand on John and said, "Do not be afraid. Write what you have seen, what is happening now, and what is to take place later. The mystery of the seven stars in my right hand and of the seven golden lampstands is this: the seven stars are the angels of the seven churches, and the seven lampstands are the seven churches."

The shining figure then told John what to write to each of the seven churches, and showed John great visions of heaven in what is known as the "Revelation".

These great visions are difficult to imagine, and even more difficult to understand. Over many centuries, countless wise people have puzzled about the things John saw, and they continue to challenge us to this day.

The heavenly host

John saw a door standing open in heaven. He was taken up and before him was a throne. God was sitting on the throne, shining with the colours of the precious stones jasper and ruby, and a rainbow glowed all around the throne. Surrounding the throne were twenty-four other thrones, and seated on them were twenty-four wise men, dressed in white with crowns of gold.

Around the central throne were four living creatures. One was like a lion, another like an ox, the third had the face of a man, and the fourth was a flying eagle. Each of the four creatures had six wings and was covered with eyes all around, even under the wings. Day and night they continuously chanted, "Holy, holy, holy is the Lord God Almighty, who was, and is, and is to come."

Then John saw a Lamb. It had seven horns and seven eyes, which are the seven spirits of God sent out into all the earth.

After this, John saw a great multitude of people from every nation and tribe, and speaking every language, standing before the throne and the Lamb. And he knew that the Lamb was Christ, who had been killed but was alive again. The multitude were clad in white robes and held palm branches in their hands. They cried out, "Healing and wholeness belong to God, who sits on the throne, and to the Lamb."

One of the twenty-four wise men said to John, "The figures in white robes are those who have overcome great pain and suffering on earth. They stand before the throne of God and serve him day and night, and he shelters and protects them.

"Never again will they hunger or thirst. The sun will not beat down on

them with scorching heat. The Lamb will be their shepherd and will lead them to springs of living water. And God will wipe away every tear from their eyes."

John recognised those words, as the prophet Isaiah had used the same words to describe a vision he had seen.

The woman and the dragon

Another great sign appeared in John's vision: a woman in heaven clothed by the sun, with the moon under her feet and a crown of twelve stars on her head. She was in pain, for she was about to give birth.

Then another sign appeared in heaven: an enormous ten-horned red dragon with seven heads wearing seven crowns. Its tail swept down a third of the stars of the sky and flung them to the earth. The dragon stood in front of the woman, waiting for the moment her child would be born, so that it might devour it.

She gave birth to a son who would rule over all the nations with an iron staff. But as soon as the child was born, he was snatched up by God to his throne, and to safety, and the woman fled into the wilderness.

War broke out in heaven. The archangel Michael and his angels fought against the dragon, and the dragon and his angels fought back. But the dragon was not strong enough and lost his place in heaven. The great dragon, who was the ancient evil spirit known as the devil or Satan, was hurled down to the earth, and all his angels with him.

John heard a loud voice in heaven say, "Now the healing and the power and the kingdom of our God have come, and the mastery of his Messiah. For the one who brings disorder day and night, has been hurled down. Therefore rejoice, you who dwell in the heavens! But woe to the earth and the sea, because the devil has gone down to you! He is filled with fury, because he knows that his time is short."

The heavenly Jerusalem

John saw a new heaven and a new earth, for in his vision the first heaven and the first earth had passed away. He saw the holy city, the new Jerusalem, coming down out of heaven from God, prepared like a beautifully dressed bride.

There was a loud voice from the throne, saying, "Look, God's dwelling place is now among the people, and he will dwell with them."

The one seated on the throne said to John, "I am making all things new! Write this down, for these words are true: I am the Alpha and the Omega, the very beginning and the far distant end." John of course knew that alpha and omega were the first and last letters of the Greek alphabet.

One of the seven angels gathered around the throne said to John, "Come, I will show you the bride, the wife of the Lamb." And he carried John in spirit away to a great and high mountain and showed him the holy city, the new Jerusalem. It shone with the glory of God, its brilliance like precious jewels.

It had a great high wall with twelve gates, each guarded by an angel, and on the gates were written the names of the twelve tribes of Israel. There were three gates to the east, three to the north, three to the south and three to the west. The wall of the city had twelve foundations, and on them were the names of the twelve apostles of the Lamb. The walls of the city were twelve thousand stadia in length and were as wide and high as they were long. (A stadion was a Greek measurement, about an eighth of a mile, or two hundred metres.)

Each foundation was decorated with a precious stone. The twelve gates were twelve pearls, each gate made of a single pearl. The great street of the city was made of pure gold, as pure as transparent glass.

John did not see a temple in the city, because he knew that the Lord God Almighty and the Lamb were its temple. And the city did not need a sun or moon to shine on it, for the glory of God gave it light, and the Lamb was its lamp.

The end of John's revelation

When John had heard and seen all these things, he was overwhelmed, knowing he had seen a glimpse of a distant future: a heavenly city on earth – perhaps the result of human work and striving to do good.

He fell down to worship at the feet of the angel who had shown them to him. But the angel said, "Do not do that! I am a fellow servant with you and with all who keep the word of God. Worship God!"

Then the angel spoke in the name of Christ, saying, "Look, I am coming soon! I am the Alpha and the Omega, the First and the Last, the very beginning and the far distant end. Blessed are those who cleanse themselves to be free of any evil, that they may have the right to the tree of life, and that they may enter through the gates of the heavenly city. I, Jesus, have sent my angel to give you this message for the churches."

Afterwards, John wrote down everything he had seen and heard in this great vision. The words he wrote onto a scroll were sent by messengers to all the Christian churches and were carefully copied many times. We now call this the Book of Revelation.

Discover the Bible

A History of the Bible

Within the lifetime of the disciples who had met Jesus, small communities of Christians spread not only throughout the Roman Empire, but eastwards as far as India, and southwards to Ethiopia in Africa. Over the centuries the communities have grown, and Christianity has spread to most parts of the world.

The Old Testament

The stories from the Old Testament were written by the Jewish people and gathered into the Hebrew Bible, which consists of twenty-four books written at different times. After the time of Christ, Christians started calling the Hebrew Bible the Old Testament in contrast to the Christian books of the New Testament.

The New Testament

Wherever Christians gathered to worship, they remembered the stories and teachings of Jesus. These were first told and retold by word of mouth, but in time they were written down and collected into the book we call the New Testament. They were written in Greek, which was the common language around the Mediterranean Sea at that time.

The New Testament consists of: the four Gospels, which were written by close followers of Jesus and tell the story of Christ; the Acts of the Apostles, which describe the early spread of Christianity; twenty-one Letters of the Apostles, many of which were written by Paul to various Christian communities; and finally John's vision in the Book of Revelation.

The Gospels

The four gospels, which describe the life of Christ, were written by:

- **Matthew**, a disciple of Jesus and a tax collector.
- **Mark**, a companion of Paul of Tarsus and later of Peter in Rome.
- **Luke**, a Greek companion of Paul of Tarsus, who also wrote the Acts of the Apostles.
- **John**, a disciple of Jesus, who also wrote the Book of Revelation.

Translations

Many Jews moved to other countries and in time they could not understand or read Hebrew, so the Hebrew Bible was translated into Greek around the third century BC. By the fourth century AD Latin became the main language in the western Roman Empire, and the whole Bible was translated into Latin. Today the Bible has been translated into around 3000 languages.

This book

This version retells the main stories of both the Old Testament and the New Testament. Sometimes background about the customs of the time or descriptions of the Holy Land has been added, which would have been familiar to people when these stories were first told.

Unfamiliar Words

Annunciation An announcement; used to describe the moment when the angel Gabriel told Mary that she would have a baby who would be God's Son.

anoint Rub with oil; a traditional way of choosing someone, or marking them as holy.

apostle A follower of Jesus who taught others.

Aramaic The language commonly spoken in the Holy Land at the time of Jesus.

ark First used to describe Noah's ark, his box-like ship; then used for the **Ark of the Covenant** – the box that contained the tablets of the law inscribed by Moses, which was later kept in the Holy of Holies in the temple of Jerusalem.

Ascension Rising up to a higher place; for example, the ascent of Christ into heaven after the Resurrection.

caravan A line of camels, roped together, that were used for transporting things through the desert.

Cherubim The second mightiest angels after Seraphim.

Christ Christians see Jesus as the Christ, or saviour. Christ or *Christos* literally means "anointed one" in Greek; the Hebrew equivalent is Messiah.

cistern An underground storage tank for rainwater, hewn out of the rock.

cubit The length from a person's elbow to their middle finger (on average about 45 cm, 18 inches).

Dagon The Philistine fish-god.

disciple A follower of Jesus during his lifetime.

The Twelve Disciples

Jesus gathered twelve disciples who followed him and helped him share the word of God:

Peter (also called Simon, or Simon Peter)
Andrew (brother of Peter)
James (son of Zebedee, brother of John)
John (brother of James, wrote the Gospel of John and the Book of Revelation. Not the same person as John the Baptist)
Philip
Bartholomew
Thomas (who doubted Jesus)
Matthew (wrote the Gospel of Matthew, was a tax collector)
James (son of Mary and Alphaeus)
Thaddaeus
Simon (known as the Zealot, meaning a "fanatical follower of God", perhaps he had been a temple priest)
Judas Iscariot (who betrayed Jesus)

Greek The most widely spoken language around the Roman Empire and Asia Minor at the time of Jesus; the language of the New Testament.

Hebrew The language of the Israelites and of the Old Testament; the name the Egyptians usually gave to the Israelites.

Holy of Holies The innermost, completely dark room of the temple in Jerusalem, which only the High Priest could enter once a year.

idol A statue of a god, often small, which was worshipped.

Israel The name God gave to Jacob; also the name of the land God gave to Jacob's descendants.

Israelites The descendants of the twelve sons of Jacob (who was also called Israel).

Jews The later name for the tribe of Judah. Many of the other tribes were lost after the Babylonian exile, as they married people from the countries they settled in and did not return.

kinsman A relative, or member of extended family.

leprosy Leprosy causes big red sores on the skin. Sometimes people can no longer feel pain in the affected areas and do not notice if they burn or cut themselves, so have large wounds that do not heal. Leprosy is hardly infectious, but in biblical times sufferers were thrown out of towns and villages to stop the disease spreading as there was no cure.

lots Casting lots was a way of choosing one out of many: a number of equal-length sticks or straws were gathered, along with one that was shorter. Each person took one stick or straw, and the person who drew the short straw was chosen. (Our word "lottery" and the expression "to draw the short straw" come from this.) In Roman times sometimes dice were thrown instead of straws being drawn.

Many Marys

In the Bible there are many different women called Mary. At that time, roughly one in every four women was called Mary.

Mary the mother of Jesus
Mary the sister of Lazarus and Martha from Bethany
Mary Magdalene, a follower of Jesus who visited his tomb on Easter Sunday
Mary, mother of the disciple James, who visited the tomb with Mary Magdalene

Messiah The Jewish people expected a saviour to come in the form of a king who would restore their kingdom. Christians saw Jesus as this Messiah, the saviour of all people. Messiah literally means "the anointed one" in Hebrew (the Greek equivalent is Christ).

myrhh A fragrant resin used in incense and perfumes.

oasis A place in the desert with water, sometimes a small pool, other times a spring.

parable Vivid story told by Jesus, with a deeper meaning that showed the workings of God.

patriarch The (grand)father or ancestor of a family.

The Patriarchs

The Patriarchs (Abraham, Isaac and Jacob) were men who spoke with God, and set out on a journey to establish a nation for God's followers, later known as Israel. Some of them had two names – their birth name and the name God gave them.

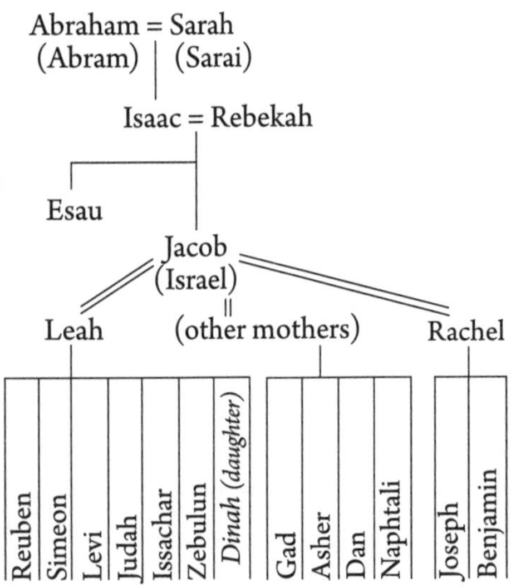

Jacob's twelve sons went on to form the Twelve Tribes of Israel.

Pharaoh The Egyptian king or emperor.

Pharisees Very religious Jews around the time of Jesus who tried to keep to every law of Moses, in particular resting on the holy day of the Sabbath. Unlike the Sadducees, they believed in angels and spirits, and that the dead would come to life at the end of time (resurrection).

Philistine Group of ancient people who lived in Canaan.

prophets People who spoke the words of God and reminded others of the ways of the Lord. They often sang and danced together in groups.

resurrection Returning to life after being dead.

Sabbath The seventh day of the week, a day of rest (in the Creation story God rested on the seventh day). It was strictly forbidden to do any work on the Sabbath. The Jewish day began and ended at sundown, not at midnight, so the Sabbath lasted from Friday sunset to Saturday sunset.

Sadducees Very religious Jews around the time of Jesus who tried to keep to every law of Moses. Unlike the Pharisees, they did not believe in angels and spirits or in the resurrection of the dead.

Samaritans Descendants of the Israelites, who followed the laws of Moses, but had their own place of worship on Mount Gerizim near Shechem. They were seen by the Jews as not following all the Jewish laws.

Sanhedrin The gathering of chief priests and teachers of the law in Jerusalem.

Satan Another name for the devil, the spirit of evil.

scribe A learned person who studied the Bible, copied manuscripts and wrote legal documents. Some were also teachers. Every town or village had a scribe.

scriptures Holy writings.

scroll Writings on long pieces of animal skin or paper (in Egypt), which was rolled up when not being used.

Seraphim The mightiest angels.
Son of Man Jesus was often called this because, as well as being the Son of God, he was the son of a human being and came to the world to help all people.
stadion (stadia, plural) A measure of length. One stadion is about 160 metres (520 feet).
synagogue A meeting house for Jews, especially in places too far from Jerusalem to visit to the temple.
teacher of the law Scribes who studied the Bible and taught.
Transfiguration A change in appearance; describes the moment when Jesus appears to his disciples in dazzling white clothes, in a more spiritual state.

Temple The first temple that Solomon built had three parts:

1. An open courtyard where the people gathered. It had a large altar on which animals were sacrificed.
2. The inner sanctuary that only the priests could enter, which had a small altar for burning incense and a table for bread.
3. At the back of the inner sanctuary, behind curtains, was the Holy of Holies. Only the High Priest could enter this completely dark room once a year. The Ark of the Covenant was kept there.

The second temple was built in the same way, but the Ark of the Covenant had been destroyed by the Babylonian king Nebuchadnezzar, so the Holy of Holies was empty. Later the courtyard was extended: anyone could enter the outer courtyard, but only Jews were allowed in the inner courtyard.

Timeline

Egyptians dominate the region 2100-1250BC

The Creation and Flood stories are not recorded in history

THE PATRIARCHS
(Abraham, Isaac and Jacob)
2000–1700 BC

2000 BC

BC *(Before Christ)*

587 BC
King Nebuchadnezzar conquers Jerusalem

721 BC
The Assyrians conquer Israel

THE TWO KINGDOMS: JUDEA 931–587 BC AND ISRAEL 931–721 BC
(Ahab, Elijah, Elisha)

EXILE TO BABYLONIA
(Daniel)
587–538 BC

Assyrians dominate the region 858-612 BC

Babylonians dominate the region 605-539 BC

538 BC
Jews return to Judea

REBUILDING THE TEMPLE
538–507 BC

Persians dominate
539-311 BC

Greeks dominate 311 BC–63 BC

AWAITING THE MESSIAH
(The Maccabees) 507 BC–1 AD

500 BC

AD (Anno Domini, meaning "in the year of our Lord" in Latin – the year Jesus was born

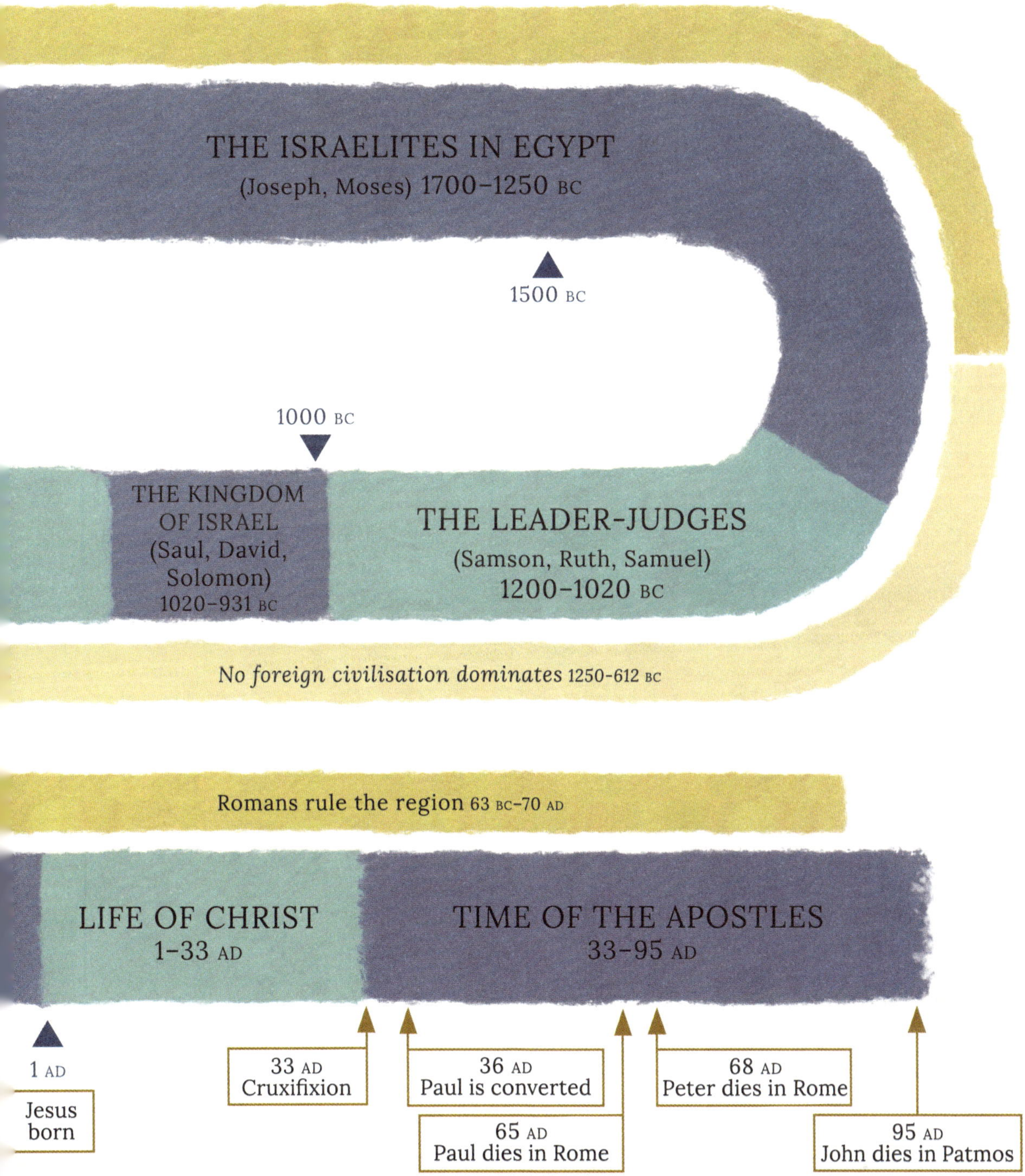
THE ISRAELITES IN EGYPT
(Joseph, Moses) 1700–1250 BC
1500 BC
1000 BC
THE KINGDOM OF ISRAEL
(Saul, David, Solomon)
1020–931 BC
THE LEADER-JUDGES
(Samson, Ruth, Samuel)
1200–1020 BC
No foreign civilisation dominates 1250-612 BC
Romans rule the region 63 BC–70 AD
LIFE OF CHRIST
1–33 AD
TIME OF THE APOSTLES
33–95 AD
1 AD
Jesus born
33 AD
Cruxifixion
36 AD
Paul is converted
65 AD
Paul dies in Rome
68 AD
Peter dies in Rome
95 AD
John dies in Patmos

THE HOLY LAND
MEDITERRANEAN SEA
Sidon
Damascus
Mount Hermon
Tyre
LEBANON
Dan
Caesarea Philippi
GALILEE
SEA OF GALILEE
Capernaum
Cana
Nazareth
Mount Tabor
Mount Carmel
Plain of Jezreel
Nain
River Jabbok
DECAPOLIS
Caesarea
Cherith Brook
SAMARIA
Jordan River
Shechem
Shiloh
Joppa
Bethel
Ai
Gilgal
Kiriath-Jearim
Ayalon
Jericho
Gibeon
Gibeah
Emmaus
Jerusalem
Mount Nebo
Keilah
Bethlehem
JUDEA
DEAD SEA
MOAB
Hebron (Mamre)
Gaza
Sodom
Beersheba
NEGEV
ARABAH
MAP LEGEND
Town
City
Mountain
REGION
Map colours:
Desert
Grassland
Mountains
Water

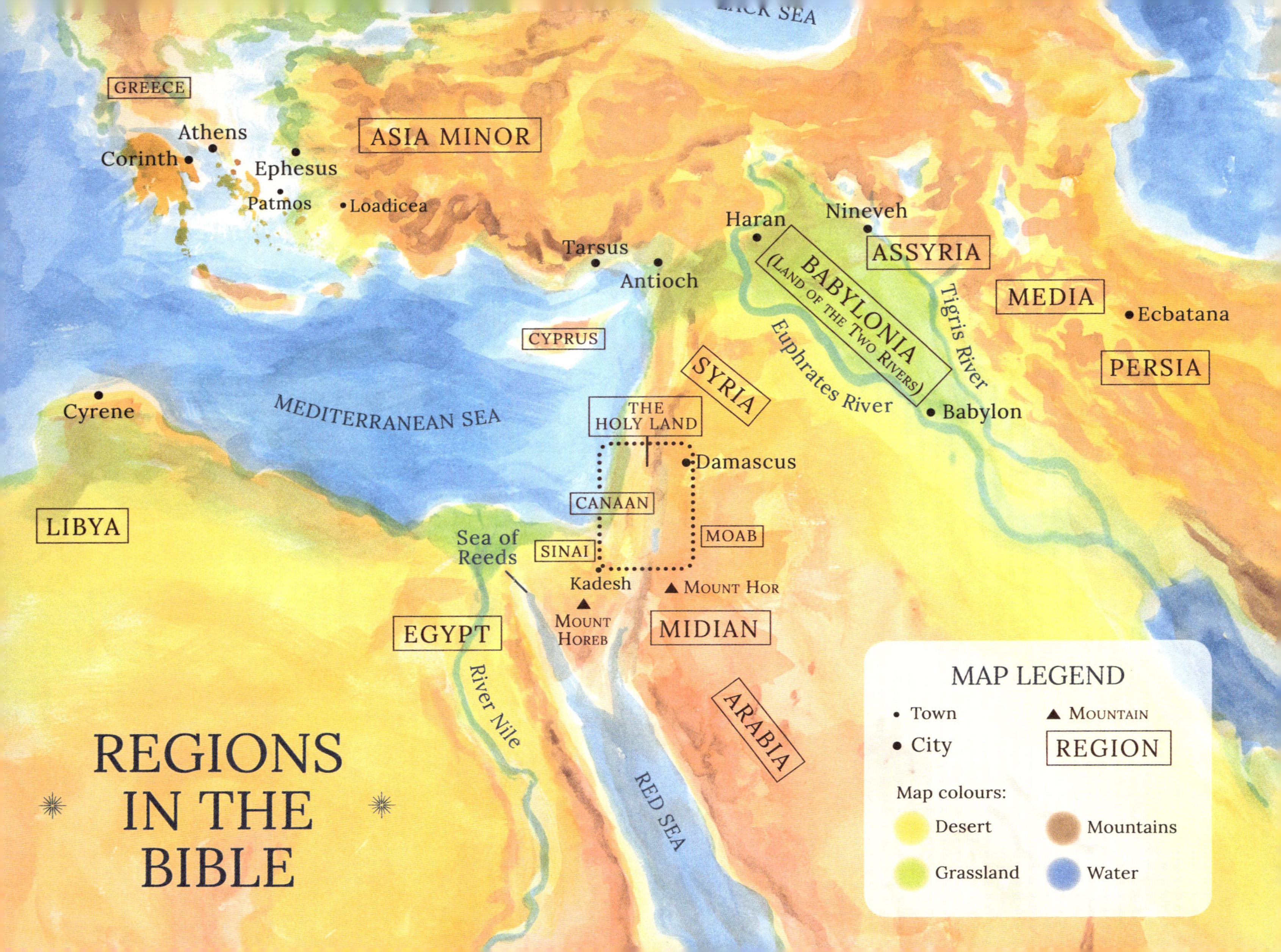
REGIONS IN THE BIBLE
GREECE
Athens
Corinth
Ephesus
Patmos
Loadicea
ASIA MINOR
Tarsus
Antioch
Haran
Nineveh
ASSYRIA
BABYLONIA (LAND OF THE TWO RIVERS)
Tigris River
Euphrates River
Babylon
MEDIA
Ecbatana
PERSIA
CYPRUS
MEDITERRANEAN SEA
Cyrene
LIBYA
SYRIA
THE HOLY LAND
Damascus
CANAAN
MOAB
SINAI
Sea of Reeds
Kadesh
MOUNT HOR
MOUNT HOREB
MIDIAN
EGYPT
River Nile
RED SEA
ARABIA
MAP LEGEND
Town
City
MOUNTAIN
REGION
Map colours:
Desert
Grassland
Mountains
Water

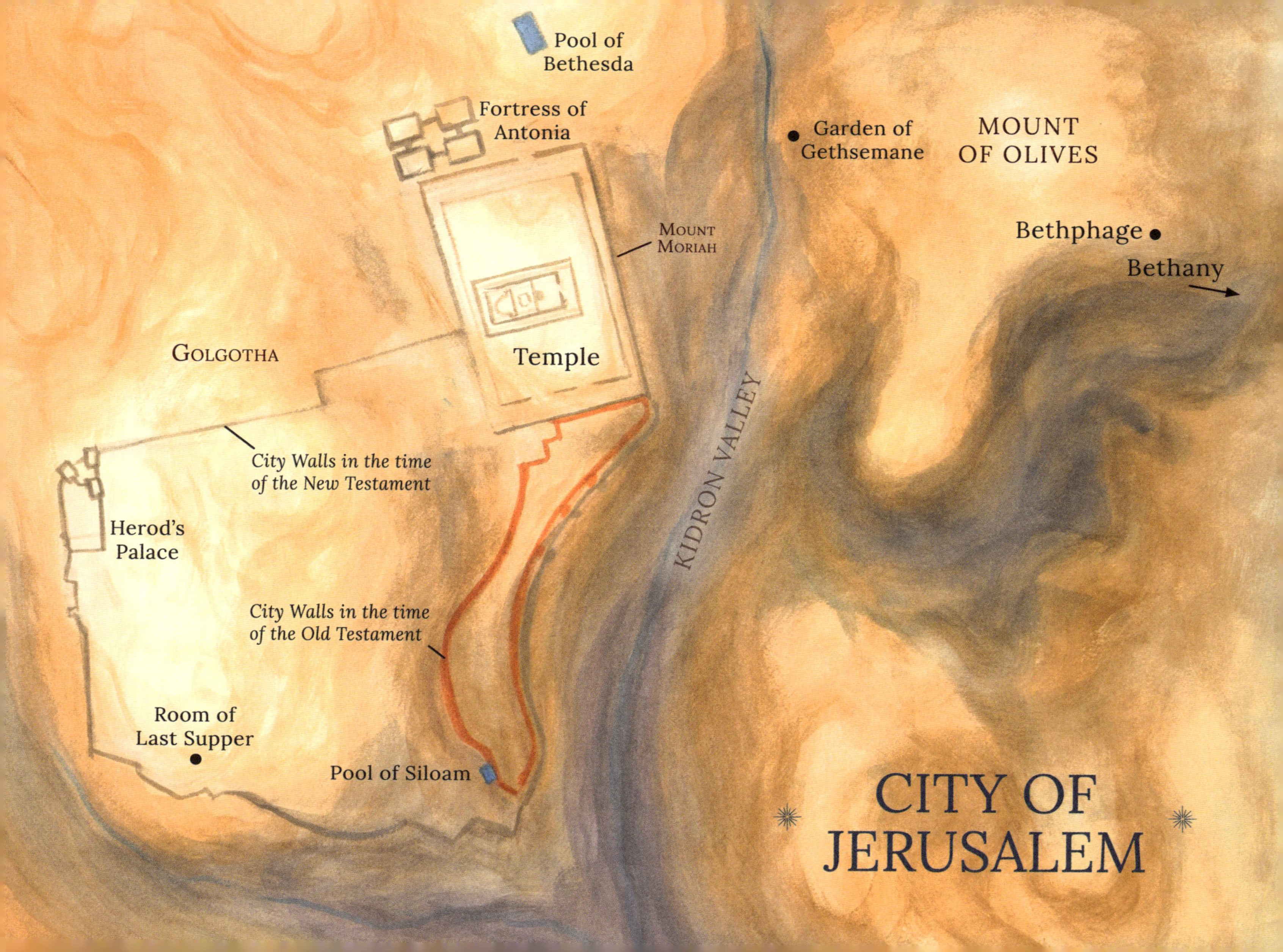
CITY OF JERUSALEM
Pool of Bethesda
Fortress of Antonia
Garden of Gethsemane
MOUNT OF OLIVES
Mount Moriah
Bethphage
Bethany
Golgotha
Temple
Kidron Valley
City Walls in the time of the New Testament
Herod's Palace
City Walls in the time of the Old Testament
Room of Last Supper
Pool of Siloam

Bible Sources

The Old Testament

Beginnings

The Creation: *(Gn 1)*
Adam and Eve: The Garden of Eden *(Gn 2)*; The Fall *(Gn 3)*; Cain and Abel *(Gn 4)*
Noah and the Flood: Noah builds the ark *(Gn 6–7)*; The Great Flood *(Gn 7–8)*; God's blessing *(Gn 8–9)*
The Tower of Babel: *(Gn 11)*

The Patriarchs

Abraham: Abram travels to Canaan *(Gn 12)*; Abram and Lot separate *(Gn 13)*; Abram rescues Lot *(Gn 14)*; God's promise to Abraham and Sarah *(Gn 17)*; God visits as three angels *(Gn 18)*; The destruction of Sodom and Gomorrah *(Gn 19)*
Isaac: The sacrifice of Isaac *(Gn 22)*; Isaac and Rebekah *(Gn 24)*
Jacob: Jacob and Esau *(Gn 25)*; Jacob steals Esau's blessing *(Gn 27)*; Jacob's ladder to heaven *(Gn 28)*; Jacob meets Rachel *(Gn 29)*; Jacob leaves Laban *(Gn 29–31)* Laban pursues Jacob *(Gn 31)*; Jacob wrestles with the angel *(Gn 32)*; Jacob returns to live in Canaan *(Gn 33–35)*
Joseph: Joseph's dreams *(Gn 37)*; Joseph is sold to Egypt *(Gn 37)*; Joseph's rise and fall in Egypt *(Gn 39)*; Jacob interprets dreams in prison *(Gn 40)*; Pharaoh makes Joseph his second-in-command *(Gn 41)*; Joseph's brothers go to Egypt *(Gn 42)*; The second journey to Egypt *(Gn 43)*; The silver cup in the sack *(Gn 44)*; Joseph makes himself known *(Gn 45)*; The deaths of Israel and Joseph *(Gn 46, 48–50)*

Moses

Moses Leads the Israelites: The birth of Moses *(Ex 1–2)*; Moses flees to Midian *(Ex 2)*; The burning bush *(Ex 3–4)*; Moses returns to Egypt *(Ex 4–7)*; The ten plagues of Egypt *(Ex 7–11)*; The Passover *(Ex 12)*; The escape from Egypt *(Ex 12–14)*
The Years in the Desert: The Israelites wander in the desert *(Ex 15–17)*; Jethro visits Moses *(Ex 18)*; The Ten Commandments *(Ex 19–20)*; Moses receives the tablets of the law *(Ex 24, 31)*; The golden calf *(Ex 32–34)*; The holy tent for God *(Ex 35–40)*; Scouts are sent to Canaan *(Nm 13–14)*; The deaths of Miriam and Aaron *(Nm 20)*; Balaam and his donkey *(Nm 22–24)*; The death of Moses *(Nm 27, Dt 34)*

Conquest of the Promised Land

Joshua: Joshua sends spies to Jericho *(Jsh 1–2)*; The Israelites cross the River Jordan *(Jsh 3–5)*; The fall of Jericho *(Jsh 6)*; The conquest of Judea *(Jsh 7–9)*; The sun stands still *(Jsh 10–11)*; The death of Joshua *(Jsh 24)*
The Leader-Judges: Deborah *(Jg 4–5)*; God speaks to Gideon *(Jg 6)*; Gideon defeats the

Midianites *(Jg 7)*; Samson's riddle *(Jg 13–15)*; Samson and Delilah *(Jg 16)*; Ruth comes to Bethlehem *(Ru 1–2)*; Ruth and Boaz *(Ru 3–4)*; Samuel's childhood *(1Sm 1–3)*;
The capture and return of the ark *(1Sm 4–7)*

The Kingdom of Israel

Saul: The Israelites want a king *(1Sm 8)*; Saul is anointed king *(1Sm 9–10)*; Saul is crowned king before the people *(1Sm 10)*; Saul loses his kingship *(1Sm 13–15)*
David: Samuel anoints David king *(1Sm 16)*; David comes to Saul's court *(1Sm 16)*;
David and Goliath *(1Sm 17)*; Saul tries to kill David *(1Sm 18–19)*; David spares Saul's life *(1Sm 23–24)*; Nabal and Abigail *(1Sm 25)*; David spares Saul again *(1Sm 26)*; The death of Saul *(1Sm 28–31, 2Sm 1, 1Ch 10)*;
David is crowned king *(2Sm 2–5, 1Ch 11)*; The conquest of Jerusalem *(2Sm 5–6, 1Ch 11, 15–16)*; David and Bathsheba *(2Sm 11–12)*; David's son Absalom *(2Sm 15, 18–19)*;
David's census *(2Sm 24, 1Ch 21)*
Solomon and Later Kings: Solomon is made king *(1K 1–2, 1Ch 28–29)*; Solomon's wise judgment *(1K 3, 2Ch 1)*; Solomon builds the temple *(1K 5–9, 2Ch 2–7)*; The queen of Sheba visits Solomon *(1K 10, 2Ch 9)*; The death of Solomon *(1K 11, 2Ch 9)*; The kingdom is divided *(1K 12, 2Ch 10–11)*; Jeroboam strays from God *(1K 12–14)*

The Prophets

Elijah and Elisha: Elijah, messenger of God *(1K 16–17)*; God sends rain on the land *(1K 18)*; God commands Elijah to find Elisha *(1K 19)*; Naboth's vineyard *(1K 21–22)*; Elijah ascends to heaven *(2K 2, 13)*
The Decline of the Two Kingdoms: Jonah *(Jon 1–4)*; Job *(Jb 1–7, 19, 38–42)*; The fall of Israel *(2K 17)*; Isaiah *(Is 6–7)*; King Hezekiah and the siege of Jerusalem *(2K 18–20, 2Ch 29, 32, Is 36–39)*; Jeremiah and the fall of Jerusalem *(2K 24–25, 2Ch 36, Jer 1, Lam 4–5)*

Babylonian Exile

Ezekiel and Daniel: Ezekiel *(Ezk 1–2, 40, 43)*; King Nebuchadnezzar's dream *(Dn 1–2)*; The men in the fiery furnace *(Dn 3)*; Belshazzar's feast *(Dn 5)*; Daniel in the lions' den *(Dn 6)*; Daniel's vision *(Dn 10, 12)*
Tobit and Tobias: Tobit becomes blind *(Tb 1–5)*; Tobias and Sarah *(Tb 6–9)*; Tobit is healed *(Tb 10–12)*
The Return from Babylon: The Jewish people return *(Ezr 1, 3–4)*; The temple is rebuilt *(Ezr 5–6)*
Esther: Esther becomes queen *(Est 2)*; Haman plans to kill the Jews *(Est 3–13)*

Awaiting the Messiah

The Maccabees: Mattathias defies the Greek rulers *(1Mc 1–2)*; Judas Maccabee restores the temple *(Mc 3–9)*

The New Testament

Jesus Christ

The Birth and Childhood of Jesus: An angel appears to Zechariah *(Lk 1)*; An angel appears to Mary *(Lk 1)*; The birth of John *(Lk 1)*; The birth of Jesus *(Lk 2)*; Wise men visit from the East *(Mt 2)*; The escape to Egypt *(Mt 2)*; The twelve-year-old in the temple *(Lk 2)*

Jesus Meets John the Baptist: John preaches in the wilderness *(Mt 3, Mk 1, Lk 3, Jn 1)*; Jesus is baptised *(Mt 3, Mk 1, Lk 3, Jn 1)*; The temptation *(Mt 4, Mk 1, Lk 4)*

The Early Work of Jesus: Jesus calls his disciples *(Mt 4, Mk 1, Lk 5, Jn 1)*; Jesus turns water into wine *(Jn 2)*; The Samaritan woman at the well *(Jn 4)*

The Sermon on the Mount: Jesus teaches the disciples *(Mt 4–6, Lk 6)*; The Lord's Prayer *(Mt 6, Lk 11)*; Treasures in heaven *(Mt 6)*; Do not judge others *(Mt 7, Lk 6)*

Miracles and Healing: Raising the young man at Nain *(Lk 7)*; Calming the storm *(Mt 8, Mk 4, Lk 8)*; Healing Jairus' daughter and the sick woman *(Mt 9, Mk 5, Lk 8)*; Healing the paralysed man at Bethesda *(Jn 5)*; Feeding the five thousand *(Mt 14, Mk 6, Lk 7, 9, Jn 6)*; Healing the deaf man *(Mt 15, Mk 7)*; Healing the ten men with leprosy *(Lk 17)*; Healing the blind man at Jericho *(Mt 20, Mk 10, Lk 18)*;

Parables: Parable of sower *(Mt 13, Mk 4, Lk 8)*; Parable of the prodigal son *(Lk 15)*; Parable of the good shepherd *(Jn 10)*; Parable of the vineyard workers *(Mt 20)*

Later Events in the Life of Jesus: Peter recognises Christ *(Mt 16, Mk 8, Lk 9)*; The Transfiguration *(Mt 17, Mk 9, Lk 9)*; The raising of Lazarus *(Jn 11)*

The Last Days of Jesus: Jesus enters Jerusalem as king *(Mt 21, Mk 11, Lk 19, Jn 12)*; The greatest commandment (Mt 22, Mk 12); Jesus is anointed at Bethany *(Mt 26, Mk 14, Lk 7, Jn 12)*; The Last Supper *(Mt 26, Mk 14, Lk 22, Jn 13)*; Jesus is arrested at Gethsemane *(Mt 26, Mk 14, Lk 22, Jn 18)*; Jesus goes on trial and Peter's denial *(Mt 26, Mk 14, Lk 22, Jn 18)*; Jesus appears before Pilate *(Mt 27, Mk 15, Lk 22–23, Jn 18–19)*; The Crucifixion *(Mt 27, Mk 15, Lk 23, Jn 19)*; The burial of Jesus *(Mt 27, Mk 15, Lk 23, Jn 19)*

The Resurrection and Ascension: Mary Magdalene at the empty tomb *(Mt 28, Mk 16, Lk 24, Jn 20)*; Jesus appears on the road to Emmaus *(Lk 24)*; Doubting Thomas *(Jn 20)*; The Ascension *(Lk 24, Ac 1)*

The Apostles

The Acts of the Apostles: The Holy Spirit at Pentecost *(Ac 2)*; The apostles are persecuted *(Ac 3–5)*; The death of Stephen *(Ac 6–7)*

Paul of Tarsus: Saul's vision at Damascus *(Ac 9, 22, 26)*; Paul's travels *(Ac 17, Ep 3, 1Cor 15)*; The armour of God *(Rm 12, 5, Ep 6)*; Paul is arrested in Jerusalem *(Ac 21–22)*; Paul is taken to Caesarea *(Ac 23–25)*

The Revelation to St John: The coming of the Son of Man *(Rv 1)*; The Heavenly Host *(Rv 4, 5, 7)*; The woman and the dragon *(Rv 12)*; The heavenly Jerusalem *(Rv 21)*; The end of John's revelation *(Rv 22)*